ENGLISH DOMESTIC CLOCKS

ENGLISH
DOMESTIC CLOCKS

by

by Herbert Cescinsky

and

Malcolm R.Webster

Antique Collectors' Club

This edition published 1976 by
Chancery House Publishing Co. Ltd.,
reprinted 1984 by the Antique Collectors' Club.
Reprinted 1991

ISBN 0 902028 37 5

Published for the Antique Collectors' Club
by the Antique Collectors' Club Ltd.

British Library CIP Data
Cescinsky, Herbert
    English domestic clocks.
    1. Clocks and watches, English—History.
    I. Title   II. Webster, Malcolm R
    681.1'13'0942   TS543.G7

Printed in England by the Antique Collectors' Club, Woodbridge, Suffolk

PREFACE

HIS book was written, primarily, to supplement another work, *English Furniture of the Eighteenth Century*, in the first volume of which certain chapters were devoted to long-case and bracket clocks, considered in the usual progression of English furniture types of the period. The larger book had the benefit of the examples of furniture of the various periods illustrated therein, which could be used for reference and comparison, an advantage obviously absent in the present work, which is concerned solely with clocks. On the other hand, this drawback is partly, if not wholly, compensated for by the greater space available, allowing of the treatment of the subject in fuller detail, and the fact that the short-comings of the larger book were useful in showing what to amplify and what to avoid. It was felt, at the time, that the clock chapters in *English Furniture of the Eighteenth Century* were not only incomplete, but also inaccurate in many points of detail, and as theories were built on many of these imperfect premises, these theories were necessarily faulty in a corresponding degree. Some of the conclusions, and one of the chapters, that on "Chippendale and Sheraton Clockcases," in the former book, have been adopted with little or no alteration in the present one. It may be remarked that some of the theories ventured at that time have been substantiated by the examination of the examples of clocks which have since been added to the specimens then illustrated. The association of authorship was rendered advisable by the fact that to properly describe the later examples (which are exclusive to this book), it was necessary to thoroughly examine the works of each clock, as many of the peculiarities which are invaluable in estimating the age of each example are not apparent in the photographs of case or dial. This examination was, obviously, the province of the practical clockmaker; hence the dual authorship.

It would appear, at first sight, that the student of the clock fashions of the period from 1665 to the present day is greatly assisted by the preserved records of the old clockmakers, and especially by the researches or lists of makers first made by Octavius Morgan and published in the *Journal* of the Archæological Institution, afterwards in Wood's *Curiosities of Watches and Clocks*, 1866, in *Some Account of the Clockmakers' Company* by Atkins and Overall in 1881, and recently by Mr. F. J. Britten. This is undoubtedly true on a large degree, and we must acknowledge our large indebtedness to Mr. Britten. When we have to consider exact periods of semi-decades, however, the extant records become very meagre, and have to be examined very closely and received very cautiously. Many of the old clockmakers had a very extended business career, and it is often a nice point to determine exactly at which point a particular specimen should be assigned. The clock itself is the only really reliable criterion, as there is no doubt that many of the long-case clocks which are met with are not in their original cases ; at any rate, this point has always to be reckoned with. Bracket clocks are, as a rule, free from this doubt, but the bracket clocks of the one maker are little or no guide in determining the characteristics of his long clocks, both as regards cases and movements. The reference here to records only covers those instances where the date of the connection of a maker with the Clockmakers' Company has been preserved. The assigning of a date to a maker from a single specimen of his work is obviously a matter of mere opinion.

An attempt has been made in this book to systematise the subject of English domestic clocks, and to avoid thereby, as far as possible, the discursiveness so common in books dealing with the technical side of our national handicrafts. If the volume does no more than to present, in interesting and readable form, the history of the development of perhaps the most characteristic of our national industries of the later seventeenth and the whole of the eighteenth centuries, and to promote an intelligent interest in the finer examples of the art of the clockmaker which are still available, it will not have been written quite in vain. These old clocks have a dual interest, as specimens of the skill of the cabinetmaker and the inventive ability of the clockmaker, and it is hardly fair to the latter to consider his productions merely as more or less decorative pieces of furniture, especially as many of the more notable examples are characterised by the extreme simplicity of their cases.

In conclusion, we desire to express our acknowledgments to Mr. Percy Webster, whose advice on many occasions has been invaluable, and whose knowledge on the subject of English clocks stands unrivalled at the present day ; and to Mr. Richard Hoffmann, who has kindly verified the mathematical calculations contained in this book.

H. C.
M. R. W.

CONTENTS

Chapter I

The Problem of the Measurement of Time

ANY have been the devices, during the historical epoch of civilised man, for subdividing and recording the two motions of the earth: its diurnal axial rotation and its orbital revolution round the sun. These time-recording instruments may be roughly divided into two classes: the passive and the active. The sun-dial is the type of the former, the clock that of the latter. On the one, the sun does its own recording, as it were, indicating its position in the heavens by the line of shadow cast by the gnomen of the dial. In the other, a force is stored, by the winding of a spring, the pulling up of a weight, or by any other contrivances, which force is released in regular fashion, so that the clock hand, or other indicator, will travel a given distance in a certain invariable time. The various methods of attaining this result do not concern us here at present, but it may be advisable to examine the nature of the attempt, and to see how much is based on natural periods and how much is purely arbitrary.

It is obvious that the subdivision of the day into twenty-four hours, of each hour into sixty minutes, and of each minute into sixty seconds, is an empirical one. It is not so obvious, however, that the calendar year of 365 days and the day itself are also not fixed astronomical periods, marking exactly the time taken by the earth to accomplish its orbital and axial revolutions respectively. The hour hand of a clock takes the same time—or should—to accomplish its path round the circle of the dial in June as in December; the length of the day—that is, the axial revolution of the earth—varies. The clock indicates approximately mean time—that is, an average for all the year; the sun-dial shows apparent solar time. Let us see how and why these differ.

The earth makes one axial revolution in 23 hours, 56 minutes, 4.09 seconds; the clock subdivides a day of 24 hours. Twelve o'clock noon, as indicated by the clock, should be the moment when the position of the earth were such that the sun appeared to be directly overhead. This moment would be the same on each day had the earth no other motion. But we know that it has an orbital revolution round the sun, and therefore the position of the earth in relation to that of the sun cannot be exactly the same on successive days, and the sun, in describing its apparent arc across the heavens, will reach the zenith sometimes before twelve o'clock noon, as marked by the clock, and sometimes later. The maximum variation each way is roughly about 15 minutes, or, to put it into exact figures, from 16 minutes 18 seconds before, to 14 minutes 28 seconds after, twelve o'clock mean time. The progression from the maximum before to the maximum after twelve o'clock is also not uniform, the problem being complicated by such factors as the inclination of the earth's axis to the plane of the ecliptic, the perturbation of its orbital path round the sun, caused by the attractions of the moon, Venus, and Jupiter (and, in an infinitesimal degree, by that of Mars), the circular movement of the pole of the earth round that of the ecliptic (known as precession), and the fact that the earth's motion round the sun is not at a uniform rate, being greater in December, when the earth is close to the sun, than in July when it is the farthest away.

In the same way as the sidereal day differs from the mean solar day, so does the year vary in like manner, and according to the standard of measurement adopted. Thus the tropical, or, as it is often incorrectly called, the solar year, is the measure of time which elapses from the appearance of the sun on one of the tropics to its return to the same position, and has a mean length of 365.2422414 mean solar days, or 365 days, 5 hours, 48 minutes, 49.7 seconds. From its historical and legal recognition as the common measure of time, this is also known as the civil year. The sidereal year is the period required by the sun to move from a given star to the same star again, and this year, affected as it is only by nutation (the oscillatory motion of the earth's axis which disturbs the circular movement known as precession), is one of the most invariable quantities in the realm of astronomy, and has a mean value of 365.2563612 mean solar days, or 365 days, 6 hours, 9 minutes, 9.6 seconds. The anomalistic year is the time which elapses between the earth's arrival at its perihelion (the point when it is the nearest to the sun) and its return to the same position. This is equivalent to 365.2595981 mean solar days, or 365 days, 6 hours, 13 minutes, 49.3 seconds.

The actual length of the day is also not a fixed quantity, owing to the moon's attraction causing tides on the earth, the effect of which is to act as a constant brake on the axial rotation. The day is thus becoming gradually longer and longer.

It follows, therefore, from the foregoing, that there exists no fixed unit of measurement by which the length of the day or the year may be determined. Nothing is constant, and consequently no system of recording or subdividing can be even approximately correct. The clockmaker is concerned with the length of the day, and recognising that this is not an uniform quantity, he takes an approximate time from meridian to meridian, which he subdivides into 24 hours, each hour into 60 minutes, and each minute into 60 seconds. He may further subdivide the second in like manner, but these subdivisions are all arbitrary, depending upon an empirical day of uniform duration. It is his business to devise an instrument for recording these arbitrary divisions in an invariable way, so that the duration of his hours, minutes, and seconds shall remain always constant. He has to contend with natural forces, with heat and cold, which, in contracting and expanding the materials which he uses, affect his regulation, and cause his timekeepers to vary. In the constant struggle with nature he is continually being worsted, but the margin of error is steadily reduced after each encounter. The perfect timepiece will probably never be constructed, but it is a part of the purpose of this book to illustrate the later stages of this warfare between the forces of nature and the inventive ability of the maker of clocks, and at the same time to show the structural and ornamental evolution of the cases in which the clocks were enshrined, and of the dials, hands, and other embellishments of the clocks themselves.

Chapter II

The Law of the Pendulum

THE history of the development of the English domestic clock practically begins with the pendulum as a regulator, and with the power obtained by the fall of a weight, although the spring barrel is almost, if not quite, co-incidental with the weight-driven clock.[1] Some exceptions must be made to the pendulum control in the rare cases of the "balance wheel" regulation; but these can be deferred to a later stage, when the mechanism of the earliest bracket clocks will be considered and examples illustrated. The "foliot" balance can be disregarded altogether, as this is never found in English clocks. For the present we can give our un-divided attention to the pendulum clock, and it is curious that although nearly everyone is well acquainted with the pendulum, the laws affecting its operation are very little understood. We can therefore commence with the following quotation from Sir Robert Ball's *Story of the Heavens*, the Astronomer Royal of Ireland being a master of the art of lucid explanation of an abstruse subject.

"For its journey to and fro the pendulum requires a certain amount of time, which does not appreciably depend upon the length of the circular arc through which the pendulum swings. To verify this law we suspend another pendulum beside the first, both being of the same length. If we draw both pendulums aside and then release them, they swing together and return together. This might have been expected. But if we draw one pendulum a great deal to one side, and the other only a little, the two pendulums still swing sympathetically. This, perhaps, would not have been expected. Try it again, with even a still greater difference in the arc of vibration, and still we see the two weights occupy the same time for the swing. We can vary the experiment in another way. Let us change the weights on the pendulums, so that they are of unequal size though both of iron. Shall we find any difference in the periods of vibration? We try again: the period is the same as before; swing them through different arcs, large or small, the period is still the same. But it may be said that this is due to the fact that both weights are of the same material. Try it again using a leaden weight instead

---

[1] The few rare spring-driven clocks engraved with English names which one meets of date prior to 1650 are invariably of foreign character. The early iron or brass wall clocks of unmistakable English origin are always weight-driven.

of one of the iron weights; the result is identical. Even with a ball of wood the period of oscillation is the same as with the ball of iron, and this is true no matter what be the arc through which the vibration takes place.

"If, however, we change the length of the wire by which the weight is supported, then the period will not remain unchanged. This can be very easily illustrated. Take a short pendulum with a wire only one-fourth of the length of that of the long one; suspend the two close together, and compare the periods of vibration of the short pendulum with that of the long one, and we find that the former has a period of only half that of the latter. We may state the result generally, and say that the time of the vibration of a pendulum is proportional to the square root of its length. If we quadruple the length of the suspending cord, we double the time of its vibration; if we increase the length of the pendulum ninefold, we increase the period of its vibration threefold.

"It is the gravitation of the earth which makes the pendulum swing. The greater the attraction, the more rapidly will the pendulum oscillate. This may be easily accounted for. If the earth pulls the weight down very vigorously, the time will be short; if the power of the earth's attraction be lessened, then it cannot pull the weight down so quickly, and the period will be lengthened."

It follows, as a necessary deduction from the above, that a clock pendulum swinging through its arc once in the space of a second must be, and can only be, of one given length. With a period of half a second the length is only one quarter that of the seconds' pendulum. Stated in actual figures, in inches and fractions of inches, a pendulum with a period of swing of $\frac{1}{4}$ second must have a length of 2.4462 inches; with a swing of $\frac{1}{2}$ second, 9.7848 inches; 1 second, 39.1393 inches; $1\frac{1}{4}$ second, 61.155 inches; $1\frac{1}{2}$ second, 88.0632 inches; and 2 seconds, 156,5572 inches.

The period of oscillation varies, however, at different parts of the globe, according to the proximity to the pole or the equator, being longer at the latter and shorter at the former, and it is even slightly altered if the pendulum be taken much below the surface of the earth, as, for example, down a coal-mine. Temperature also affects the time of swing of the ordinary clock pendulum, and this in a twofold way. In the first case the resistance of the atmosphere is lessened, and the time in consequence slightly shortened, if the air be heated; whereas, as an irregular compensation, heat expands, and lengthens the metal of which the pendulum rod is made, and thus protracts the time of the swing.

Quoting again from Sir Robert Ball :—

"It is possible to determine the time of vibration of the pendulum with great accuracy. Let it swing for 10,000 oscillations, and measure the time that these oscillations have consumed. The arc through which the pendulum swings may not have remained quite constant, but this does not appreciably affect the *time* of its oscillation. Suppose that an error of a second is made in the determination of the time of 10,000 oscillations : this will only entail an error of the ten-thousandth part of a second in the time of a single oscillation, and will afford a correspondingly accurate determination of the gravity.

"Take a pendulum to the equator. Let it perform 10,000 oscillations, and determine carefully the *time* that these oscillations have required. Bring the same pendulum to another part of the earth, and repeat the experiment. We have thus a means of comparing the gravitation at the two places. There are, no doubt, a multitude of precautions to be observed, which need not here concern us. It is not necessary to enter into details as to the manner in which the motion of the pendulum is to be sustained, nor as to the effect of changes of temperature in the alteration of its length. It will suffice for us to see how the time of the pendulum's swing can be measured accurately, and how from that measurement the intensity of the gravitation can be calculated.

"The pendulum thus enables us to make a gravitational survey of the surface of the earth with the highest degree of accuracy. We cannot, however, infer that gravity alone affects the oscillations of the pendulum. We have seen how the earth rotates on its axis, and we have attributed the bulging of the earth at the equator to this influence. But the centrifugal force arising from the rotation has the effect of decreasing the apparent weight of bodies, and the change is the greatest at the equator, and lessens gradually as we approach the poles. From this cause alone the attraction of the pendulum at the equator is less than elsewhere, and therefore the oscillations of the pendulum will take a longer time there than at other localities. A part of the apparent change in gravitation is accordingly due to the centrifugal force ; but there is, in addition, a real alteration. At a hasty glance it might be thought that, as there was a protuberance of matter at the equator, there ought to be a greater attraction there than elsewhere. This is not so. The effect of the additional matter is more than compensated by the greater distance of the pendulum from the centre of the earth. Indeed, a moment's reflection will show that the pendulum at the pole is, on the whole, nearer to the mass of the earth than when it is at the equator. It illustrates, in a marked way, how the researches in different branches of science are interwoven, when we find that, by observing the swing of a pendulum at different parts of the earth, we are enabled to determine the *shape* of our globe as accurately as by the elaborate measurements of the arcs of the meridian."

As the period of swing of a clock pendulum varies at different latitudes, it is necessary to qualify, somewhat, the foregoing statements regarding the different lengths for the various periods. To be exact, a pendulum with a swing of 1 second must have a length of 39.1393 inches, *in the latitude of London ;* but this measurement would vary at other parallels, being its longest at the pole, where the greater attraction causes the clock to go more quickly, and the shortest at the equator. The famous clockmaker John Ellicott devised an instrument for calculating the effective lengths of pendulums at different parallels of latitude from equator to pole.

With a seconds' pendulum, the clock simply records the number of the oscillations in terms of seconds, minutes, and hours. The power stored in the wound-up weight or spring is used merely to keep the pendulum swinging. Remove the weights, or allow the spring to run down, and the arc of swing will gradually lessen until the pendulum ceases to oscillate. Gravitation has overcome the initial impetus given to it. In a general way, the size of the weights or the power of the spring will not affect the time of the pendulum's swing ; it will cause it to describe a wider or narrower arc ; but, as we have seen, this does not affect the periodic time. Actually, a very wide arc of swing will affect the time slightly, owing to the increased resistance of the atmosphere. There are other considerations which have also to be taken into account with a pendulum driven by power. An over-weighted or over-sprung clock is said to "govern the pendulum," instead of the pendulum governing the clock. The power exerted should be just sufficient to keep the pendulum at its work, no more nor less.

It is misleading, and hardly correct, to regard a pendulum as regulating a clock, as the inference is that the clock records the time and the pendulum causes it to do this in a regular fashion, which is only approximately true. Really, it is the pendulum which actually marks the time, which is recorded in terms of single swings and multiples of such on the dial of the clock. If the clock goes, and fails to keep accurate time, it is always the pendulum which is at fault, never the clock itself if it be properly constructed. We are so generally accustomed to regard a clock dial as a circle on which is recorded the lapse of hours—twelve or twenty-four, according to the way in which the dial is divided—which for greater convenience is subdivided into minutes or seconds. The tendency to consider a clock in this way is even greater in the case of the early lantern or sheepshead types, where minute hands are exceptional or unknown. As a matter of fact, this way of regarding a clock is really beginning from the wrong end. What the clock actually does is to maintain a power sufficient to keep the pendulum on the swing, and to record the number of the oscillations. What we mean when we speak of a clock keeping time is that the pendulum swings once in a certain invariable fraction of the total length of the horological day of twenty-four hours, which, as we have seen in the first chapter, is the nearest we can get to a natural period of time, as distinct from an empirical one, such as a week, an hour, a minute, or a second. Thus the pendulum of a clock with a seconds' dial oscillates 86,400 times in the 24-hour day if the clock records exact horological time—that is, if each swing takes exactly one second to accomplish. Supposing, however, we find that the clock has gained five minutes in this period: this means that the pendulum has oscillated 86,700 times instead of 86,400, or, in other words, each swing has taken a fraction less than a second—to be exact, $\frac{287}{288}$ths of a second—and to adjust the clock the pendulum must be lengthened. If the pendulum length were directly proportional to the time of swing, it would be almost impossible to correct a margin of error such as this; but as the times of vibration are as the square roots of the lengths, a much smaller margin of error than five minutes in the 24-hour day can be corrected by the small turning screw under the pendulum bob.

The next point to be considered is how the effective length of a clock pendulum can be calculated. It is obviously not the total length which is required, as this always remains constant. When we "shorten" the pendulum, we really screw the disc a trifle nearer to its point of swing. Again, it would be thought that the centre of the arbor, or horizontal rod on which the pendulum crutch swings, would be one point of measurement. This is not so, however, as although the pendulum in its swing carries the crutch with it, the two do not describe exactly the same arc. If the crutch were prolonged, and the bob of the pendulum fixed to the end, at exactly the same level as it usually is on the pendulum itself, the arc of swing would take less time than with the pendulum. Again, if the points of measurement were exactly defined, there would be no need to keep on adjusting the length of the pendulum (variations of temperature not being considered for the moment), as the clockmaker or repairer has to do to ascertain the exact length for the clock to keep accurate time. With a seconds' dial clock he could measure the pendulum, adjust it exactly to 39.1393 inches in length, and the clock would keep accurate time as a logical necessity. The fact that this length has to be found by experiment is sufficient to show that one at least if not both of the points of measurement cannot be exactly determined.

Let us first consider the disc end of the pendulum. It would be thought at first that the point of measurement here would be the centre of the bob or disc, but this is not the fact. What we have to find is the centre of gravity, *not of the disc, but of the entire pendulum*. It is obvious that this central point must be somewhat higher up than the exact centre of the disc. The first point of measurement, therefore, cannot be found by calculation, but only by experiment. To verify this fact : if we add a small weight to the pendulum rod immediately above the disc, we do not shorten the pendulum, but we raise its centre of gravity, and the pendulum will oscillate more quickly and the clock will gain in consequence. If, on the contrary, we add the weight *below* the disc, the clock will lose.

Let us now turn our attention to the other end of the pendulum, the second point of measurement. Here the pendulum is held from the "jaws" by a flexible piece of steel—the "suspension," as it is termed. It is the bending point of this suspension which constitutes the other point of measurement. The steel does not bend at a sharp angle, however, but in a bow, more or less acute according to the size of the arc of swing. It is obvious that there is here no exact point which can be indicated, although such a point does exist. To find this it is necessary to set the clock in motion, measure the length of the pendulum as nearly as possible, and to correct the remaining inaccuracy by the adjusting screw. The length of a clock pendulum, therefore, with a swing of one second, is 39.1393 inches, measured from the centre of gravity of the entire pendulum to the exact bending point of the flexible suspension. This latter can be of steel, or, as is sometimes the case, of string or gut ; the problem remains the same.

We know that if we lower the pendulum bob by means of the adjusting screw, the pendulum will take longer to perform its arc of swing. It would be thought, therefore, that if we were to remove the bob altogether, the pendulum would be lengthened to its utmost limit, and the clock would lose the maximum amount in consequence. This is not the case, however, as the following explanation will show, apart from the question of the alteration of the centre of gravity just referred to. If we suspend a rod, or wire, 39.1393 inches in length from its point of swing to its centre of gravity, and cause it to oscillate in pendulum fashion, it will take approximately one second to swing once through its arc. If to each swing we add an impetus with the finger, we enlarge the arc, but without altering the periodic time. A swing through an arc of one foot and another through six inches will each take one second to accomplish. If, however, we take the wire between the thumb and finger, exerting force in both directions, we can make the pendulum swing through any arc, and in any time we please, according to the degree of force which we exert. In other words, we are using a greater power than the pendulum can control, and the laws governing its swing are temporarily abrogated. This is precisely what occurs when the pendulum disc is removed. The pendulum no longer governs the clock: it is the clock which controls the pendulum ; and the heavier the weight which we put upon the going train, the quicker will the pendulum oscillate. The weight of the pendulum disc, therefore, must be sufficient to overcome the pull of the weight which drives the clock—or the force of the spring, as the case may be—as transmitted from the main to the escape wheels, so that the latter is just enough to maintain the necessary power to prevent the pendulum from ceasing to oscillate.

We can briefly summarise the whole problem thus : the effective length of the pendulum is calculated from the bending point of the suspension spring to the centre of gravity of the entire pendulum. The centre of gravity is that point in a body or system of bodies rigidly connected, upon which the body or system acted upon only by the force ot gravity will balance itself in all positions. The effective length being, therefore, from the point of swing to the centre of gravity, it is obvious that when we remove the disc we shift the centre of gravity higher up the pendulum rod, and by so doing shorten its effective length, causing the clock to go faster in consequence.

Another problem has now to be considered. We will take two clocks, both weight-driven, for simplicity of explanation, which have lost their pendulums. The one has a seconds' dial, the other has none. We have now to calculate the length of these missing pendulums. The problem is, of course, the same in both cases, but in the one it is simplified by the presence of the seconds' dial—that is, if the finger of this dial be directly actuated by the swing of the pendulum. The answer here is, as we have already seen, 39.1393 inches, from the bending point of the suspension to the centre of gravity. In the case of the other clock, however, we have no such guide, and the length has to be calculated in the following way. It is presumed that the reader has some acquaintance with the mechanism of a clock, although it is intended to explain this in a later chapter.

Count the number of teeth on the centre wheel and multiply by the number of those on the third wheel. Multiply the result by twice the number of teeth in the escape-wheel. Multiply the number of leaves, or horizontal serrations, in the third pinion by the number of leaves in the escape pinion. Divide the result of the wheels by the result of the pinions. Divide the result by 60. Take the square of this result, and divide it into the number 140,904; the result is the length of the pendulum in inches. Fractions which occur in the result can be disregarded, as slight margins of error can be corrected by subsequent adjustment.

To prove this calculation, we will take the train of a clock with a seconds' dial where the length of the pendulum is known, and see whether the method justifies the result. Trains differ, even in seconds' pendulum clocks, and we have taken one at random, the George Allett clock illustrated in Fig. 198 of this book.

The number of teeth on the centre wheel is 60, on the third wheel 48, and on the escape-wheel 30. Then $60 \times 48 = 2880$; $2880 \times 30 \times 2 = 172,800$.

The number of leaves on the third pinion is 8, and on the escape pinion 6; $6 \times 8 = 48$. Divide 172,800 by 48: the result is 3600; 3600 divided by 60 equals 60; the square of 60 is, again, 3600. The number 140,904 divided by 3600 gives $39\frac{151}{900}$ as a result, which is practically 39.1393 inches. The fraction of difference—roughly about $\frac{1}{35}$th of an inch—is left to be regulated by the adjusting screw.

Chapter III

The Regulation of Domestic Clocks

I N the previous chapters we have considered the pendulum, and the laws relating to its function, at some length. There is, however, another problem with which the clockmaker has to contend when dealing with clocks of great precision : namely, the lengthening or shortening of the pendulum rod by the expansion of heat, or the contraction of cold, with concomitant alteration of the position of the centre of gravity of the pendulum and loss of accuracy in its measurement of time. The clock, consequently, goes faster in cold, and slower in hot weather. The adjusting screw at the base of the pendulum disc is useless in a case of this kind, as the derangement may vary from hour to hour. Many devices have been suggested, and adopted, for the correction of this error, but they have all one principle in common, and it is only necessary to consider two forms here, the mercurial pendulum of George Graham (1673–1751) and the "gridiron" pendulum of John Harrison (1693–1776). Both are of the type known as compensated pendulums, the object in each being to use the different coefficients of lineal dilatation possessed by two metals, so that in the one, if the bob be lowered by expansion under heat, this may be compensated by raising it in an equal degree by the expansion, in the opposite direction, of the other. In the mercurial pendulum (Fig. 1), the rod A B, and the stirrup, B C, are of steel. Inside this stirrup is a cylindrical glass jar, D, nearly filled with mercury. The adjusting screw, E, is used to raise or lower the jar, but this does not concern us at present, as it is only used to adjust the pendulum to the proper length. With an increase of temperature the combined lengths of the rod A B and the side of the stirrup B C are increased by a proportional amount—the co-

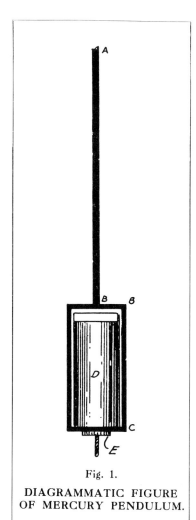

Fig. 1.

DIAGRAMMATIC FIGURE OF MERCURY PENDULUM.

efficient of lineal dilatation and the change of temperature conjointly—and the centre of gravity is lowered. Leaving out as a negligible quantity the expansion of the glass jar, the mercury rises in the jar by an amount proportional to its bulk—its coefficient of cubical dilatation and the change of temperature conjointly —and if the quantity of mercury be accurately proportioned to the length of the rod and its stirrup, the centre of gravity is restored to its original position, and the function of the pendulum is unaffected by the change of temperature.

The same principle is embodied in the "gridiron" pendulum in the next illustration (Fig. 2), which has been shown in modified form for convenience of understanding. The rods A, B, and C are of steel, those marked D and E of brass or other suitable metal. For the sake of greater simplicity, we may concern ourselves only with the rods A, C, and D ; B and E being provided only for symmetry, and to hold the pendulum rigid. We can also, for the same considera- tion, neglect the suspension G, and the tie bars J and F. The coefficients of lineal dilatation of steel and brass respectively are, approximately, as 100 to 60. If, therefore, the combined lengths of the rods A and C, in comparison with the length of D, are as 5 to 3, increase of temperature will cause the steel rods, by expansion, to lower the bob H, and the brass rod to raise it in an equal degree, and thus its position will remain unchanged. This is, however, acting on the supposition that the weight of the framework can be ignored in comparison with that of the disc ; if this be taken into account, the adjustment is greatly com- plicated, and involves abstruse problems which would be out of place in a book of this character.

It is found, however, that a strip of dry, well- seasoned pine is very little affected by changes of temperature, and this is frequently used, in regulator clocks, in lieu of the elaborate contrivances described above. With astronomical clocks, however, the greatest precision is required, and here the gridiron has been found more suitable than the mercurial pendulum,

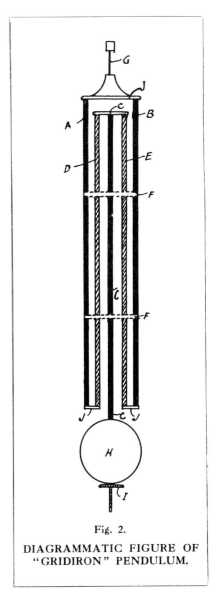

Fig. 2.

DIAGRAMMATIC FIGURE OF "GRIDIRON" PENDULUM.

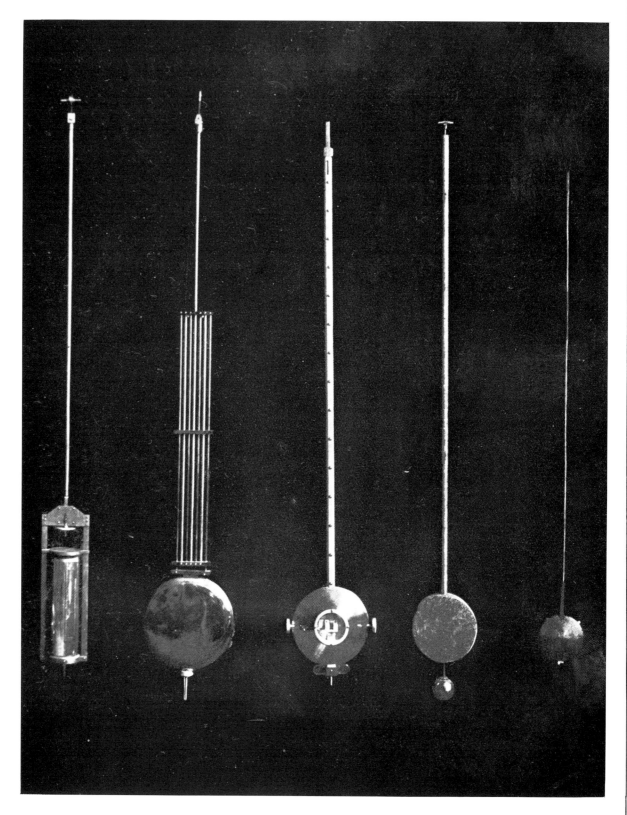

TYPES OF LONG-CASE CLOCK PENDULUMS.

Fig. 3.	Fig. 4.	Fig. 5.	Fig. 6.	Fig. 7.
Mercurial Pendulum.	"Gridiron" Pendulum.	Ellicott's Compensated Pendulum.	Wood-rod Regulator Pendulum.	Ordinary Seconds' Pendulum.

by reason of the fact that differences of temperature—inconceivably minute, of course, but enough to cause a clock to vary in a sufficient lapse of time—occur at different parts of the clock, which may cause the rod to expand and yet leave the mercury unaffected, or vice versa; whereas the steel and brass rods of the "gridiron" pendulum, running side by side practically throughout the length of the pendulum, are affected in equal degree.

A complete range of pendulums generally used for long-case clocks is shown in Figs. 3 to 7. The first two are the mercury and "gridiron" types before referred to. Fig. 5 is the compensated pendulum invented by John Ellicott (1706–1772). In this device the bob rests on two levers, unequally balanced, the shorter ends being acted upon by the expansion of the brass fillet attached to the front of the pendulum rod by slotted screws. As the brass fillet expands and presses on the shorter arms of the two levers, the latter are depressed and raise the pendulum bob in equal degree. The two milled screws on either side of the bob are for adjusting the bearing of the two levers. This Ellicott compensated pendulum is occasionally found in clocks of the regulator type, frequently made for

use in the timing shop of a clockmaker. Fig. 6 is a wood-rod pendulum of the regulator clock type, dry pine being usually found to be little affected by changes of temperature. Fig. 7 is the usual long-case clock "seconds" pendulum, which demands no explanation.

In the next chapter it is intended to examine the mechanism of clocks and to show how the power generated by the uncoiling of a spring or the fall of a weight is distributed in various directions, with the one end in view: to make the clock hands traverse the dial in the space of 1 and 12 hours respectively.

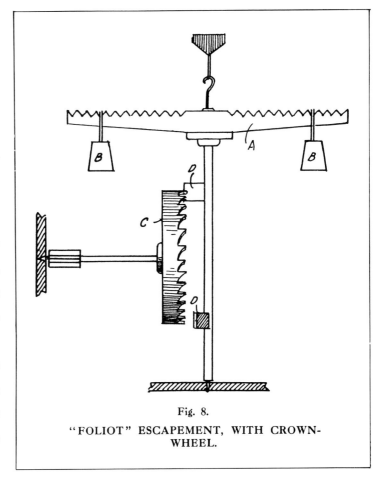

Fig. 8.

"FOLIOT" ESCAPEMENT, WITH CROWN-WHEEL.

The governing of this power is the escapement in its various forms, or the devices adopted for checking the fastest wheel in the train of the clock—*i.e.* the one which requires the least power—so that the revolutions of all the wheels shall be even and constant, performing one revolution in a fixed, measurable period of time.

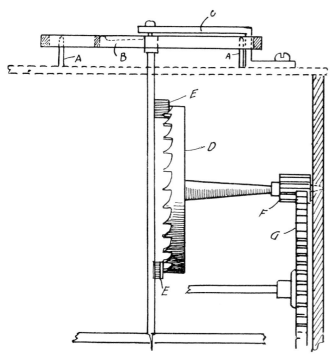

BALANCE ESCAPEMENT, VERTICAL VIEW.

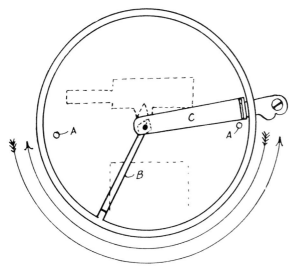

BALANCE-WHEEL, VIEWED FROM ABOVE.

Fig. 9.

As before stated, the pendulum is the most efficient regulator, and the history of the English domestic clock almost begins with its introduction. The earlier devices have to be considered, as in a later chapter on brass lantern clocks it will be found that these were frequently converted from the balance-wheel form of control, and that the pendulum, especially in the early examples, was seldom, if ever, original, or known, when these lantern clocks were made.

Had the power-driven clock been an English invention, we could at once have commenced with the balance-wheel, which is the oldest form of regulation known to English horology. The balance, however, is already a developed form, and we have to look to Germany and Switzerland to find its prototype. This is the "foliot" balance, shown in Fig. 8, which is never found on English clocks. Here the crown-wheel C is checked by the oscillating cross-bar A, which swings in a more or less determined period of time, and with each oscillation releases one tooth of the crown-wheel. Regulation is effected by the two small weights B B, which can be placed farther towards, or away from, the centre, in the notches provided for this purpose, thereby causing the cross-bar to oscillate quicker or slower. The pallets attached to the vertical arbor are shown by the letters D D, the upper one engaging the teeth of the contrate-wheel in the illustration.

The principle of the balance-wheel (Fig. 9) is almost identical with the foregoing, the wheel oscillating in the same way as the "foliot" cross-bar. In both illustrations the wheel has a single spoke, B, which strikes against the pins, A A, and limits the arc of the swing. Regulation was effected by adding to, or diminishing the driving weight. C is the overhanging bar to which the wheel is pivoted, D is the contrate-wheel, F its pinion, and G the third wheel. E E are the two pallets attached to the vertical arbor of the balance-wheel.

The escapement or control is attached directly to the arbor of the balance-wheel, but with the introduction of the pendulum a separate device became necessary. The escapement known as the "verge" or "crown-wheel" (Fig. 10) has the disadvantage of requiring a wide swing of the horizontal pendulum arbor for the pallets to free the escape-wheel—which acquires its name from its resemblance to a crown. Owing to the wide arc of swing of the pendulum it is usually reserved for bracket clocks with short pendulums. It is obvious that the enclosure of a seconds' pendulum with a crown-wheel escapement in a trunk of the usual long-case variety would be impossible, and, despite certain fanciful theories applied to provincial clocks, it is doubtful if it was ever attempted. The invention of the "anchor" escapement (Fig. 11) is

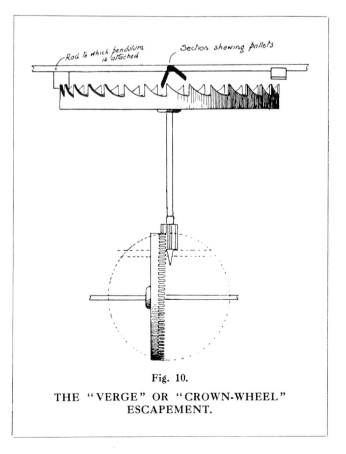

Fig. 10.

THE "VERGE" OR "CROWN-WHEEL" ESCAPEMENT.

Fig. 11.
"ANCHOR" ESCAPEMENT,
RECOIL TYPE.

almost coincidental with the introduction of the pendulum itself, and is the universal fashion with long-case clocks. The usual type of anchor escapement is known as the recoil, from the slight backward impetus usually given to the escape-wheel—and also to the finger of the seconds' dial, to which it is directly connected—as each tooth is released. To correct this recoil, and to make for greater precision in timekeeping, George Graham devised the "dead-beat" escapement (Fig. 12), where the one tooth is firmly locked until the next is released. The "dead-beat" escapement has the drawback of being difficult of lubrication, but this is a technical matter which need not concern us here. It is incomparably superior to the recoil type, as far as precision is concerned.

This chapter has been concerned solely with the regulation of clocks, without reference to the question of their mechanism. It is a debatable point whether it should have been placed after, rather than before, the next chapter, but the two can be taken in conjunction for the purpose of a better understanding of the subject of the mechanism of clocks.

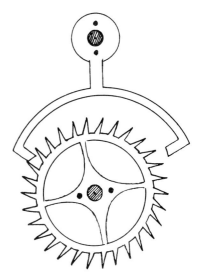

Fig. 12.
GRAHAM'S "DEAD-BEAT"
ESCAPEMENT.

Chapter IV

The Mechanism of Clocks

HERE are many who have a keen appreciation for the case-work of the finer specimens of English clocks of the eighteenth century to whom a simple explanation of the mechanism of the clock movements themselves, devoid, as far as practicable, of technical terms, may be of service. The practical clockmaker can afford to ignore this chapter.

We can begin by taking an 8-day clock with a seconds' pendulum (Fig. 13) of the type which is usually found in the early square-dial "grandfather" cases until the close of the seventeenth century. From this we can proceed to the later kind, and at the same time be able to revert to the earlier lantern clock without needless recapitulation or redundancy of explanation.

As a beginning, it will be as well to divide the movement of the clock we are examining into two parts, the "going" and the "striking" trains respectively. In both instances we proceed from the wheels attached to the barrels on which the gut lines are wound—the "great" or "main" wheels—to the "escape" wheel with its "anchor" in the going, and the "fly" wheel in the striking trains. The collection of wheels in each case is known as the "train." The two are connected—as the going has, obviously, to govern the function of the striking so that the clock will sound the hours at the proper times—in this instance when the minute hand points to the XII at each revolution. We are not concerned, at present, with half- and quarter-hour striking clocks, or with any other forms of striking mechanism than the simple hour-striking.

We have seen in Chapter II that the going train of a clock merely provides a set of wheels so geared that they will record, with the assistance of the dial and hands, the swings of the pendulum in terms of seconds, minutes, and hours. The power which keeps the pendulum at its work is obtained from the fall of the weight attached to the gut line which is wound round the barrel. In the earlier lantern clocks, as we shall see later, a cord is used instead of a gut line, which is pulled over a grooved wheel instead of being wound on a barrel. In both kinds the fall of the weight pulls the barrel or the wheel round in its descent, and thus supplies the motive power of the clock. The great- or main-wheel is attached to the barrel with a ratchet and check—or "click"—as indicated in Fig. 13, so that the barrel can be wound in the one direction only—the reverse way to which the wheel revolves when the clock is going. The motion is transmitted from the main- to the escape-wheels, with increased speed and concomitant lessening power.

It is obvious from the outset that if the escape-wheel were not checked in some way, the weight would fall as quickly as the combined retarding friction of all the wheels and pinions would allow. It is also obvious that the weight would gather power as it descended, and the fall would gradually get quicker and quicker. The escape-wheel is the one which is selected for the checking, as being the one which revolves the quickest and requiring, therefore, the least power. Without entering here into the various devices which have been adopted for this checking or "escapement," we will confine ourselves to the vertical escape-wheel and the "anchor" check, as shown in the illustrations.

We have now to seek for a starting point—an uniform movement, occupying a measurable division of time for its accomplishment. In this clock illustrated here there are four such points: the pendulum, which swings once in a second; the minute wheel, which revolves once in an hour; the hour wheel, which has a revolutionary period of 12 hours; and the "day-of-the-month" wheel, which has a period of 24 hours. We will select the pendulum as the most convenient starting point. The pendulum here is carried in a "crutch," which is attached to a horizontal "arbor" or rod. To this arbor is fixed the anchor, the pallets of which engage with the escape-wheel as the pendulum swings, two oscillations of the anchor—*i.e.* two seconds of time—releasing one tooth of the escape-wheel. In speaking of revolutions of clock wheels, we are only concerned with the number of teeth in each; the size of the wheel itself can be disregarded. The escape-wheel having 30 teeth, and each requiring two swings of the pendulum to release it, the wheel must make one revolution in 60 seconds. To a prolongation of the escape-wheel pinion, beyond the face of the dial, is attached the finger of the usual seconds' dial, each swing of the pendulum impelling it forward one space on the dial.

To the escape-wheel is attached a pinion of 6 "leaves," engaging with a wheel of 48 teeth, known as the "third" wheel. The time of revolution of the 6-leaf pinion—*i.e.* the escape-wheel—being one minute, that of the third wheel is in

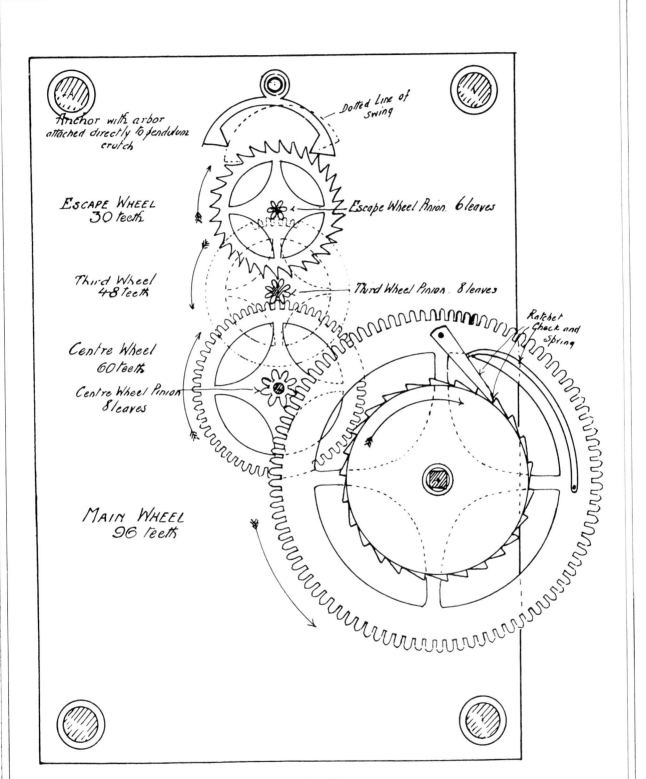

Fig. 13.

EIGHT-DAY, LOCKING-PLATE, STRIKING CLOCK.   GOING TRAIN.   (STRIKING TRAIN REMOVED.)   (ACTUAL SIZE.)

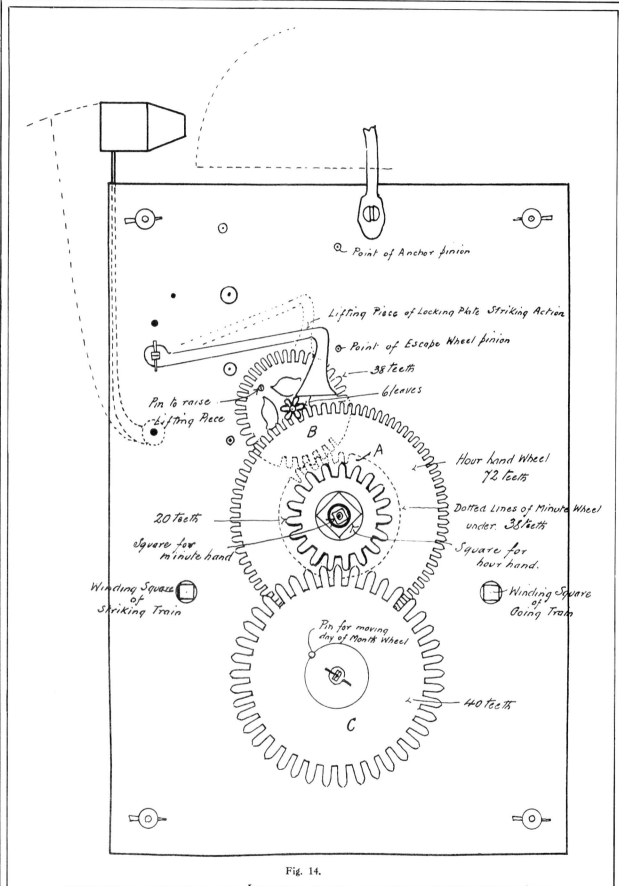

Point of Anchor pinion

Lifting Piece of Locking Plate Striking Action

Point of Escape Wheel pinion

38 teeth

6 leaves

Pin to raise Lifting Piece

B

A

Hour hand Wheel
72 teeth

20 teeth

Dotted Lines of Minute Wheel under. 38 teeth

Square for minute hand

Square for hour hand.

Winding Square of Striking Train

Winding Square of Going Train

Pin for moving day of Month Wheel

40 teeth

C

Fig. 14.

EIGHT-DAY, LOCKING-PLATE, STRIKING CLOCK. "MOTION WORK" UNDER DIAL.
(DIAL REMOVED.) (ACTUAL SIZE.)

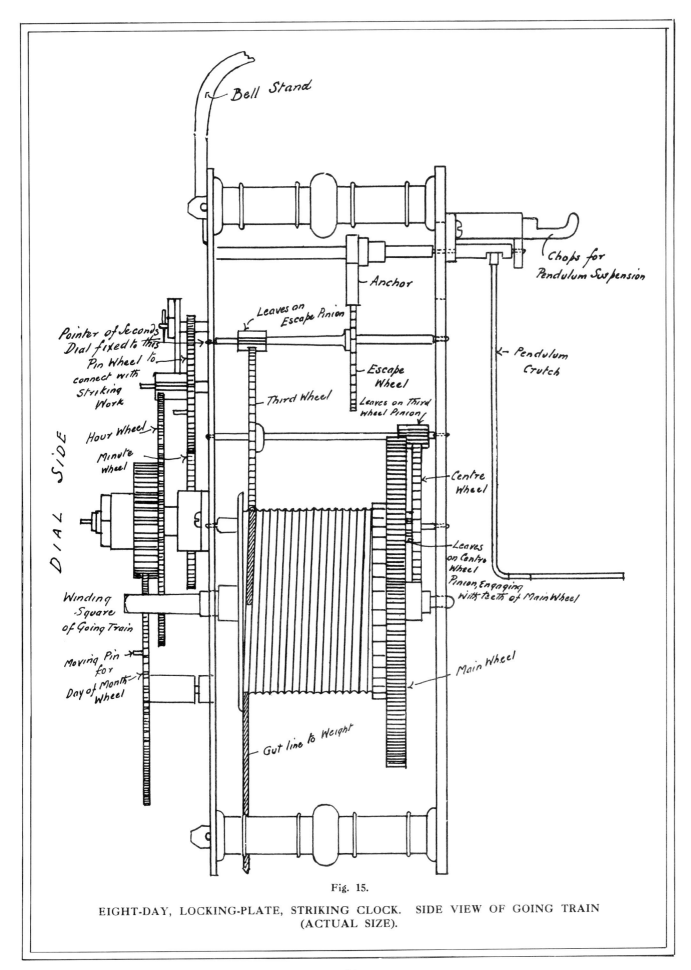

Bell Stand

Anchor

Chops for
Pendulum Suspension

Leaves on
Escape Pinion

Pointer of Seconds
Dial fixed to this
Pin Wheel to
connect with
Striking
Work

Escape
Wheel

Pendulum
Crutch

Leaves on Third
Wheel Pinion

DIAL SIDE

Third Wheel

Hour Wheel

Minute
Wheel

Centre
Wheel

Leaves
on Centre
Wheel
Pinion, Engaging
with teeth of Main Wheel

Winding
Square
of Going Train

Moving Pin
for
Day of Month
Wheel

Main Wheel

Gut line to Weight

Fig. 15.

EIGHT-DAY, LOCKING-PLATE, STRIKING CLOCK.   SIDE VIEW OF GOING TRAIN
(ACTUAL SIZE).

the proportion of 6 to 48, and is, therefore, eight minutes. The third wheel pinion has 8 leaves, engaging with a centre-wheel of 60 teeth; 60 is to 8 as $7\frac{1}{2}$ is to 1; the centre-wheel, therefore, makes one revolution in $8 \times 7\frac{1}{2} = 60$ minutes. It is obvious that this must be the wheel to which the minute hand of the clock is attached, which makes one revolution round the dial in an hour. Before, however, considering this centre-wheel further, we will trace the progression of wheels to its conclusion—the main-wheel. The centre-wheel has a pinion of 8, engaging with the main-wheel of 96; the latter, therefore, makes one revolution in 12 hours. Supposing that the barrel be wound with the gut line to its fullest capacity, and that the space for the fall of the weight be ample, the clock will go for a period of 12 hours multiplied by the number of complete turns of the gut line on the barrel. This latter is grooved to facilitate the even winding of the line, and, having 16 spiral grooves in its length, the clock will go, therefore, for 8 days of 24 hours each between windings.

We will now return to the centre or minute wheel, which is shown, taken through the plate, in Fig. 14, and indicated by the dotted lines in the centre, and also on the left-hand side of Fig. 15. The axis pin is prolonged through the barrel, or "pipe," of the hour wheel, and the minute hand is fixed to its square. In Fig. 14 the minute wheel A engages with another, B, both of 30 teeth, and therefore both with a time of rotation of one hour. This second wheel has a central pinion of 6, engaging with the hour-hand wheel of 72, the latter, consequently, making one revolution in 12 hours. To the square of this wheel's axis the hour hand is attached. Both hour and minute hand shafts or pipes are merely "friction-tight"—*i.e.* fitted over the arbors without fixing, so that while they are held securely enough to revolve with the wheels without slipping, the hands can be moved without turning the wheels of the clock. The hour-hand wheel has a smaller one fixed to its face, and having 20 teeth. This engages with the wheel C, of 40 teeth, which, therefore, rotates once in 24 hours. On the face of this wheel is a projecting pin which pushes forward the large day-of-the-month wheel behind the dial plate once in 24 hours. The numerals on this wheel are seen through the small square aperture under the hands on the usual grandfather-clock dial.

We have now considered the going train from the pendulum to the main-wheel, but before leaving this collection of wheels under the dial, technically known as the "motion-work," we have to examine how the going is connected with the striking train

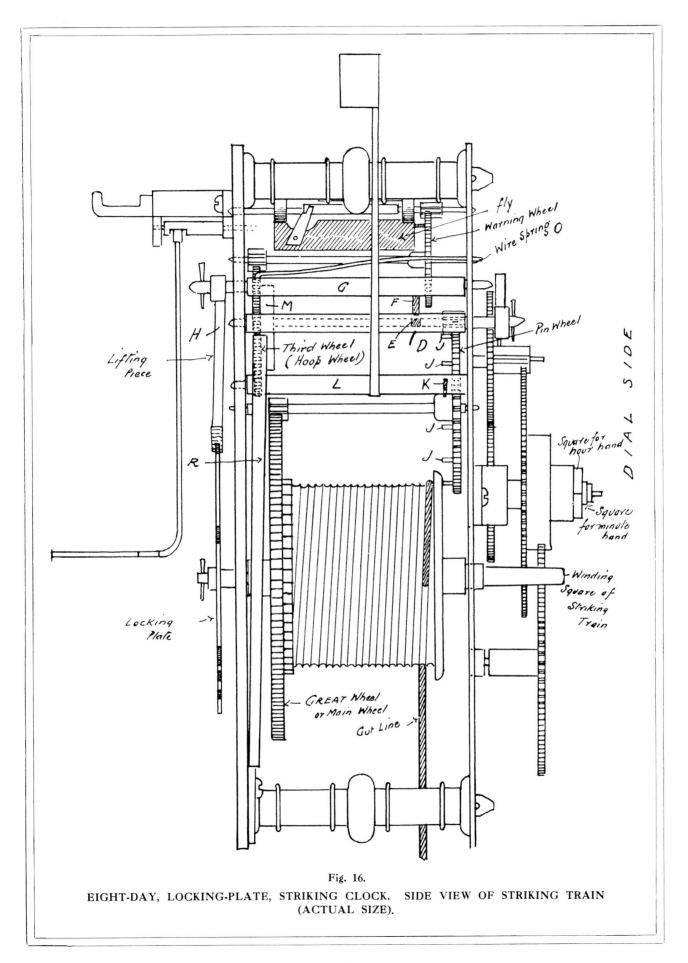

fly
Warning Wheel
Wire Spring O
G
M
F
H
Third Wheel
(Hoop Wheel)
E I D J
Pin Wheel
J
Lifting
Piece
L
K
J
Square for
hour hand
J
R
Square
for minute
hand
Winding
Square of
Striking
Train
Locking
Plate
GREAT Wheel
or Main Wheel
Gut Line
DIAL SIDE

Fig. 16.

EIGHT-DAY, LOCKING-PLATE, STRIKING CLOCK.   SIDE VIEW OF STRIKING TRAIN
(ACTUAL SIZE).

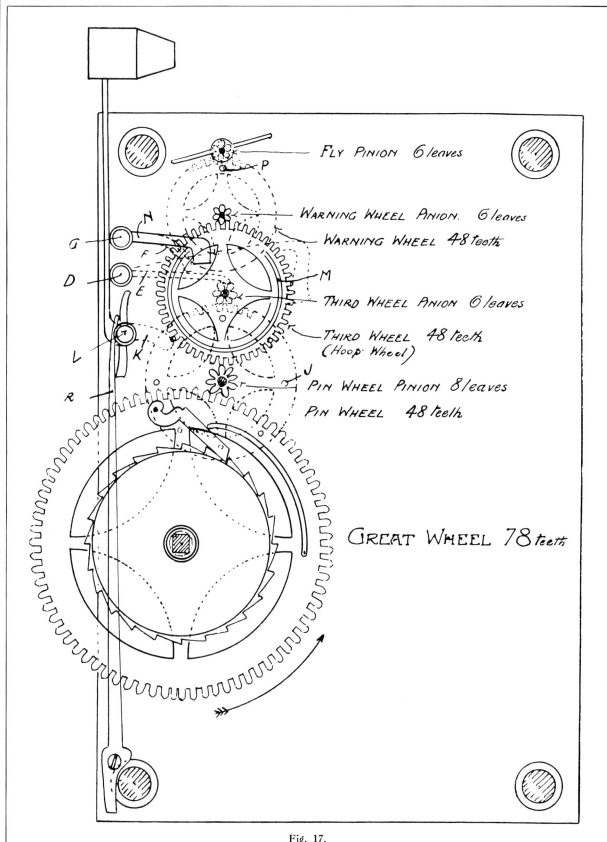

Fig. 17.

EIGHT-DAY, LOCKING-PLATE, STRIKING CLOCK. STRIKING TRAIN. (GOING TRAIN REMOVED.) (ACTUAL SIZE.)

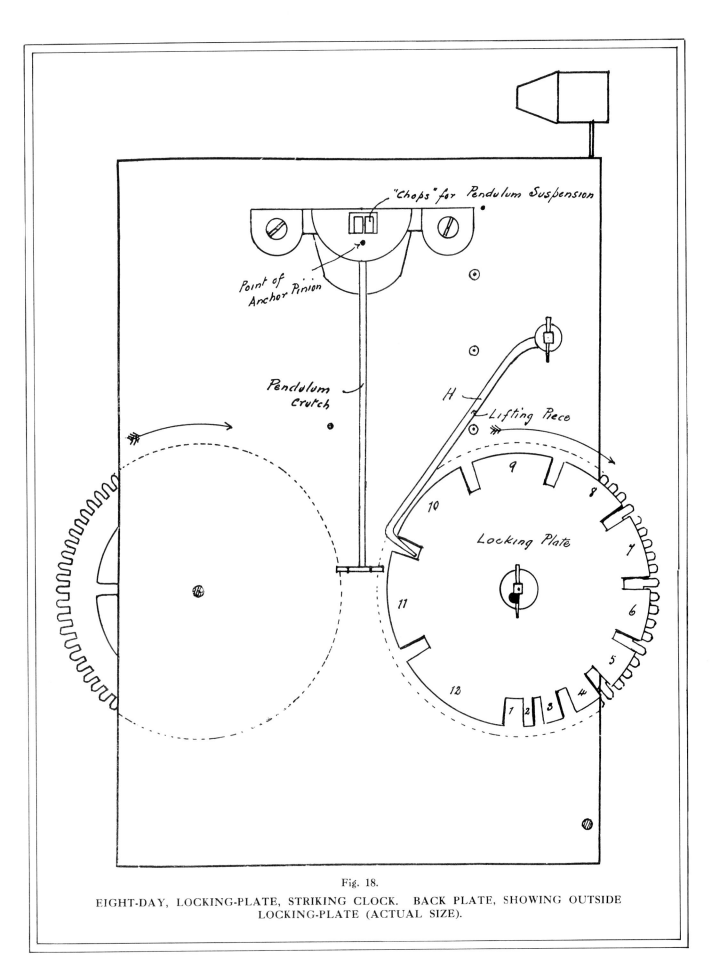

Fig. 18.

EIGHT-DAY, LOCKING-PLATE, STRIKING CLOCK. BACK PLATE, SHOWING OUTSIDE
LOCKING-PLATE (ACTUAL SIZE).

of the clock. Referring again to the wheel, B, Fig. 14, which makes one revolution in an hour, it will be observed that this has a projecting pin, in the same way as the day-of-the-month wheel, and this, once in every hour, raises the "lifting-piece" above. This lifting-piece is connected with an arbor, D, in Figs. 16 and 17. To this arbor is attached another lifting-piece, E, Figs. 16 and 17, on which another piece, F, Figs. 16 and 17, rests. When the lifting-piece on the outside is raised by the pin of the wheel, B, Fig. 14, that on the arbor, D, is raised in a corresponding degree, and, carrying the one F, resting on E, with it, causes the arbor above, C, to make a partial revolution. To this arbor, carried through the back plate, is attached the lifting-piece of the "locking-plate," H, in Figs. 16 and 18, which in turn is raised, thus releasing the locking-plate. The power stored in the great-wheel of the striking train is thus liberated, as the locking-plate is directly attached to the same arbor as the great-wheel, which is carried through the back plate as shown in Fig. 16. Returning now to the great-wheel of the striking train : this engages with the pinion of the pin-wheel, the latter making 39 revolutions to 4 of the great-wheel. Attached to the pin-wheel are 8 projecting pins, J, Figs. 16 and 17, which, each in turn, as the wheel revolves, raise the lifting-piece, K, Figs. 16 and 17, causing the arbor, L, to make a partial revolution. To this arbor is fixed the tail of the bell-hammer, which is raised until the pin on the wheel releases the lifting-piece on the arbor, L, when the hammer falls and strikes the bell. The spring, R, Figs. 16 and 17, is provided to secure the forcible return of the hammer when it is pushed outwards. The motion of the released great-wheel carries round the locking-plate with it until the next serration is reached, when the lifting-piece, H, drops into the notch next in order, and the striking ceases. The space between the notches in the locking-plate regulates the time taken in the striking, and the pins on the pin-wheel the number and the progression of the blows. The locking-plate in Fig. 18 is shown in the position for the next hour—eleven—to be struck.

The remainder of the striking mechanism has now to be explained. Let us consider this absent, for the moment, and the locking-plate in its position as illustrated, and see what would happen. The lifting-piece, H, being raised from its notch in the locking-plate, the full power of the weight on the great-wheel would be released, and as the tendency would be for it to gather power, the pin-wheel would be whirled round as fast as the friction would allow, and before the hammer had fallen on the bell the next pin would have arrived at its lifting position. The result would be that the clock would not strike at all. It is here that the remainder of the striking work comes into play. The next wheel, which corresponds to the third in the going train, is known as the "hoop-wheel," by reason of the brass "hoop" or band projecting from it, running round for about three-quarters of its circumference. This hoop is shown in profile in Fig. 16, and in lateral view in Fig. 17, and indicated by the letter M. Locking into the aperture in this hoop is the locking-piece, N, Fig. 17, which is acted upon by the wire spring, O, Fig. 16. While the outside locking-plate is travelling round from notch to notch, the lifting-piece, H, is temporarily raised, and, being on the same arbor as N, it lifts it in the same way. The pin-wheel having 8 pins and 48 teeth, and the pinion of the hoop-wheel having 6 leaves, the latter makes one complete revolution in the time taken for the one pin to engage the hammer-tail and the next to come round to the same position. The hoop-wheel therefore locks each stroke, by the piece N engaging with the hoop, and thus prevents the pin-wheel from gathering power. The "warning-wheel"—the next in order—is fitted with a pin, P, Fig. 17, which gives the "fly" a preliminary impetus as the clock begins to strike. The warning-wheel is usually adjusted so as to warn the hour one or two minutes before it is actually struck.

The striking work is now controlled by the hoop-wheel between each blow of the hammer, but a further regulation is necessary to prevent the train from gathering power during the time which the hammer takes to rise and fall. To this end the fly-wheel is provided, which acts as a governor, by the resistance which it offers to the air. For the purpose of making the fly effective, speed has to be gained so that power can be lost in the same ratio, so that the resistance of the air to the fly shall be adequate. Calculating the striking in the same way as we did with the going train, we will take the revolution of the great-wheel as 4, and, as we have seen, that of the pin-wheel, having 48 teeth, and engaging with the hoop-wheel pinion of 6, gives 312 for the latter. The 48 teeth of the hoop-wheel engage with the warn-wheel pinion of 8: $312 \times 8 = 2496$. The warn-wheel of 48 engages with the fly 6-pinion of 8; therefore 2496×8 gives a result of 19,968 revolutions of the fly- to 4 of the great-wheel, or 4992 to 1.

We can conclude by calculating the time through which the striking train will run without rewinding, in the same way as we did with the going train. The unit of measurement here in the pin-wheel, which being furnished with 8 pins makes one complete revolution in causing the hammer to strike eight blows. The bell is struck 156 times in the 24 hours; the pin-wheel revolves, therefore, $19\frac{1}{2}$ times in that period. The revolution of the great-wheel, as compared with that of the pin-wheel, is as 4 to 39; therefore as $39 : 4 : : 19\frac{1}{2} : 2$. The great-wheel consequently revolves twice in the 24 hours, and, having 16 grooves, the period corresponds with that of the main-wheel of the going train.

The striking movement we have been considering is that known as the "outside locking-plate" type. In another variety the locking-plate is placed on the great-wheel arbor between that wheel and the back plate. This is known as a "locking-plate on main-wheel." The locking-plate system is early, and was rarely used on high-class long-case clocks after about 1705. This is, however, an unsafe indication of date, as some makers were very conservative in their work. The locking-plate has the disadvantage of striking the hours in regular progression, irrespective of the position of the hands. If these, therefore, are turned round without allowing the clock to strike at each hour, the striking work is thrown out of gear, and the lifting-piece of the locking-plate has to be raised and the clock allowed to strike until the locking-plate agrees with the position of the hands. The later development is the "rack-striking" device, which we have now to consider. This, being regulated by the position of the hands, is a marked improvement on the locking-plate system, and was generally adopted for long-case clocks after about 1705.

Before leaving the explanation of the going train of an 8-day clock, it may be as well to explain that another wheel placed between the main and centre wheels, and geared as 1 to 4, will transform the 8-day into a month clock. The additional requisite power for the longer performance is, of course, understood. Eight-day clocks are said to have a "train of four" and month clocks a "train of five" wheels from main to escape. A year clock can be calculated in like manner.

Fig. 19 shows the motion-work of a rack-striking clock between the front plate and the dial, the latter being removed. To the disc of the hour-wheel a helical plate, or "snail" (Figs. 19 and 20, A), is fixed, which is slipped over the arbor and secured by the small screw as shown. The snail therefore revolves with the hour wheel and the hands, and in the position indicated in the illustration Fig. 20, the hands would point to twelve o'clock. The rack has an L-shaped piece or arm, C, fixed to it, and this has a pin, D, which comes into contact with the various faces of the snail in its revolution and regulates the distance to which the rack will fall when released. The rack, being pivoted at E, and the pin D coming into contact with the edge of the snail as the rack falls, it is obvious that the snail, in turning with the hour wheel from one o'clock to twelve, offers a gradually decreasing circumference to the pin D, thus allowing the arm C to rise on its pivot, and by so doing to throw the rack farther outwards as it falls. The rack is in the position as shown at twelve o'clock, when it has fallen ready for the striking, and in that indicated by the dotted lines at one o'clock. The wire spring, F, is provided to keep the pin of the rack against the snail, and to ensure the rack falling as soon as it is released.

As in the case of the locking-plate action previously described, in the rack-striking we have the power, put upon the train by the fall of the weight, held in check, and released only at each hour for the striking to take place. The knife-edged pinion, or gathering-pallet, H, being fixed to the arbor of the pallet-wheel, would turn with that wheel if it were not held in check by its "tail" being stopped by the rack-pin when the latter is up. This pin projects on the inside face of the rack, towards the back-plate. The rack-pin, holding the tail of the gathering-pallet, locks the whole striking train through the pallet-wheel until the fall of the rack releases the train. Above the rack, however, is the lifting-arm, G, the spear-point of which locks into the rack teeth and prevents it from falling. The illustration, Fig. 19, is really incorrect, as with the rack back on its pin, and the tail engaging with the edge of the snail, as shown, the lifting-piece, C, would be raised in the position indicated by the dotted lines.

Reverting now to the hour wheel: this engages with the pinion of the motion-wheel, the teeth of which, in turn, engage with those of the minute wheel in equal ratio, in the same way as with the locking-plate action, with the exception that the motion-wheel is there on the left, whereas here it is on the right. The motion-wheel is fitted with a pin, K, and, having a 60-minute revolution, once in every hour this comes into contact with the tail of the warning-piece, L, Figs. 19 and 20.

This warning-piece is taken through an aperture in the front plate at H, and when the pin, K, begins to lift it, the piece comes into the path of, and eventually into contact with, the pin of the warning-wheel, Fig. 20, N, and the recoil gives that wheel a slight impetus which is communicated to the fly, and the clock "warns" the hour. As the motion-wheel continues to revolve, the pin K, lifting the warning-piece L, raises the arm C with it, and lifts the point of the arm out of the teeth of the rack. The spring, F, pressing on the tail of the rack causes it to fall, and the tail of the gathering-pallet being released, the train is free. The rack falls as far back as the position of the snail, A, and the pin, D, in the rack-tail will allow, and in the striking, the pallet-wheel in its revolution takes the pallet, H, round with it, the knife-edge of which "gathers" up the teeth of the rack until the round of hours has been sounded. When the number of hours has been struck, and the motion-wheel is past the end of the

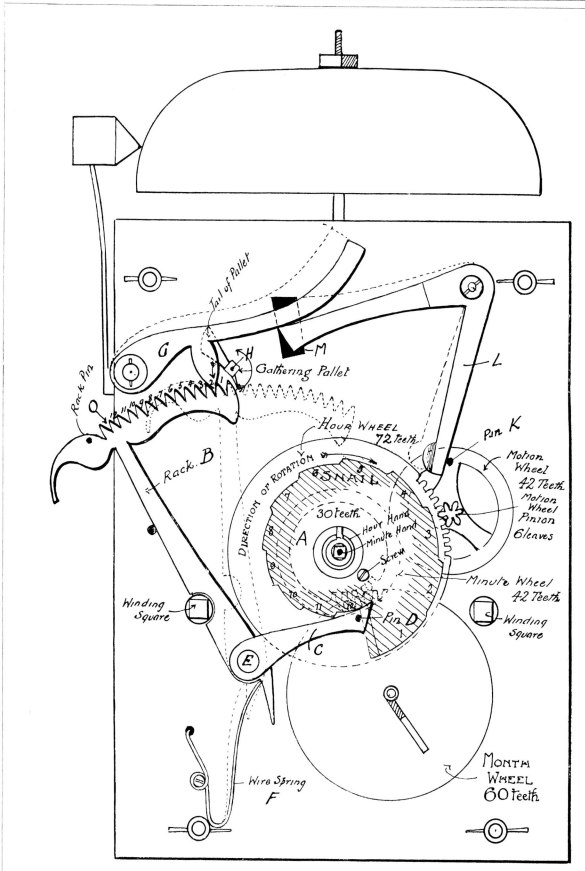

Fig. 19.

EIGHT-DAY, RACK-STRIKING CLOCK.   MOTION-WORK UNDER DIAL.   (DIAL REMOVED.)
(ACTUAL SIZE.)

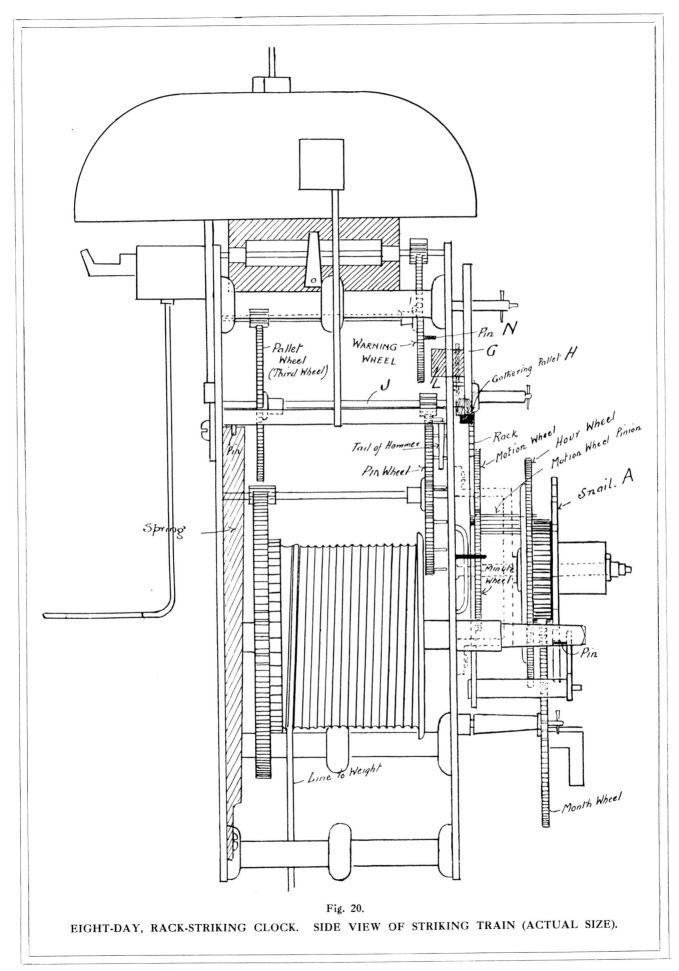

Fig. 20.

EIGHT-DAY, RACK-STRIKING CLOCK.   SIDE VIEW OF STRIKING TRAIN (ACTUAL SIZE).

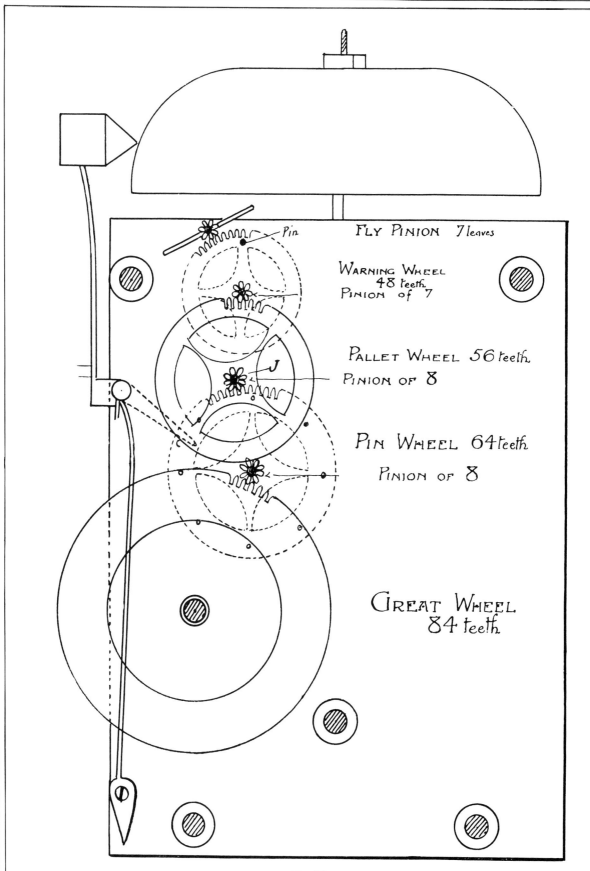

FLY PINION 7 leaves

WARNING WHEEL
48 teeth
PINION of 7

PALLET WHEEL 56 teeth
PINION OF 8

PIN WHEEL 64 teeth
PINION OF 8

GREAT WHEEL
84 teeth

Pin

J

Fig. 21.

EIGHT-DAY, RACK-STRIKING CLOCK. STRIKING TRAIN. (GOING TRAIN REMOVED.)
(ACTUAL SIZE.)

lifting-piece, L, the point of the arm, G, falls into the last notch of the rack at C. The gathering-pallet always begins at the extreme right-hand end of the rack at twelve o'clock, as indicated in the illustration. At eleven o'clock its position of rest is one notch farther in, and at one o'clock it is at rest in the notch numbered 11. For convenience of understanding, the hours have been numbered both on the rack and the snail. The train is shown in Fig. 21, and the side view with the position of the wheels and parts in Fig. 20. It will be noticed that the train is "planted" differently, and that the number of teeth and leaves vary, in comparison with the locking-plate striking action previously considered. There appears to have been no rule beyond that of relation of the wheels to the pinions, as defined in the previous chapter, for regulating the numbers of teeth and leaves. Frequently, with the same length of pendulum and the same train of four or five, as many as a dozen formulæ are possible. Certain of the proportions are necessarily fixed; thus with a seconds' pendulum the escape-wheel has always 30 teeth, and with a $1\frac{1}{4}$ second's length 24 teeth. The gearing in all clocks is also arranged to give the minute wheel a period of rotation of one hour, and the hour wheel a period of twelve times as much. Beyond this the relation of teeth to pinions depends a good deal on the original formula adopted, the size of the dial with the position of the seconds' dial, the winding squares (in other words, the centres of the escape- and main-wheels respectively), and perhaps the individual fancy of the maker of the clock. Generally speaking, a month clock has the winding holes lower in the dial than in the case of an 8-day, but even this has a good deal to do with the planting of the train.

Having now examined the movement of 8-day weight clocks in some detail, we can revert to the older form—the lantern clock—without needless explanation of details and technical terms which have already been fully described in the foregoing.

Fig. 22 shows the side view of a lantern clock with a verge escapement and a direct bob pendulum. As many modifications, in points of detail, are to be found in various specimens, especially during the seventeenth century, it is very unsafe to instance isolated features as evidences of early date. It may be stated as a general rule, however, that these brass lantern clocks have a duration of approximately 30 hours between each winding, and that the two trains are invariably planted the one behind the other—the going train in front and the striking train at the back. The only point of interest at present, for the purpose of completing this chapter and avoiding recapitulation of the previous subject-matter, is the duration of

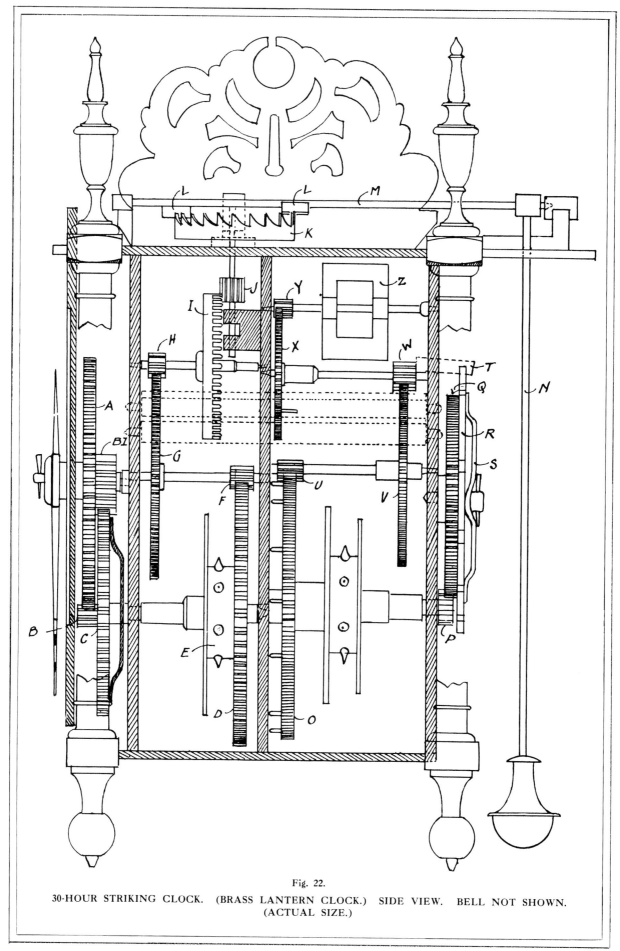

Fig. 22.

30-HOUR STRIKING CLOCK. (BRASS LANTERN CLOCK.) SIDE VIEW. BELL NOT SHOWN.
(ACTUAL SIZE.)

these lantern clocks between windings. We have already fully described an 8-day movement: it only remains to subject the lantern clock illustrated in Fig. 22 to a similar examination.

In the same way as was followed with the 8-day clock, with the 30-hour we have to find a fixed point—that is, a wheel the revolution of which occupies a measurable division of time—from which to make our calculations. In the case of the 8-day clock we had a pendulum with a swing of exactly one second as a starting point, but in the lantern clock this is absent, the pendulum being about a quarter the length of that of the 8-day. We have, therefore, to look elsewhere for our fixed unit. It is obvious that this is to be found in the wheel to which the hour hand is attached, Fig. 22 A, which revolves once round the dial in twelve hours. This wheel, in the example we are considering, has 60 teeth, and engages with a pinion of 15, B, which is directly attached to the arbor of the main-wheel, D. The clock illustrated here has been fitted, at a later date, with a minute hand, hence the wheel C attached to the pinion B, which engages with the small wheel B1, of 18 teeth, behind the hour wheel. The main-wheel makes one revolution in three hours (hour wheel of 60 engaging with pinion of 15; :60:15::12:3), and carries the wheel C, of 54 teeth, with it. This engages, in turn, with the minute wheel B1, of 18 teeth, which makes, therefore, one revolution in an hour. This minute-hand wheel has been shown here, although it is no part of the original clock, to illustrate an early example of dual-hand motion-work.

The duration of these lantern clocks depending entirely on the length of cord or chain attached to the weights —as compared with the later grooved barrels cut for a definite length of gut line—we can only make approximate calculations. The main-wheel, as we have seen, makes one revolution in three hours, and as the

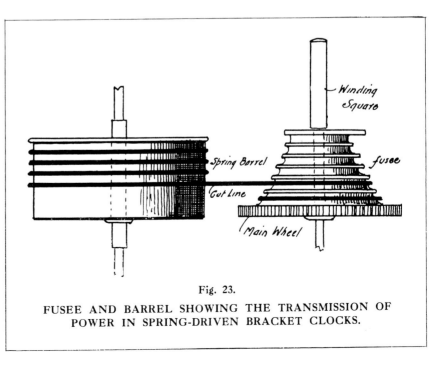

Fig. 23.

FUSEE AND BARREL SHOWING THE TRANSMISSION OF POWER IN SPRING-DRIVEN BRACKET CLOCKS.

net diameter of the grooved wheel, or drum, E, is $1\frac{1}{4}$ in., if we allow for a cord of $\frac{1}{4}$ in. in thickness, it requires a fall of about 5 in. of line for each 3 hours' going of the clock, or a total drop of 4 ft. 6 in. for the full run of 30 hours. The drum, E, is spiked, to hold the cord tight and to prevent it from slipping as the weight descends. Some makers used an open-linked chain in lieu of a plaited line, with a gain in strength but a loss in flexibility. In this case the spikes on the drum were spaced so that each engaged, in turn, with the links of the chain as the weight descended.

To calculate the train from the main-wheel to the escape, we have a former with 72 teeth and a 3-hour revolution, engaging with a centre-wheel pinion of 7, F, which gives $3\frac{3}{7}$ revolutions of the latter in one hour. The centre-wheel, G, has 64 teeth engaging with a contrate-wheel pinion of 6, H; $64 \times 3\frac{3}{7} \div 6 = 36\frac{4}{7}$, the number of revolutions of the contrate-wheel, I, in the same period. This latter has 48 teeth, and on the crown-wheel (escape) pinion there are 6 leaves; therefore $48 \times 36\frac{4}{7} \div 6 = 292\frac{4}{7}$. The crown-wheel consequently makes $292\frac{4}{7}$ revolutions in one hour, and, having 15 teeth, the pendulum—two swings of which free one tooth of the crown-wheel—makes $8777\frac{1}{7}$ oscillations per hour, or a fraction more than $2\frac{3}{7}$ oscillations per second. We have already seen that a pendulum of 39.1393 in. in length from the point of swing to its centre of gravity has a swing of exactly one second at the meridian of London. The pendulum of Fig. 22 has a *total* length of $7\frac{3}{8}$ in.; it is a nice calculation, from the figures of the train given above, to determine its exact length from swing-point to centre of gravity.

With the striking train of Fig. 22 it will be noticed that the pin-wheel and the great-wheel are one and the same, the pins, O, lifting the hammer-tail as the wheel revolves. R is the locking-plate, and from this we can make another calculation, in two ways. The locking-plate in one complete revolution takes the same time—or very nearly so—as the pins on the great-wheel take to lift the striking-hammer 78 times—*i.e.* the numbers from 1 to 12 added together. There are 12 pins on the great-wheel, and the revolutions of this to the locking-plate are, therefore, in the relation of 78 to 12, or 13 to 2. We can now examine how the gearing of the one wheel into the other verifies this calculation. The wheel attached to the locking-plate, Q, has 48 teeth, engaging with the pinion of 8, P, which gives a ratio of 6 to 1. The difference between this 6 to 1 and the former result of 13 to 2 is accounted for by the partial revolution of the great-wheel during the time that the lifting-piece is falling into the successive notches in the locking-plate.

The remaining lettered indications on Fig. 22 are as follow :—S is the spring which keeps the locking-plate in position, T is the lifting-piece in its notch, U and V are the wheel and pinion corresponding to those of the hoop-wheel in the 8-day clock, W and X those of the warn-wheel, and Y and Z the fly-wheel pinion and the fly respectively. The two transverse arbors carrying the lifting-pieces, the one from the motion-work on the left and the other for the locking-plate on the right, are indicated by dotted lines.

A comparison of this movement with those of the 8-day clocks previously illustrated will show how the two trains are connected so that the striking acts in unison with the going train.

So far, this chapter has been devoted solely to weight-driven clocks, which demand, as a necessary condition, an adequate space beneath the dial for the fall of the weights. The lantern is really the true bracket clock by reason of this fact, although the term has, through custom, been used to designate the spring-driven, small, wood-cased clock of the types with which we are all more or less familiar. It is obvious that the functions of the weight-driven and the spring clocks being identical, the principles involved must also be similar. There is one point, however, which merits description. The fall of a weight suspended from a line wound round a drum is more or less constant in quantity, hence the pull on the main-wheel of the long-case clock is about the same whether the clock be fully wound or nearly run down. With a spring coiled inside a barrel, the uncoiling of which supplies the motive-power to drive the clock, this is not the case ; the spring is more powerful when fully wound than when nearly exhausted. It is here where the system of the barrel and fusee comes into play. The principle involved can be readily understood from the following illustration ; if we take two drums fitted on to shafts or axles so that they will revolve, the one twelve inches in diameter and the other only three, and wind a line round each, it will be found that a greater pull will be required to unwind the line by pulling the drum round in the case of the smaller than in the larger one. It is on this principle that the barrel and fusee of the spring-driven bracket clock is constructed. The winding of the clock pulls a gut line—or in the later examples a fine-linked bicycle chain—from the barrel on to the spiral fusee. The winding begins from the large end and finishes on the smaller one. When the power of the clock is at its greatest—when fully wound

—the line has to be pulled from the smaller end of the fusee, but as the spring grows weaker the fusee offers an ever-increasing diameter to the lessening power, and so the rate of the going of the clock remains approximately uniform. An example of a barrel and fusee, looking down on the clock, is shown in Fig. 23.

The remaining points which demand consideration in the mechanism of clocks have already been referred to in Chapter III.

Chapter V

Brass Lantern or "Birdcage" Clocks

HE lantern or "Cromwellian" clock is the direct progenitor of the long-case on the one hand, and the bracket clock on the other. The latter term is a misnomer; it is the lantern which is the true bracket clock, as, whether standing on a bracket or spiked to a wall, an elevated position was demanded by the fall of the weights, and sometimes by the swing of a long pendulum, in contradistinction to the wood-cased, spring-driven clock, which is better described by the term "table clock" employed by Thomas Chippendale in the *Gentleman and Cabinetmakers' Director*.

It is a popular and erroneous idea that these brass lantern clocks are always of early date, and it is quite usual to find examples attributed to a period varying from one to two centuries before they were actually made, simply on account of the general style. It is true that the lantern is the earliest description of case which was made in England, but the manufacture was by no means confined to the seventeenth century, lantern clocks being produced, especially in country districts, until well into the nineteenth, until the era of machine production and Birmingham methods duplicated them wholesale to supply the growing demand in the antique market.

Even with the noted London makers of the later seventeenth century, the introduction of the wood-cased clock by no means ousted the brass case from popular favour, and it is not exceptional to find a lantern clock by a leading maker of later date than a long-case or wooden "table-clock" from the same hand.

As it would be out of place, in a book of this kind, to concern ourselves with forgeries and spurious examples of any kind, we can consider only genuine specimens of lantern clocks, although the term "genuine" cannot be held to imply that the clock is in the same state as it was in the original instance, when it left the maker's hands. The general convention is that the date of the pendulum, as applied to English domestic clocks, is approximately about 1660, and the honour of the innovation has been variously attributed to Richard Harris, Christian Huygens, Ahasuerus Fromanteel, or Robert Hooke. There is very little, if any, accurate data, however, regarding the actual introduction of the pendulum, as a controller of clocks, into

England. It is certain that its use was common in Germany and Italy at an earlier period of the seventeenth century than 1660.

It is sufficient for our purpose to assume an approximate date of 1660 for the introduction of the pendulum into England, and it is reasonable to assume, considering the greater accuracy of this form of control over that of the balance-wheel, that the latter was quickly superseded after the former became generally known. Evelyn the diarist records, in April 1661, the fact that he dined "with that great mathematician, Mr. Zulichem [Christian Huygens of Zulichem—a confusion of name and birthplace not uncommon with John Evelyn], the inventor of the pendule clock"; and from a later entry we can gather that these "pendule clocks" were a novelty at this date, and were exhibited at the shop of the elder Fromanteel —at this period the most renowned of London makers, being referred to by Evelyn as "our famous Fromanteel."

Taking the period of 1660 as a reasonably accurate one, we are justified in assuming that in the case of lantern clocks of earlier date which are fitted with pendulums, this control has been converted from the original balance escapement, and one would expect to find indications of this conversion. This is precisely what is apparent in every genuine lantern clock of date prior to 1660, the screw holes left by the removal of the cross-bar against which the balance-wheel strikes in its oscillation being usually left and a separate fixing provided for the supports of the pendulum arbor.

Lantern clocks differ so little the one from the other, excepting in such details as size, character of engraving, and the like, that a multiplicity of illustration would serve no useful purpose. The examples shown here have been chosen as strictly representative of the various patterns into which nearly all the genuine specimens which are encountered can be resolved. We are concerned only with lantern clocks from about 1600 up to the period when they were superseded either by the long-case or the "table" clock, which covers the first three-quarters of the seventeenth century. Earlier examples are too exceptional, and later ones merely repeat former characteristics, generally in a very depraved fashion. Certain rules may be stated regarding the period we have chosen here. The first is that these clocks are invariably one-handed, the minute hand, when it occurs, together with its "motion-work," being always a later addition. The second is that the two trains are invariably planted the one behind the other—the striking at the back—and

Fig. 24.

WM. PAYNE IN EAST SMITHFIELD.

30-hour, Brass Lantern Striking Clock.
Balance-wheel control.
Unique example.

$15\frac{1}{4}$ ins. high over all × $6\frac{1}{4}$ ins. wide
× $5\frac{3}{4}$ ins. deep.
1 in. hour circle.

Date 1618.

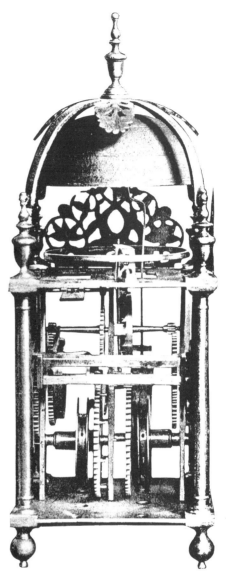

Side view showing the balance-wheel.

The balance wheel viewed from above.

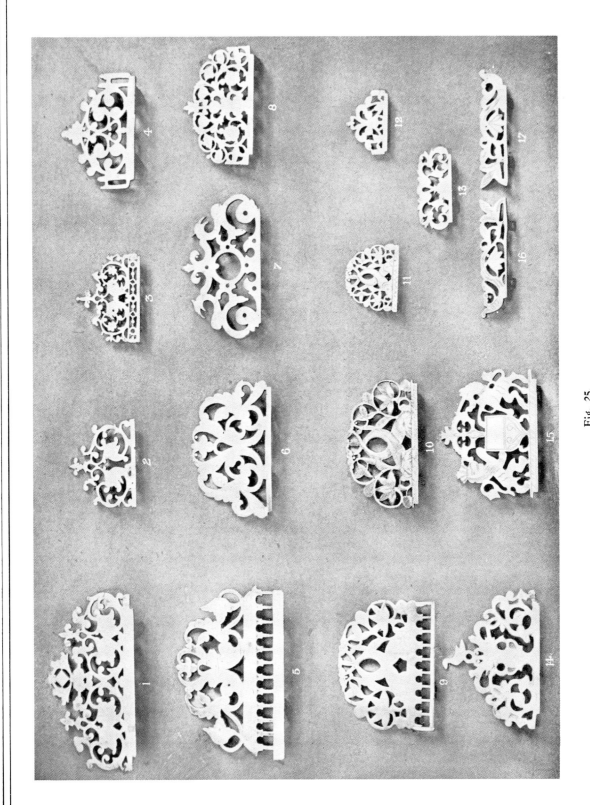

Fig. 25.

EXAMPLES OF FRETS OF BRASS LANTERN CLOCKS.

Fig. 27.

ANONYMOUS.

30-hour, Brass Lantern Striking
and Alaruming Clock.
Anchor pendulum, with curious
wings at side.
Alarum dial numbered 1 to 6 in
Roman and Arabic numerals,
7 to 12 in Roman only.

14 ins. high × 5 ins. wide × $5\frac{1}{2}$ ins.
deep.
Dial $6\frac{1}{8}$ ins. diameter.

Date about 1670.

Fig. 26.

ANONYMOUS.

30-hour, Brass Lantern Striking Clock
with Alarum.

$14\frac{1}{4}$ ins. high × $5\frac{1}{4}$ ins. wide × 5 ins. deep.

Date about 1630.

Fig. 28.

JOHN CRUCIFEX, LONDON.

30-hour, Brass Lantern Striking Clock.

$10\frac{1}{2}$ ins. high × 5 ins. wide × $4\frac{1}{2}$ ins. deep.

Date about 1680.

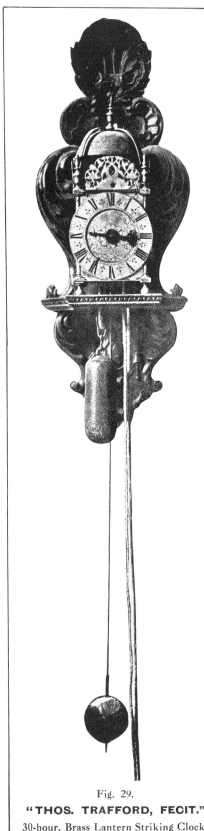

Fig. 29.

"THOS. TRAFFORD, FECIT."

30-hour, Brass Lantern Striking Clock.
15 ins. high × 5⅞ ins. wide (under hour-ring)
6 ins. deep.   1¼ in. hour circle.

Date about 1660-70.

are generally of 30-hour duration. The power is always gained from the fall of a weight suspended from a plaited line or an open-linked chain. It is hardly necessary to point out that a spring-driven lantern clock is a modern production.

The obvious superiority of the pendulum to the balance-wheel, admitting as it does of more or less accurate regulation, accounts for the fact that original balance-wheel clocks are exceedingly rare. Fig. 24 is one of these exceptional clocks, signed inside the hour-ring and dated 1618 on the movement. The whole is in original state, with the exception of the hour hand, which is of somewhat later form. The pattern of the frets is some indication of date, although not an invariable one, makers having their own predilections in this regard. In Fig. 25 a series of these frets is illustrated. Nos. 13 and 14 are always primitive, but the dolphin fret, No. 10, is also frequently found as early as 1610-20. The heraldic fret (No. 14) was, however, the favourite device at this period. The frets were frequently signed with the name or initials of the person for whom the clock was made, in the original instance. They were nearly always finely engraved, especially in the early examples. It would be useful if these patterns could be regarded as indications of period, but this is the fact only in a very general degree. Certain makers appear to have favoured particular types, but examples are too rare to enable a rule to be stated, especially as the style of these frets was probably dictated by a distinct trade, which produced and finished them for the leading clock-makers of the period. Some general fashions certainly did prevail at various dates, but the habit of the later copying of earlier forms has rendered these hopelessly confused at the present day.

The dolphin fret is the one which persisted for the greatest length of time, and is usually found on clocks from 1650 to 1670.

Fig. 26 is an early example of about 1630, shown by the very narrow hour-ring and the thick arrow-headed hand. The turning of the pillars and terminals is also typical of the Charles I. period. The lantern clocks of the first quarter of the seventeenth century were invariably clumsy in detail and proportions, the large bells flat and coarse in section. It is not until after about 1640 that the members of the columns and terminals began to be more refined.

Figs. 27 and 28 are curious: the first by reason of the side-wings or boxes, glazed on the fronts, inside which the anchor-shaped pendulum swings. The second has many of the characteristics of an early clock, in the pattern of the

Fig. 30.
ANONYMOUS.
30-hour, Brass Lantern Striking Clock.
15 ins. high × 5¾ ins. wide × 5¾ ins. deep.
Width across hour-ring 6¼ ins.
Circle 1⅚ in. wide.
Date about 1630.

Fig. 31.
ANONYMOUS.
30-hour, Brass Lantern Striking Clock.
15 ins. high × 5⅝ ins. wide × 5⅝ ins. deep.
1 5/16 in. circle. 6⅛ ins. across hour-ring.
Date about 1640.

Fig. 23.
ANONYMOUS.
30-hour, Brass Lantern Striking and
Alaruming Clock.

15½ ins. high × 5¾ ins. wide × 5¾ ins. deep.
7 ins. wide over hour-ring. 1¾ in. circle.

Date about 1650-60.

frets and the turning of the pillars. The minute hand, with its motion-work, is here original, the date of the clock being approximately about 1680.

The usual position for these lantern clocks was on a wooden bracket, holes being cut in the shelf for the weight cords and pendulum. The long, or "royal," pendulum is in itself, however, a late device, although older than the anchor escapement which permitted of the enclosure of these long pendulums in the narrow cases of the long clocks of a later period. Fig. 29 is a lantern clock on its bracket, of approximately the date of the Great Fire of London.

Fig. 30 is a lantern clock of about 1630, with the hour-ring very narrow, and the hand thick and clumsy, arrow-headed, and with the usual spiked tang projecting beyond the collet. Both in this and Fig. 31, a somewhat later specimen, the dolphin fret has been adopted. The latter exhibits evident signs of its conversion from the original balance escapement, the recoil spikes being left in the top plate, and the "pottons" being pierced for the vertical pinion of the balance-wheel. Fig. 32 has a curious form of recoil escapement, and a long pendulum. The case is spiked behind, for attaching to a wall without a supporting bracket. The signing of clocks was not a general practice at this date, and it was not until the Clockmakers' Company became firmly established that it became more or less obligatory.

Figs. 33 and 34 are two views of an elaborate chiming lantern clock, of unusually early date. These clocks are exceedingly rare before about 1670, and the signing of the case and the elaborate engraving of the dial show the importance of this specimen at the time it was made. Inside the hour-ring are three skeletons, the one in the centre standing on a coffin, those on the sides holding hour glasses; a somewhat macabre reminder of the flight of time. Above, and on either side of the central skeleton, is inscribed " Nobilem ex Rustico distingue," " Talis eram qualis es," and " Talis eris qualis sum." The side view of the striking work shows how the hammers are actuated. The weights are supported on chains in lieu of the usual cords.

It was remarked, at the outset of this chapter, that these brass lantern clocks were nearly always of 30-hour duration. That

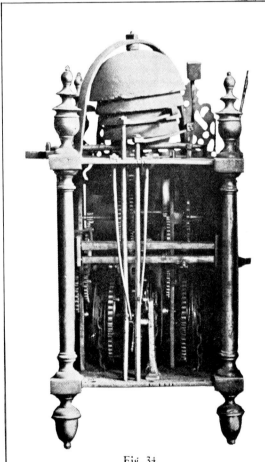

Fig. 34.

The side view of Fig. 33, with door, fret, and large bell removed to show the striking work.

Fig. 33.

DAN^l. HOSKINS, LONDON (?).

Brass Lantern, 30-hour, Striking and Chiming Clock. Chiming on four small bells and striking on one large bell.

16 ins. high × 6¼ ins. wide × 6 ins. deep. Hour-ring 1¼ in. wide. Centre engraved with three skeletons. Centre standing in a coffin, on sides with hour-glasses. Inscribed " Nobilem ex Rustico distingue,"
" Talis eram qualis es,"
" Talis eris qualis sum."

Date about 1630.

Front view.

Side view showing the engraving of side door.

Fig. 35.

"EDUARDUS EAST, LONDINI, FECIT."

Eight-day Miniature Striking Lantern Clock.
Finely engraved brass and water-gilt case.
Chased frets.   Unique specimen.
Direct crown-wheel pendulum.

8 ins. high over all × 3⅗ ins. wide × 3½ ins. deep.

Date about 1660.

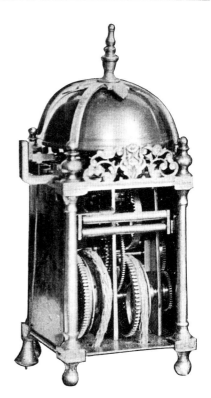

Side view with door removed showing the eight-day work.

this was not the invariable custom is shown by the beautiful little miniature clock illustrated in Fig. 35. The side view shows the train of four of the 8-day clock. The case is finely engraved on three sides, and water-gilt. The pendulum is of the short bob type, and the clock was evidently intended to be supported by the

Fig. 36.

THOMAS WHEELER,

Near yᵉ French Church.

30-hour, Brass Lantern Striking Clock.

In the possession of Percival Griffiths, Esq.
Height 17½ inches.

Date about 1675.

Fig. 37.

NATHˡ. HODGES, LONDON.

30-hour, Brass Lantern Striking Clock.

1 ft. 2¾ ins. high.
9 in. dial.

Date about 1675.

Fig. 38.

JOHN BOWYER, LONDINI, FECIT.

Brass Lantern, 30-hour, Striking and Musical Clock,
playing on ten bells from barrel.

15¼ ins. high × 6 ins. wide × 6¼ ins. deep.

Hour circle 1⅛ in. wide.

Finely engraved frets.

Date about 1685.

Fig. 39.

Side view of Fig. 38, with side door and fret removed to
show the musical work.

L-piece behind, shown in the side view. The exceptional character of this unique specimen is probably responsible for the unusual pattern of the frets. The hand is curiously simple for this comparatively late date and the elaborate case of the clock, although there are evidences beyond that of the 8-day movement to show that this is not an early specimen of Edward East's work. It has been specifically made for the crown-wheel escapement; in fact, the whole clock is as nearly as possible in its original condition.

Figs. 36 and 37 are of the date of the long-case clock, although both are one-handed, Fig. 37 having been converted, and the winding-square holes pierced in the dial at a comparatively recent date. Late lantern clocks are generally ungainly in size, with the turning of the pillars and terminals very roughly cut.

Figs. 38 and 39 are two views of a brass lantern clock fitted with a striking and musical work, the latter actuated by a spiked drum directly attached to the main-wheel. The clock has three weights, the musical work being separately driven, the drum having a species of locking-plate attached to it, equally divided into twelve divisions, so that the musical work is set into operation at each hour. The minute hand is here also a subsequent addition, in spite of the late date of the clock itself. There is no doubt that even at the close of the seventeenth and well into the eighteenth centuries some fashion dictated that two-handed movements should be reserved for wood-cased clocks.

Further consideration of these brass lantern clocks would merely resolve itself into a repetition of examples. There are very few important details which vary, and after the long-case clock became firmly established in popular favour, the lantern declined in a corresponding degree. Sufficient has been indicated here to show the general character of the earlier examples; in fact, these could be accurately described as true bracket clocks, in contradistinction to those after 1700, which merely repeat the older forms with later anachronisms super-added.

Chapter VI

The Development of Long-case Clock Dials

T is an unquestionable fact that the trade of the clockmaker was ruled, in a very arbitrary way, by the dictates of fashion. This is especially the case during the earlier periods, when the Clock-makers' Company was a powerful and autocratic guild. The forming of a craft into a species of "close preserve" has the inevitable tendency of confining production within narrow limits and of fostering the growth of fashions, which act as restrictions on spontaneity or originality of form. The purpose of the clock itself, as a recorder of time, being paramount to all other considerations, would also tend to fetter the artistic licence of the clockmaker, as compared with the trade of the joiner, for instance, where purpose, although important, was not pre-eminent. Thus in London, where the influence of the Clockmakers' Company was the more direct and effective, we find certain fashions followed very closely; it is only in the smaller country districts where they are disregarded. In the former case we find the 10-, the 11-, and the 12-inch square dials following each other in fairly orderly progression, as far as long-case clocks of the usual type were concerned. To these, again, succeed the various forms of the arch-top, until towards the end of the eighteenth century types tend to become depraved, and definite fashions dissipated in conse-quence.

In addition to sizes, we have also fashions in the embellishment of dials, as in corner-pieces, hands, patterns of winding holes, and the like, and a similar evolution with regard to the cases of these long clocks also takes place. Generally speaking, these various phases indicate earlier or later dates for the clocks them-selves, but it is very unwise to accept the evidence of any single detail, unless supported by that of others. With the exceptions to be hereafter specified, it is advisable to assign a period to a long-case clock *by the date of the latest character-istic which it exhibits.* The same also applies, in somewhat more general fashion, to the earlier bracket clocks, although the latter, as a rule, are marked by greater freedom in their development, as compared with the long-case variety.

Some qualification of the above is obviously necessary in the case of a clock where the component parts are actually of different dates. Thus, a replaced corner-piece of a late fashion must not be taken as an indication of a similarly late period for the clock itself. The same applies, with equal force, to the hour and minute hands, which were always liable to break, from rust or ill-usage, and to be replaced by others of a subsequent type. It must also be remembered that it has only been during the last twenty years that these masterpieces of the art of old clockmakers have been greatly esteemed and cherished; they were frequently relegated to lumber-rooms during the Victorian era, to moulder or rust, the cases broken up, and the movements sold as scrap-metal. With such barbarism, it is a matter for wonder that so many examples have survived to the present day as to render the adequate illustration of a book such as this a possibility.

The dials of long-case clocks up to about 1760 are reliable indications of the dates of the clocks themselves, if all the various details are considered in relation. The movements will usually supply the necessary corroborative evidence, if such be necessary. Isolated points, however, are unreliable, as, apart from the possibility of later additions—which should always be expected—in details such as the patterns of corner-pieces, hands, ringing of winding holes, engraving of dial plates, and the like, the individual fancy of the maker of the clock has always to be reckoned with. These details will be more fully considered in the subsequent chapters, on the development of hands and corner-pieces. Bracket clocks can also be disregarded, for the moment, as these are always more sporadic in character, their smaller size, and consequent greater portability rendering the question of the suitability of design to purpose one of lesser importance than in the case of the long-case clock.

So far, no reference has been made to the evidence afforded by the cases of these " grandfather " clocks. We enter here on a matter requiring the nicest discrimination and judgment, combined with a practical knowledge of the technical side of the trades of the cabinetmaker and the marqueterie cutter. The subject of these cases will be considered, at greater length, at a subsequent stage, but the difficulties of the problem can be briefly indicated here. In the first place, it is more than doubtful whether any of these long cases were made under the direct superintendence of the clockmaker, as a general rule. This applies, with especial force, to the early square-dial clocks with seconds' pendulums. The size of the dial being known—say, 12 in. × 12 in., for example—the length of the pendulum, and therefore the position of the lenticular glazed aperture in the lower door to show the pendulum-bob in its swing, being fixed, no further measurements were required. When the arch dial came into vogue, the matter was somewhat more complicated, by the height of the arch of the dial-top and the fact that dials were sometimes irregular in size ; but even here we have no authentic evidence to show that the case was made to fit the clock, instead of the reverse process. If, as was exceedingly probable, the earlier cases were ordered from Holland—and the evidences for this will be adduced later on — individual fancy must have played a greater part than the arbitrary dictates of fashion, as far as the clockmaker was concerned, although we may transfer the influence of the latter from the maker of the clock to that of the case itself.

Granting all these problems successfully solved, we have another, and a still more formidable difficulty to surmount : we have no reliable evidence, especially with the square-dial clocks, to show that the clock is in its original case. Dials were nearly always signed, and later additions can usually be detected on careful examination, but we have no signature on the cases to guide us. Thus clocks in two 12-inch cases, for example, can be transposed without the slightest incongruity being apparent, as a general rule, and although one cannot anticipate a subsequent fashion, there is nothing to prevent a reversion to an earlier type. Charming as many of the early simple panelled cases were, such as Fig. 90, in the opinion of many they would not bear comparison with those elaborately inlaid with gaudy marqueterie. Given a fine clock, such as the Tompion here referred to, in a simple black panelled case, and another of inferior merit, but in a fine marqueterie case, there is every probability that the clocks might be changed, and the value of the Tompion thereby enhanced, in the eyes of the greater majority of collectors. The question of actual forgeries is beyond the scope of this book, otherwise the possibility of cases made up from various parts of several specimens would also have to be considered. The only safety from this apparently inextricable confusion consists in the changes in the sizes and shapes of dials at the various periods rendering the cases of the earlier type unsuited to contain the clocks of a later period, and in the fact that the amount of time and labour lavished on these early cases, as compared with the market value of the clock in its case, renders the making of forgeries a very dubious speculation. Considering the question in its entirety, however, there is no doubt that the dials of "grandfather" clocks, for many reasons, are much more reliable criteria than the cases in which they are contained, and it is now proposed to trace the former, in orderly progression, from the earliest types until the close of the eighteenth century, after which defined fashions, which have guided us hitherto, may be said to disappear, or to become so diffuse as to render them unreliable indications of date. In almost every instance London-made clocks have been selected for illustration, and nearly each type has a tendency to radiate into others which would occupy too much space to show here. The important characteristics will be pointed out as they occur, together with their relation the one to the other.

Fig. 40 is, perhaps, the earliest known type of long-case dial. The hour circle is exceedingly narrow, the Roman numerals small and squat, the minute divisions on the extreme outer edge of the hour-ring with Arabic numbers inside the circle—a usual indication of an early clock—and the dial centre very closely "matted." The spandrel corners are engraved instead of having brass corner-pieces attached, and although the movement is an 8-day, with the barrels cut for gut, Edward East had already applied the extra 8-day wheel to a lantern clock of an earlier date than this example, as we have seen in the previous chapter. The maker's name is signed on the bottom of the dial, and in Latin, "Eduardus East, Londini." The word "fecit" was frequently added. The winding holes are quite plain, and the squares are nearly flush with the face of the plate, an indication that a "bolt-and-shutter" maintaining power has not been originally fitted to the clock and afterwards removed. The maintaining power, of which the bolt-and-shutter type is the earliest known variety, is an instance of the pride which the early makers took in the accuracy of the clocks which they made. The device is shown in Fig. 43, where it will be noticed that the winding holes are closed by shutters. It is obvious that the power which drives the clock being derived from the fall of a weight, this power is temporarily removed while the clock is being wound, the weight being then supported by the winding-key. The action of winding, therefore, in the ordinary way, would cause the clock to stop, or in the case of a very accurate movement, to "trip," or go backwards. It is here where the "bolt-and-shutter" maintaining power comes into play. To open the winding holes it is necessary to move the shutters, by the depressing of a lever or the pulling of a string—according to the device adopted—and this action puts a spring on the going train, of power sufficient to drive it in lieu of the weight while the latter is inoperative during the process of winding. The left-hand shutter, on the striking side, is not really necessary, being added merely for symmetry. When the winding is accomplished, and the key removed, the swing of the pendulum gradually closes the shutters again, and the spring having exhausted its power, the weight resumes its function. The whole operation usually persists from two to three minutes, the shutters closing automatically.

To conclude with Fig. 40: it will be noticed that there is no seconds' dial or aperture for the usual "day-of-the-month" wheel, and that the hands

Fig. 40.
1665.

Fig. 41.
1670.

Fig. 42.
1675.

Fig. 43.
1680.

TYPES OF LONG-CASE CLOCK DIALS.

are almost of the late lantern-clock type. In Fig. 41 the hour circle is broader, the spandrels ornamented with cherub-headed corners, and the centre of the dial is engraved. The name, Thomas Tompion, is shown on the engraved scroll between the winding holes. The hands are of similar form to those on Fig. 40, the hour hand of the double-loop form, the minute hand slender and joining to the collet with a simple scroll. In the development of clock hands it is always the hour hand which is first elaborated, the simple minute hand persisting until about 1695, after which the scrolling is ornamented to accord with its more ornate fellow.

Fig. 42 is an early type, indicated by the square-top bell and the aperture for the day-of-the-month wheel above, instead of below, the hands. The cherub-corners are simple (which is not an infallible sign of an early dial), and are also finely chased and gilded—a much more reliable indication. The hands are a development from the late lantern-clock style, and are elaborately filed up, or "carved" as it is termed. The hour circle has broadened, but the engraved minute divisions are still on the outer edge.

Fig. 43 has the Tompion cherub-headed corner, the head in high relief and the butt of the wings scrolling down to the edge of the hour circle. The name, "Thomas Tompion, Londini," is engraved on the bottom edge of the dial plate, in the same position as in Fig. 40, the hour circle is narrow, with the minute divisions on the outer edge. At a superficial glance Fig. 43 might be referred to an earlier date than Fig. 42, but the presence of the "bolt-and-shutter" maintaining power, the elaborate piercing of the hour hand, and the seconds' dial are later signs. The seconds' dial, however, is of a very early type, with an engraved ring outside in addition to the seconds' divisions on the inside. The Arabic numerals are kept very small in consequence, and this feature, together with the unusual size of the circle of the small dial, are characteristic only of the very early clocks. The engraving of the numerals on the month wheel, as in Figs. 41 and 43, is also of early character.

Fig. 44 illustrates the next development. The corner-pieces are of later type— which are no reliable indications of date—although, taken in conjunction with the broader hour circle, the cramped Roman numerals, and especially the ringed winding holes, these suggest a later date than the Tompion dial. The hour hand is still plain in character, the minute hand simply scrolled, and the centre of the dial plate carefully matted. The absence of a seconds' dial is here no indication, as the train was not always calculated for a pendulum of sufficient length, owing to the small size of some of these cases. The month aperture is quite plain, and the whole style of the dial

Fig. 44.
1685.

Fig. 45.
1690.

Fig. 46.
1690–95.

Fig. 47.
1695.

TYPES OF LONG-CASE CLOCK DIALS.

Fig. 48.
1695–1700.

Fig. 49.
1695–1700.

Fig. 50.
1700–5.

Fig. 51.
1705–10.

TYPES OF LONG-CASE CLOCK DIALS.

Fig. 52.
1710.

Fig. 53.
1710–15.

Fig. 54.
1720–5.

Fig. 55.
1725–30.

TYPES OF LONG-CASE CLOCK DIALS.

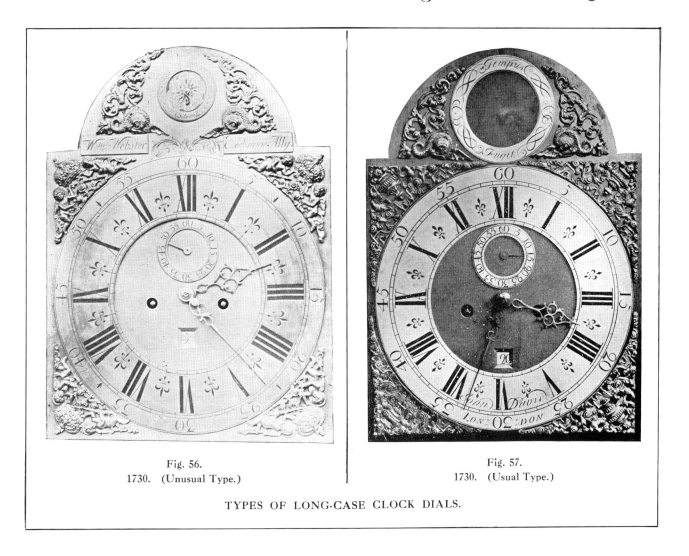

Fig. 56.
1730. (Unusual Type.)

Fig. 57.
1730. (Usual Type.)

TYPES OF LONG-CASE CLOCK DIALS.

exceedingly simple and refined.   It is very exceptional to find the "bolt-and-shutter" maintaining power fitted to a dial with ringed winding holes as in this example.   In dials of early form, where the winding squares are set back from the inside face of the dial plate, it is usually found, on examination of the movement, that the original shutters have been removed (probably by ignorant clock jobbers, in the process of cleaning), together with the maintaining power.

Fig. 45, although possessing the same pattern of corner-piece as on Fig. 44, is of a later type.   The dial is larger—11 inches square instead of 9 or 10—the hour-ring is broader, with a more florid style of engraving, particularly in the half-hour divisions, and the name is engraved on the circle between the V and VII.   The winding holes are ringed and the day-of-the-month aperture engraved.   The hour hand is of the broad spade pattern, and the scroll finish to the minute hand is larger and more ornate.   The seconds' dial has large Arabic numerals and a ringed centre.   The

Fig. 58.
1730–5.

Fig. 59.
1735.

TYPES OF LONG-CASE CLOCK DIALS.

minute divisions are still on the outer edge of the hour circle, but they are deeper, in proportion with the greater width of the ring.

From 1690 to about 1705 a fashion appears to have set in for the elaborate engraving of clock dials. The practice was rarely carried to such excess as in Fig. 46, where nearly the whole of the exposed face of the dial is covered with scrolled ornamentation. This dial is from a country-made clock, which may account for the unusual amount of the engraving, especially round the winding holes—which were nearly always ringed at this date, probably as some protection against scratching the dial face with the key—the name on the engraved valance above the day-of-the-month aperture, the crudely finished corner-pieces, and the clumsy style of the hands. As an example, however, showing to what extent this fashion of engraving dials was carried, Fig. 46 is useful.

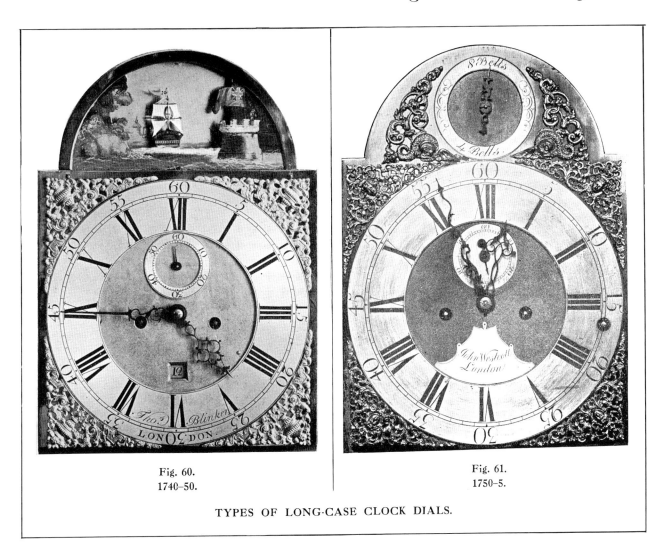

Fig. 60.
1740–50.

Fig. 61.
1750–5.

TYPES OF LONG-CASE CLOCK DIALS.

Fig. 47 marks the next departure, the minute divisions being set in from the outer edge of the hour circle, with a separate ring outside for the Arabic numerals. This fashion had already been foreshadowed, as it were, in the minute-numbered dials, which were sometimes made by fine early makers such as Christopher Gould and Joseph Knibb, where the separate numbering of each minute from 1 to 60 necessitated this outer ring with the minute division set inside. In Fig. 47 the space between each corner-piece, on the outer edge of the dial, and the day-of-the-month aperture are all engraved, and the same fashion has been followed with the dial centre, which is ornamented with a Tudor rose in imitation of the older form of lantern clock with central alarum disc. The hour hand is broad, well pierced, and carved, and of a pattern very much favoured by Dan Quare. It is curious to note the attention which was paid to trifling details in these early clocks. The general form of the hands was dictated by the idea of making the one as different as possible, in general appearance, from the other. The steel hands did not stand out prominently against the background of silvered ring and brass centre, and this dissimilarity was very necessary to facilitate instant recognition. With the later form of enamelled dial, this precaution became no longer so urgent, and both hour and minute hands were then made after the same pattern, the one merely a smaller edition of the other. With the early clocks, however, this fastidiousness was carried still further; the minute hand was made of just sufficient length to trench on the minute divisions when these were on the outer edge—as in Fig. 45—and when these were set in from the edge of the dial, the hand was made correspondingly shorter, as in Fig. 47. If Figs. 45 and 47 were of the same size across the circle, the minute hand of the former would appear too long if fixed to the latter. For the purpose of observing the progress of the slower moving hand, the hour divisions on the inside of the ring were also divided into four—the half-hours by an engraved device—and this fashion persisted, without exception, until about 1735–40, after which date these hour divisions were usually omitted. It is hardly necessary to point out that an hour circle, with the four subdivisions on the inside and no minutes on the outer edge, was originally made for a clock with an hour hand only, and probably as a wall clock, to stand on a bracket. One continually meets with these specimens, however, engraved with makers' names from obscure country villages—which have been since fitted with a minute hand and a grandfather case, so that this caution may not be quite unnecessary. These clocks are usually of the "pull-up," 30-hour type, with grooved wheels for rope instead of barrels cut for gut. Masquerading as long-case clocks, they should deceive no one with the slightest knowledge.

Figs. 48 and 49 show the fashions of 1695–1700. The dials are larger, the hour hands more ornate, and there is a growing tendency to make the outer ring for the Arabic numerals on the hour circle larger and the minute divisions less significant. This tendency is shown, in a further stage, in Figs. 50 and 51. At this date the name of the maker is nearly always found engraved between the V and the VII on the hour circle. In Figs. 48, 49, and 50 the corner-pieces are of almost identical pattern, but in Fig. 51 we get the crown surmounted by a Maltese cross and flanked by winged boys, an indication that the first decade of the eighteenth century has been reached. Another indication is in the corner-piece being kept small to allow of the engraved band round the edge of the dial plate. It is not the fact, as has been suggested, that this band of engraving was required to fill the space left by using an 11-inch circle and corners on a 21-inch dial, as the Maltese crosses on the corners project right over this engraved band, and with an 11-inch dial would hang over the edges. In the last phase of the square dial, Figs. 52

and 53, the outer ring with the Arabic numerals has become so large as to permit of the name being engraved between the 35 and the 25, instead of between the Roman VII and V. The hour hand, having reached its maximum size by about the end of the seventeenth century, begins now to decline and become smaller. The fashion of engraving the centre of the dial also begins to disappear, as in Fig. 53. The two favourite patterns of corner-pieces of the period will be noticed in Figs. 52 and 53.

The arch-top appears to have superseded the square form of dial as early as 1720-5, but intact specimens of this date are very rare. The fashion had, however, already set in at this period, although the usual custom appears to have been to take the former square dials and to add separate arched tops to them. Fig. 54 is one of these composite dials where the arch and the corner-pieces are nearly twenty-five years later in character than the other parts of the dial. The original bolt-and-shutter maintaining power has been preserved—a rare feature with arch-dial clocks—and there are two apertures, above and below the hands, for the day of the week and the month respectively. It will be noticed, as showing the early character of this example, that the minute divisions are on the outer edge of the hour circle, and the hands are of the type of 1695-1700.

Fig. 55 is a complete and very early arched dial. It is unusual in having no day-of-the-month aperture, although in the later forms, after 1750, the day was often indicated by a finger on a subsidiary dial in the arch, sometimes in conjunction with "moon-work." Fig. 55 has a similar boss in the arch, engraved with the name of the maker, as in Fig. 54.

Fig. 56 is of unusual type, the arch being added, and the join covered by two plates of brass engraved with the maker's name. The case of this clock is one of the very rare examples which were made in England and sent to China to be lacquered, and the lapse of time involved—probably as much as ten years— for the journey out and home, and for the work to be executed, may account for the mixture of characteristics of several periods in the dial.

It will be noticed that in these early arched dials the arch is usually very low, being considerably less than half a circle. Fig. 57 is a good type of about 1730. The arch has a subsidiary dial, serving no purpose, being merely engraved with the words "Tempus Fugit." The inside of the hour-ring has still the quarter divisions as in the earlier clocks. The name is engraved on the circle between the VII and the V. Fig. 58 is very similar in character, but the hands are later;

Fig. 62.
1760   (Earlier Type.)

Fig. 63.
1760-5.

TYPES OF LONG-CASE CLOCK DIALS.

and at this date it became the fashion for the maker to engrave his name on a separate oval of brass attached to the dial centre below the hands. This is missing in Fig. 58, but is shown in the next example. In the arch of Fig. 59 is a subsidiary dial curiously engraved in two circles, the outer one divided into 36 divisions, from 1 to 12 repeated three times and marked in Roman figures, and the inner into 30 spaces. numbered from 1 to 29½—the age of the lunar month. The hand, carrying with it the blue and white disc on which the moon and sky are depicted, shows the age of the moon in the aperture, the days of its age on the inner circle, and the hour at which this is taken on the outer. Thus the reading is at one o'clock on the twelfth and twenty-seventh day of the lunar month. The position of the moon on the former of these days and hours is that shown in the illustration. The day of the calendar month is shown, in the usual way, in the aperture below the oval disc on which the maker's name is engraved.

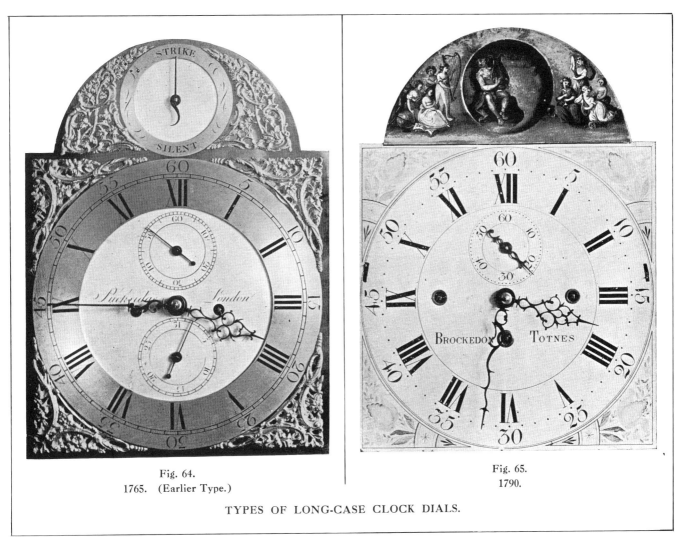

Fig. 64.
1765. (Earlier Type.)

Fig. 65.
1790.

TYPES OF LONG-CASE CLOCK DIALS.

A familiar device, rare in London clocks but frequently met with in those of provincial origin, after 1745, was a moving figure in the arch, attached to the pendulum arbor and oscillating with it. Fig. 60 has a rigged ship, giving the illusion of approaching a castle which it never reaches. It will be noticed that the hour divisions on the inside of the circle have disappeared. The flamboyant minute hand of Fig. 61 indicates the middle of the eighteenth century, and is usually associated with the pattern of the hour hand shown here. Fig. 62 has the silvered dial which came into vogue shortly after 1750, although the minute hand is of earlier type. In this and the next example two pictorial treatments used in the decoration of these arches are illustrated. Fig. 63 has the characteristic hands of the period. The silvered hour-ring on a matted brass ground was seldom used at this period, excepting for chiming clocks or others with elaborate movements. Fig. 64 is a typical dial of the middle Chippendale period, nearly always associated with oak cases veneered with finely-figured curl

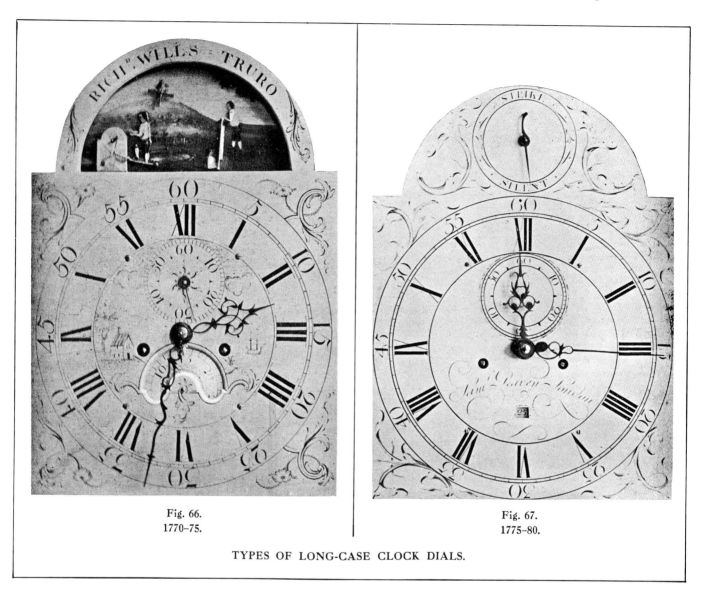

Fig. 66.
1770–75.

Fig. 67.
1775–80.

TYPES OF LONG-CASE CLOCK DIALS.

mahogany. Fig. 65 is the country type of appropriate period, allowing the usual margin of twenty years for provincial rendering of London fashions. It is painted white, with the hour-ring and seconds' dial quite flat, and edged with black lines. Figs. 66 and 67 are also the provincial and London renderings of the popular fashions, although, after about 1770, any defined vogue which had formerly existed in the decoration of clock dials tends to disappear. Fig. 68 is a nineteenth-century dial showing the persistence of earlier features, although the pattern of the corner-pieces indicates a very late date. The engraving of the dial centre is also of equally late character.

Figs. 69, 70, and 71 are regulator dials, and consequently occupy a class apart from the others which we have hitherto considered. Regulator clocks, being made more for use in clockmaker's shops than in private houses, do not follow any

Fig. 68.
1800-5. (Showing persistence of early character.)

Fig. 69.
Type of Regulator Dial of 1800–5.

Fig. 70.
Regulator Dial of 1810–15.

Fig. 71.
Regulator Dial of 1820–30.

defined fashions in their development. The cases also were frequently of a rough and unfinished character, although the clocks, being especially constructed for exact timekeeping, are usually of the highest class. This especially applies to clocks of the type of Fig. 71, although even these circular-dial regulator clocks are often found in cases which, while of simple form, are frequently veneered with the choicest mahogany—an illustration of the pride which was taken by the leading clockmakers in their work from the latter part of the seventeenth century until the mid-Victorian era. The former careful attention was no longer paid to trifling details; thus the two hands of Fig. 70 resemble each other so closely in general form that it is easily possible to mistake the one for the other. The former high standard of workmanship, however, had not entirely departed by the end of the first quarter of the nineteenth century, although the number of high-class makers had become greatly diminished, and the general level of the trade had fallen to a very low ebb. Generally speaking, the "Golden Age" of English clockmaking may be said to extend from 1670 to 1770—a century full of fine traditions, when high-class workmanship was the rule and shoddy the exception. The years from 1770 to 1810, and from 1865 to the present day, have witnessed a gradual reversal of these conditions, and in these days of machinery and com-mercialism, practically all the individuality has departed from a trade which formerly occupied an unequalled position in the history of English handicrafts. It is curious, and inexplicable, that the years from 1810 to 1865 should have witnessed a revival of the former high traditions, but such is the case. It is rare to find a clock of the early and mid-Victorian epoch of poor quality. The general style, both of case and dial, was usually distinguished by a lack of taste, but the same may be said of nearly everything else which was produced at this date.

Chapter VII

The Development of Clock Hands

E have seen, in previous chapters, that the trade of the clock-maker was governed, in a very marked way, by the fashions of various periods. Clock hands form no exception to the rule, but there are certain factors governing these which are absent in the remaining parts of a clock. Until almost the close of the eighteenth century, when clock hands began to be stamped out from thin steel, the usual way was to file up from the rough metal. This circumstance obviously favoured variation in a marked degree; it was easier to depart from a given pattern than to adhere closely to it. Again, it is the rule of all trade fashions that the craft has to develop to a considerable extent before it becomes influential enough to create a fashion of any kind for itself. Thus with the early lantern clocks; while the general form of the square brass case surmounted by the large bell becomes a fixed type at a very early period, details such as the turning of pillars and spires or the design of the hand is usually very sporadic. Generally speaking, however, lantern-clock hands can be resolved into four types which follow each other in more or less regular progression. These are (1) the arrow-head, (2) the spear, (3) the open loop, and (4) the spade hand. Examples of the first are shown in Plate I, No. 1, of the second in Nos. 2, 3, 4, and 5, of the third in No. 8, and of the fourth, in various stages of development, in Nos. 6, 7, 9, 10, 11, and 12. Nos. 13, 14, and 15 show the evolution into later forms, which persist, in country districts, until nearly the close of the eighteenth century.

With the introduction of the long-case clock and the seconds' pendulum, the early type of hand was nearly always a development of the spade form, or rather of the double loop shown in Nos. 7, 9, 10, 11, and 12 of Plate I. In Plates II and III, Nos. 1 to 10 are early hands from 1670 to about 1690, all taken from high-grade clocks with narrow hour circles, and with minutes engraved on the extreme edge of the ring. Nos. 11, 12, and 13 are 1690–1700 types of the pierced spade hand, usually filed up in relief or "carved," to use the general term. No. 14 is exceptional, the boss of the hour hand enlarged and beautifully pierced and carved. This boss revolves with the hour hand. A pair of hands such as this would probably represent three to four weeks' work, and would be used only on a clock

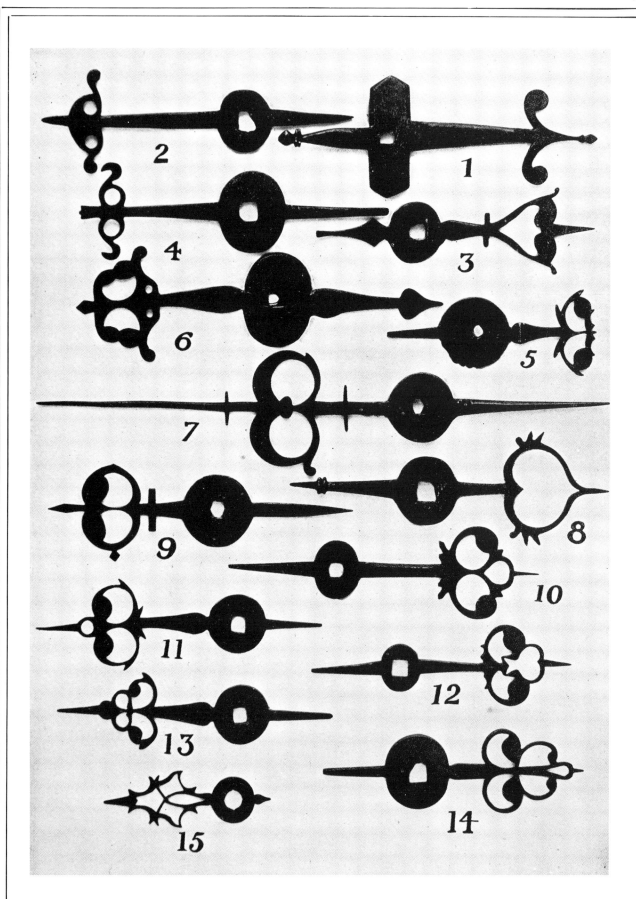

PLATE I.—LANTERN CLOCK HANDS.

84

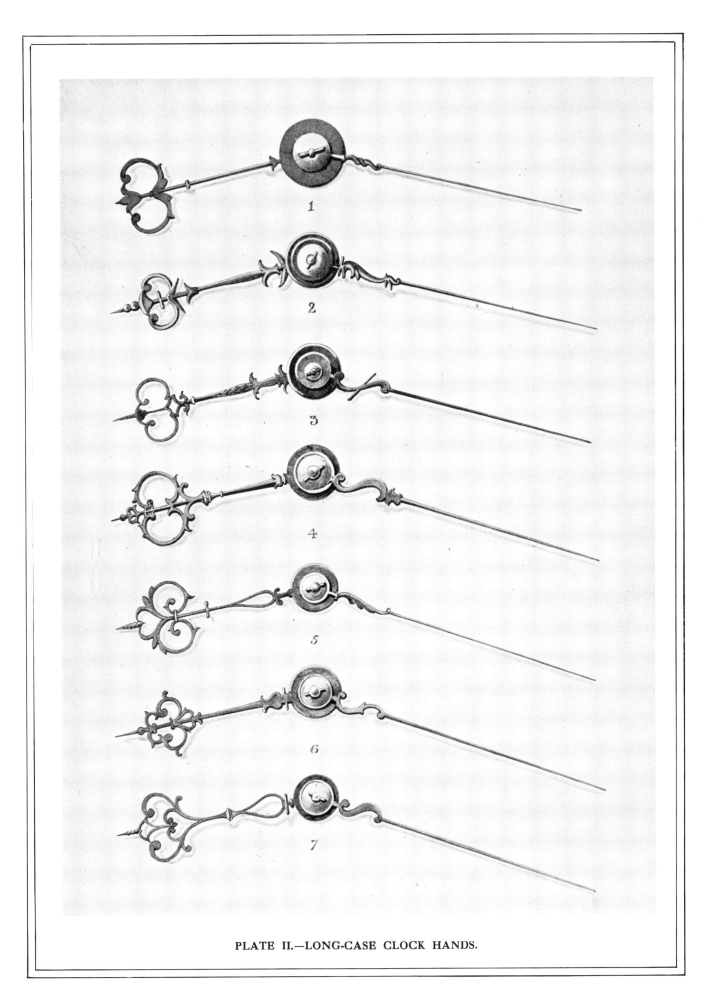

PLATE II.—LONG-CASE CLOCK HANDS.

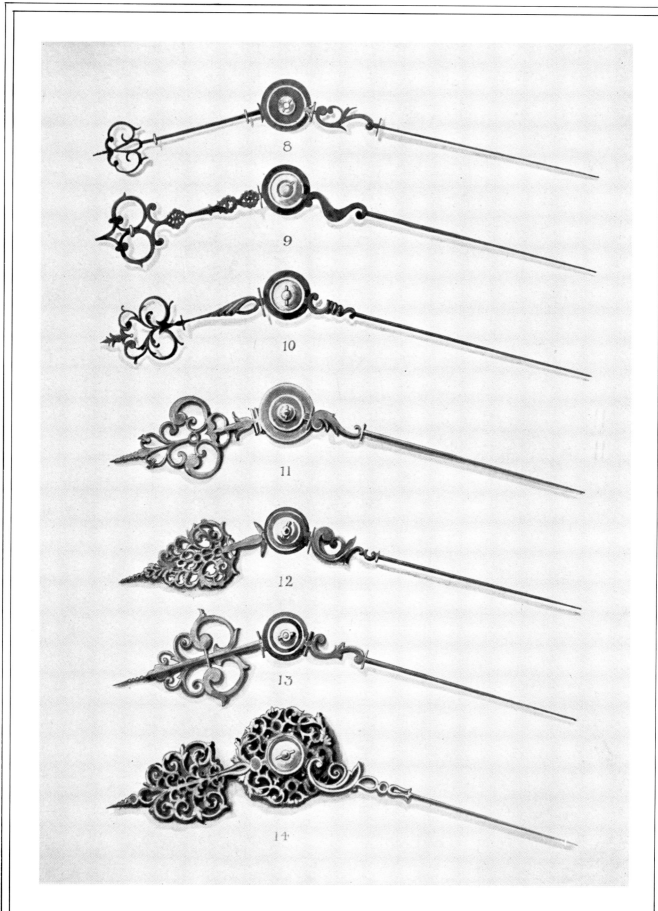

PLATE III.—LONG-CASE CLOCK HANDS.

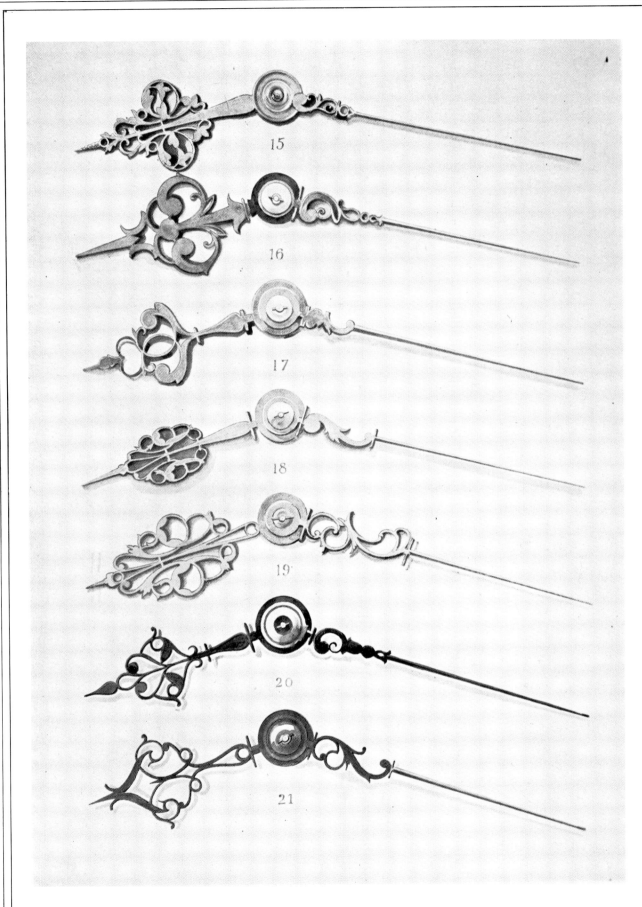

PLATE IV.—LONG-CASE CLOCK HANDS.

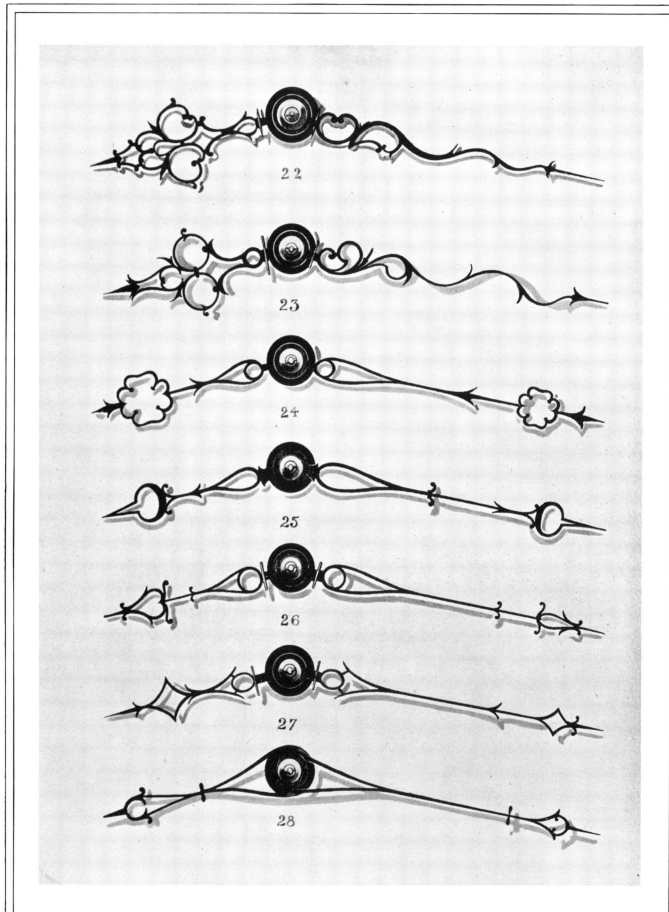

PLATE V.—LONG-CASE CLOCK HANDS.

of the finest quality. Nos. 15 to 19, Plate IV, are good examples of the hands of the later type of square dial, and Nos. 20 and 21 of the earlier kind of arch. Nos. 22 and 23, Plate V, date from 1750 to 1760, and No. 24 is some fifteen years later in character. Nos. 25 to 28 are from silvered arch dials, and were used from about 1790 until the middle of the nineteenth century.

It will be noticed that the marked distinction between the hour and the minute hands tends to disappear as they develop—or degenerate. In the earlier clocks the hour-ring was always divided on the inside into four subdivisions of the hour, and the point of the large hand just entrenched on this circle. The minute hand reached to the outside of the dial ring in the very early kinds, where the minute divisions were engraved on the extreme outer edge, and when these minute spaces were set inside, with a separate circle for the Arabic numerals, the minute hand was correspondingly shortened. With a good clock, in original condition, this detail should persist until the close of the eighteenth century, but clock hands, from their delicate nature, were exceedingly liable to breakage, either from careless usage or from rust, and when replaced by others, this detail was frequently overlooked.

The design of clock hands varying almost with each clock, and certainly with each maker, to attempt to give even a representative selection is almost hopeless within the compass of a book such as this. The examples shown here are instructive, however, in one particular: they show the relating design of the minute to the hour hand. The former, being the one used to alter the position of the hands, was necessarily most prone to breakage, apart from its more fragile character, and in replacing, it was not unusual to fix another of a different period to its fellow. Thus the flamboyant minute hand of Nos. 22 and 23, or the open loop of Nos. 24 to 28 would be entirely out of character if paired with hour hands of the earlier types, although it is not exceptional to find clocks which here suffered this indignity at the hands of uncultured "restorers." As a general rule, the circumstances governing the regulation of long-case clock hands apply also to bracket clocks, with such modifications as the smaller size of the latter would facilitate.

Chapter VIII

The Development of the Spandrel-corners of Clock Dials

HE brass spandrel-corners of long-case clock dials are frequently cited as significant indications of the date of the clocks themselves, and this evidence is, in some measure, reliable, but is subject to certain reservations. These corner-pieces differ, in their nature, from any other part of the clock, in the sense that, although the finishing of chasing and gilding is the work of the craftsman's own hand, the original design was governed by the patterns of the moulds from which they were cast. There is no question that with these brass spandrel-corners we enter the domain of another trade than that of the clockmaker—namely, that of the brassfinisher. Clock hands, for instance, had to be elaborately filed out from a piece of steel, with little or no preliminary patterns, certainly none which would tend, in any degree, to fetter the design. The result is, that although the devices adopted resemble each other to a certain degree, no two pairs of hands are ever exactly alike, unless the one has been deliberately copied from the other. This absence of exact correspondence is so general, that when two pairs of hands are of exactly the same design, the one is almost always a later copy. With the brass corner-pieces the circumstances are the exact opposite of those regulating the patterns of clock hands. The same mould being used over and over again, and four times for the one dial, the one design inevitably tends to become stereotyped. There is no doubt that these corner-pieces, in the rough state, were held in stock by the brassfinishers of the eighteenth century in considerable quantities, and the custom was, in all probability, for country makers to lay in a supply when in London. That the makers of corner-pieces were comparatively few in number is suggested by the small variety of the patterns which are found on clock dials during the eighteenth century, and the fact that these designs are usually the same on London or provincial-made clocks. For the same reason we can infer that these corner-pieces were made, as a general rule, in London or the immediate vicinity. Some slight distinction must be made, however, between those spandrel-pieces which were cast direct from the original mould, and those which were duplicated from pre-existing specimens. It is generally known that moulds taken from finished castings always lose something of the original model, especially if this be badly finished. The loss intensifies with

succeeding duplications—mould from casting and casting from mould, and so on in regular progression. It is this feature, in particular, which ear-marks many of the country-made clocks of the latter half of the eighteenth century; the corner-pieces are obviously taken from others of earlier types rather than from the original moulds.

With a centralised sphere of manufacture for these corner-pieces, the tendency would obviously be for each particular clockmaker to select those patterns which pleased his own taste, without regard to fashions of the moment. He would also regulate the time spent upon the chasing and the expense of gilding or lacquering by the value set upon the clock they were intended to adorn, and by the elasticity of his conscience as a tradesman. Such fashions as existed would be regulated more by the brassworker than by the clockmaker. The principal factor which would tend to effect a change in this regard, and to necessitate the making of new moulds or patterns, would be a change in the size of the clock-dials or a modification of shape, such as from the square to the arch form. The very earliest type of long-case clock dials—which are exceedingly rare, and of which one example is illustrated in the chapter on the development of clock-dials—have the spandrels of the dial-plate engraved in lieu of attached corner-pieces, but as early as 1670 the trade of the brassfinisher had become an adjunct to that of the clockmaker.

It will readily be understood that the conditions under which these corner-pieces were made would tend to restrict the number of patterns. The forty-five examples shown here are the result of a collection of years, and although there are one or two designs not included, it is surprising how complete the collection really is. Some hundreds of clocks passed in review will be found to nearly all have one or the other of the patterns illustrated here fixed to the dials. Had each clockmaker, however, possessed his own stock of patterns, which were used only on his own clocks, there is no doubt that ten times the number of the examples shown here would have been inadequate.

It will be seen, from the foregoing, that the design of a corner-piece is necessarily a doubtful indication of the date of a clock, excepting in a general way. There are several other factors which have also to be mentioned. The corner-pieces, being generally fixed with a small screw or rivet, were liable to work loose, and to fall off and be lost. In such cases, if the original pattern were not available, the only course was to remove the other three, and to replace

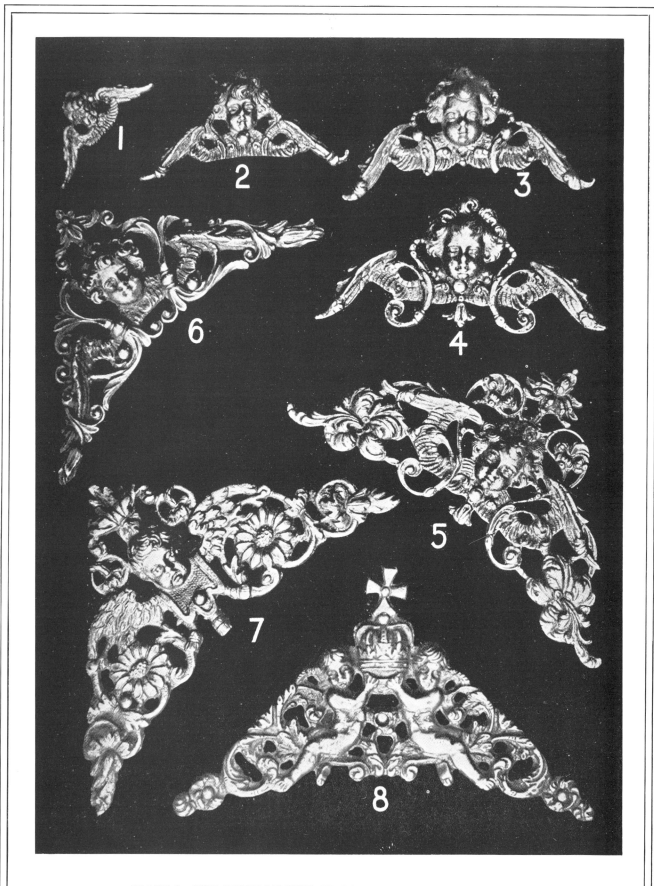

PLATE I.—THE DEVELOPMENT OF LONG-CASE CLOCK CORNERS.

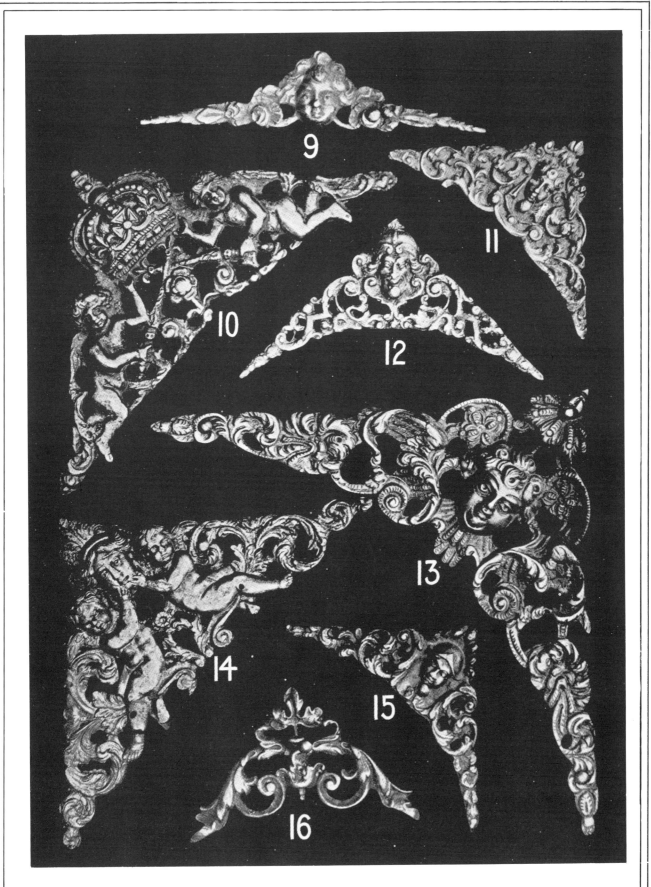

PLATE III.—THE DEVELOPMENT OF LONG-CASE CLOCK CORNERS.

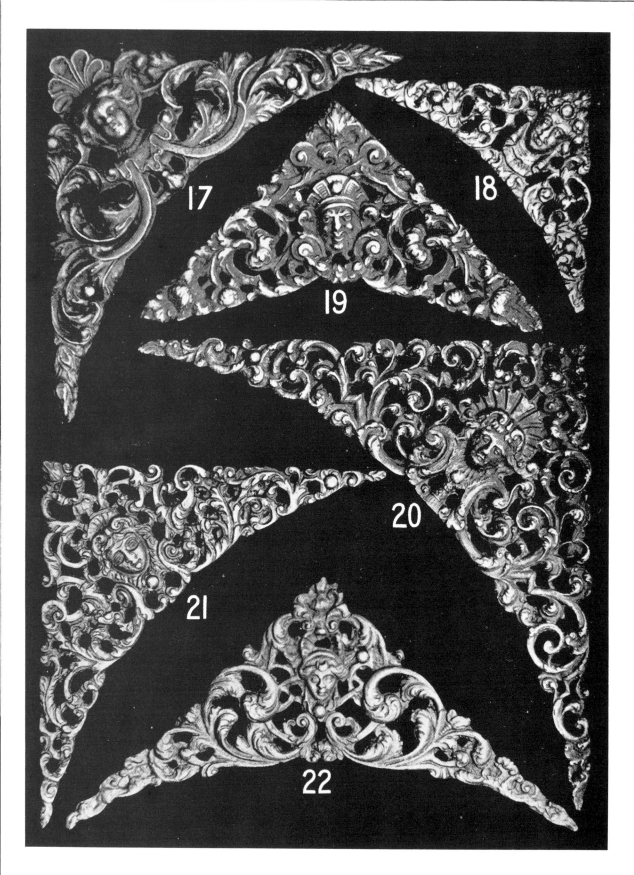

PLATE II.—THE DEVELOPMENT OF LONG-CASE CLOCK CORNERS.

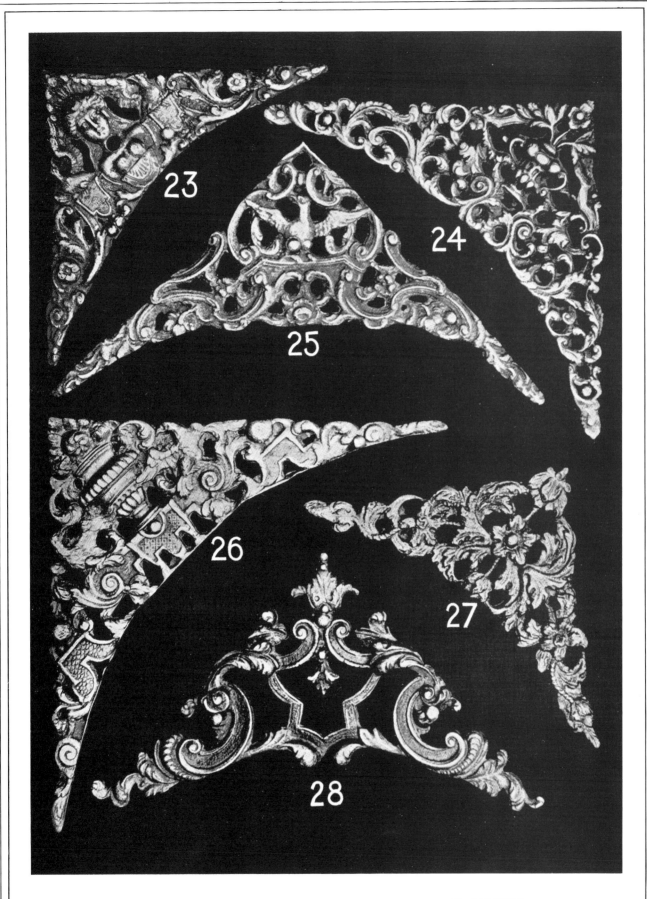

PLATE IV.—THE DEVELOPMENT OF LONG-CASE CLOCK CORNERS.

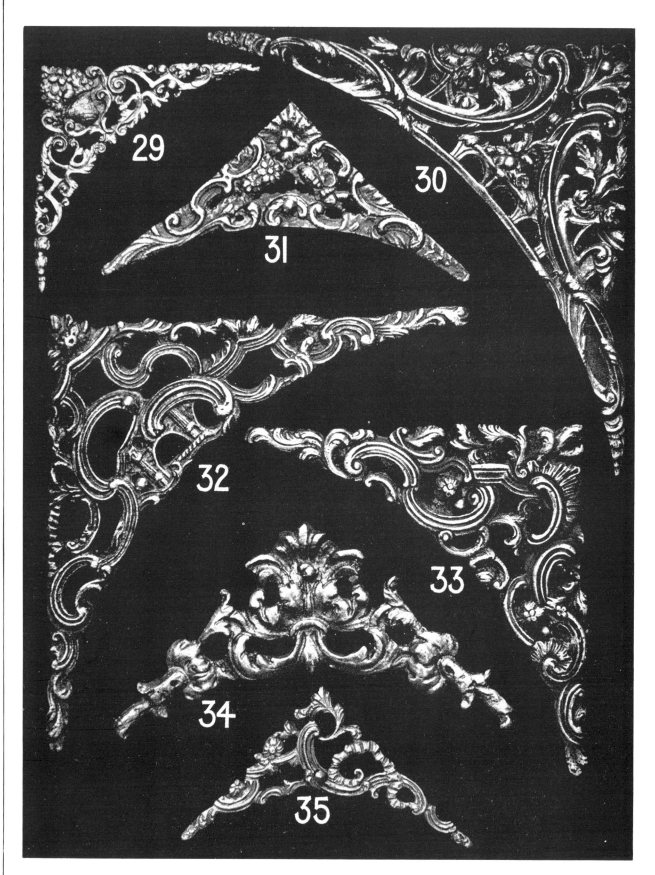

PLATE V.—THE DEVELOPMENT OF LONG-CASE CLOCK CORNERS.

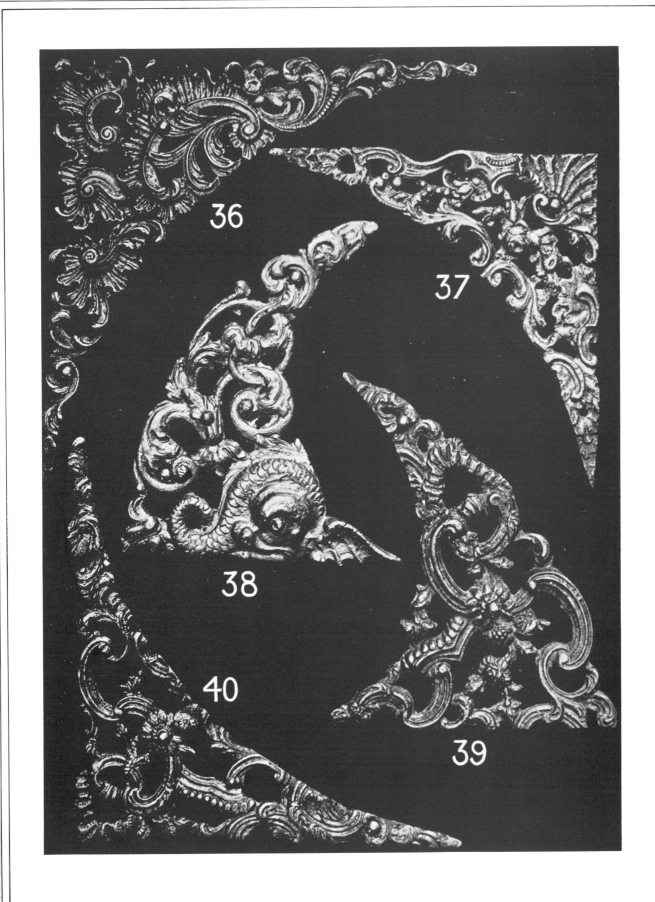

PLATE VI.—THE DEVELOPMENT OF LONG-CASE CLOCK CORNERS.

PLATE VII.—THE DEVELOPMENT OF LONG-CASE CLOCK CORNERS.

with a new set of another design. One continually meets with clocks where the corner-pieces have been changed in this way, and probably from this cause. Added to this, while the arch had superseded the square dial by about 1725, and dials became larger at about the same period, it was not unusual to find a country maker, working at the very close of the eighteenth century, and still using the 10- or 11-inch square dial of a century before, and to make the confusion worse, omitting the minute hand, and with it the minute divisions on the outside of the hour-ring. The pattern of the spandrel-corner adopted was usually as obsolete as the remainder of the dial; often the corners were engraved in the fashion of 1665–70, and this as late as 1800.

With long-case clocks of normal size—as distinguished from miniature or "grandmother" clocks—the usual size of the dials was 10 inches square up to about 1685, after which we find the 11-inch as a general rule, until about the end of the seventeenth century. From 1700 to about 1720–25 dials are nearly always 12 inches square, and this size does not alter appreciably even for some years after the introduction of the arch-top. In Plate I, Nos. 1 and 2 are bracket-clock corner-pieces; No. 3 is from a 10-inch dial of 1670-75, No. 4 being rather later in character, and from an 11-inch dial. No. 5 is the usual corner-piece of high-class 12-inch dials from 1695 to 1710, and was an especial favourite with Christopher Gould and Charles Gretton. No. 6 is a more exceptional type of about the same date. No. 7 is the corner found on clocks by the early apprentices of Thomas Tompion—the "Father of English Clock-making"—such as Graham, Allett, and others. No. 8, two angels supporting a small crown, surmounted by a Maltese cross, was a familiar pattern after about 1705, No. 10 being a later form. No. 9 is from the top-rail of a door in the hood of a square-dial Tompion clock of 1695, but this embellishment is rare. No. 14 is also exceptional, and is probably the last pattern found on square dials by high-class makers. No. 13 is from a 14-inch square dial clock nearly 10 feet in height, with a subsidiary dial in the lower door showing the equation of time. No. 16 is from the base of the hood of a long case in panelled ebony. Nos. 17, 19, 20, 21, and 22 are from early arched dials of 1730–35, Nos. 25, 26, and 28 being some years later in date. After about 1750 we get the types of No. 30, or the irregular corner such as Nos. 32 and 33. No. 36 is the corner-piece of a 14-inch dial of the later arch type, and Nos. 38, 39, 41, 42, 44, and 45 are the spandrel-pieces flanking the usual subsidiary dial or boss in the arch. No. 38 is, perhaps, the earliest, but shortly after the introduction of the arch dial any defined fashions which had formerly existed in the patterns of clock dials tended to become dissipated. There was also a very frequent habit of copying the earlier fashions in numberless points of detail which renders any attempt at chronological arrangement futile. There is, however, one almost infallible indication of an early clock, or an equally reliable criterion as to whether it possesses its original corners. With good makers, these spandrel corner-pieces were always carefully chased and frequently water-gilded. The time and care expended on the early dials, such as in the matting of the centre with a small punch, and the engraving of winding-holes and the edges of the dial plate, would have made the addition of a roughly cast corner-piece almost a species of sacrilege. After about the middle of the eighteenth century, however, the former high standard was rarely maintained, and towards the end it is not unusual to find corner-pieces used almost as they must have emerged from the mould, untouched even by the file, and innocent of the engraver's punch or graving tool. With high-class clocks, however, particularly those of London makers, some attempt at finishing was always made, although lacquering was usually substituted for gilding. Before the end of the eighteenth century, however, the fashion for the flat silvered dial, engraved and waxed, had ousted the former type, with silvered hour-ring on a matted ground, from favour, and brass corner-pieces, thus becoming unnecessary, were relegated to the minor makers in provincial towns and villages.

Chapter IX

Long-Case Clocks from 1670 to 1740

HE divergence of the development of the "bird-cage" or lantern clock into the long-case on the one hand and into the bracket clock on the other is easily accounted for, on logical principles. The "grandfather" case is a reasonable evolution, as, with the adoption of the pendulum as a controller, it would soon be discovered that the greater the length, and consequently the slower the oscillation, the more accurate would be this control. The desirability of a subsidiary dial for recording seconds would also follow the use of an additional hand for marking the minutes. The early lantern clocks had always the hour hand only—in fact, with country makers especially, single-handed clocks were made until almost the close of the eighteenth century. On the dials of these clocks the outer or minute divisions on the external edge of the hour-ring are, of course, absent.

The adoption of the seconds' dial as an addition to the minute hand regulated the length of the pendulum to 39.1393 inches, as we have already seen. These long, or "royal" pendulums, when attached to lantern clocks, necessitated an additional hole cut in the brackets on which they were placed to allow of the long pendulum to swing through its arc. In the earlier lantern clocks the usual custom was to fix the clock to the wall by spikes attached to the back, but the bracket was afterwards found to be the more convenient method. The long pendulum originally fitted to a lantern clock was an extremely rare proceeding, and is only found in specimens after about 1675. The "grandfather" case would probably have become an accomplished fact even earlier than it did, had it not been that the "crown-wheel" or verge escapement—where the escape-wheel was placed horizontally—necessitated so wide an arc of swing to free the wheel, that the enclosing of the pendulum in a trunk case of ordinary proportional width was impossible. With the invention of the anchor escapement—the principle of which has already been described—this difficulty was removed, and the long case became practicable. Many other factors must also have operated in the direction of the long case and its favourable reception. It enhanced the appearance and value of the clock—no mean consideration when the status of the early clockmakers and the importance of the industry is remembered—and transformed the hitherto insignificant brass lantern clock into a handsome piece of furniture.

It removed one of the principal objections to the lantern clock as a timekeeper, its liability to be affected by the fall of dust on the exposed works—a disadvantage which the large bell on the top hardly removed—and it permitted of a greater amount of work to be profitably expended on the dial and hands, which were now protected from the corroding effects of the atmosphere of the glazed hood. The influences which affected the evolution from the lantern to the wood-cased bracket clock will be indicated at a later stage when this branch of the subject is considered.

The development of the grandfather clock has already been dealt with in some detail, and we can devote our attention, for the moment, to the cases in which the clocks were placed. It is here where we have to leave the domain of absolute fact and to enter that of speculation and deduction. The inherent difficulty of the problem is, that as the early cases contained the clocks of English makers, who would, undoubtedly, have ordered the cases to be made to fit their clocks, instead of the reverse proceeding, and as the so-called English cases undeniably differ from the generality of those made on the Continent at the same period, they have been forthwith accepted, by nearly every authority, as being of English manufacture, and have been instanced as examples in the dating of furniture of similar detail and decoration. In some instances the clock cases have been cited as authorities for the dates of furniture of corresponding make, and sometimes the furniture has been used to date the clock cases. To adduce satisfactory evidence, in such detail as the subject demands, of the erroneous nature of these comparisons, it would be necessary to consider the subject of English furniture of the later seventeenth and the early eighteenth centuries at greater space than the scope of this book would permit. We can, however, instance one or two significant facts which are beyond dispute, although they are too frequently neglected. The first is, that the preserved records of the old clockmakers enable accurate periods to be assigned to their work, as we have not only the dates and extent of their careers, but also the progression of their clocks from the earlier to the later types—and consequently of the cases in which they are contained, where the clock is still in its original state. The dates of clocks by noted makers, therefore, can be postulated with certainty by an experienced clockmaker. We are dealing with fixed periods, not those dictated by a judgment which can err, or a mere opinion where too often the facts are tortured to square with a preconceived theory. In the second place, when we reach the non-debatable period of English furniture, from the commencement until almost the close of the eighteenth century, it is significant that long clock cases never exactly tally with the furniture of the same period. In the earlier clocks they anticipate fashions, sometimes by ten or fifteen years, whereas after about 1735–40 the maker of clock cases is always from twenty to thirty years later than the cabinetmakers in adopting ruling fashions. Marqueterie clock cases persist long after the furniture of plain walnut had ousted the marqueterie of William and Mary from general favour. We do not find plain walnut cases until mahogany had effectually superseded walnut as the fashionable wood for furniture, and mahogany cases coincide almost with the early Heppelwhite period, when mahogany had declined in favour, and the

Fig. 72.

GERMAN CABINET INLAID WITH MARQUETERIE. Dated 1656.

An example of the high degree of perfection which had been attained in the art of laying marqueterie in veneer, at this period, on the Continent.

use of the lighter woods—satin-wood, "hare-wood," chestnut, and sycamore—had taken its place.

There can be no doubt that had these early long clock cases been made in England, the work must have been done by the cabinetmaker or "joyners" of the period. The age of specialisation had not yet been reached, when certain makers confined their efforts solely to one or two articles of furniture. The cabinetmaker was a general practitioner, although there is evidence that the trade of the chairmaker was distinct. It is only after about 1780, however, that we find makers confining themselves exclusively to such pieces of furniture as sideboards, tables, knife boxes, and the like, and this is the case only in rare instances, and solely with cabinetmakers working in London.

The third point we have to consider is, that every reliable authority, tracing the orderly progression of English furniture from Tudor times, is compelled to place pieces of furniture such as Fig. 73, not earlier than the reign of James II—1685. We have here an inlay of crude marqueterie, but the piece is not veneered, and the inlay is chopped into the solid wood. Although the art of the marqueterie cutter was in a primitive state in England at this period, it had reached a high stage of development on the Continent, as is evident by the German cabinet, which is dated 1656, illustrated in Fig. 72. In Holland, especially, the laying of marqueterie in veneers had reached an extraordinary degree of excellence at this period. It is curious that English marqueterie suddenly appears as a full-blown art in the country. We find very few, if any, experimental pieces, with the exception of articles such as Fig. 73, and here the *method* is so different that such examples can be disregarded altogether. This sudden degree of perfection coincides with the accession of the Dutch Stadtholder to the English throne as William III, and it is well known that many of the artisans of Holland fol-

Fig. 73.

OAK CHEST INLAID WITH MARQUETERIE OF HOLLY, IVORY, AND MOTHER-OF-PEARL.

A typical example of "chopped-in" marqueterie of the period 1685-90.

lowed in his train, bringing to this country their native arts and crafts. The art of cutting and laying marqueterie in veneers bristles with technical difficulties and pitfalls for the unskilled, and although stray specimens of Dutch marqueterie had found their way into this country at an earlier date, and also a few emigrant cabinetmakers from Holland were domiciled in the East Anglian counties as early as the first years of Charles II, there is every reason to suppose that the methods of the marqueterie cutter's craft were kept a jealously guarded secret. In the actual laying of the marqueterie veneers we do find instances of 'prentice work by the English cabinetmakers in the case of furniture, but never in that of clock cases. From the most simple to the most elaborate the workmanship is always perfect; there are no signs whatever of inexperience. This subject has already been so exhaustively treated in the first volume of *English Furniture of the Eighteenth Century*, that it is not necessary to recapitulate the evidence given in that book in the present instance. We can confine ourselves to the consideration of specimens, as they arise in the ordinary progression of examples, where they have a bearing on this phase of our subject. For the present, we are concerned with the gradual development of the long case, with such regard to the clock contained therein as is necessary to establish the priority of date of the case itself and its position in this orderly progression. We have first to distinguish between an actual long-case clock—one which has been originally and specifically made as such—and a converted wall clock which has been fitted with a tall case at a later period. We have seen that lantern clocks have all certain constructional features in common. They

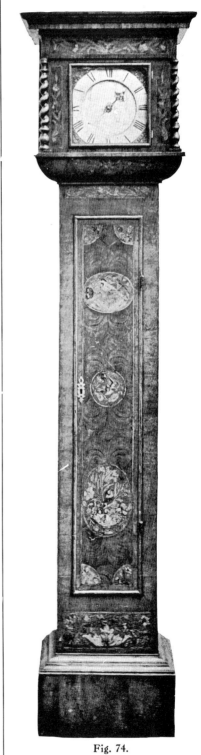

Fig. 74.
**THOS. FOWLE,
EAST GRINSTEAD.**
30-hour Striking Clock, 10-in. Dial.
An example of a wall clock fitted to
long case at a later date.

Fig. 75.

Fig. 76.
Enlarged Dial of Fig. 75.

Fig. 75.

"JOHANNES FROMANTEEL, LONDINI."

30-hour Striking Clock.
Ebonised case.

6 ft. 8 ins. high.   Waist 10 ins. wide × 6¾ ins. deep.

Dial 8⅞ in. square.   1⅝ in. hour circle.

One of the very earliest types of an original
long-case clock.

Date about 1670-5.

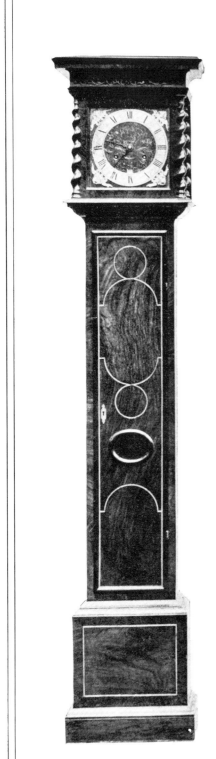

Fig. 77.

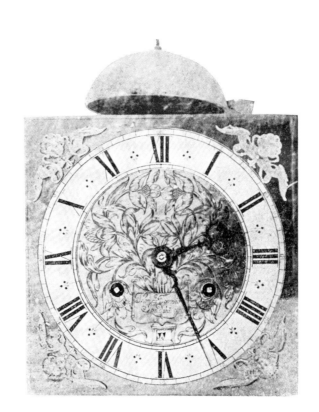

Fig. 78.
Enlarged Dial of Fig. 77.

Fig. 77.
THOMAS TOMPION, LONDON.
30-hour Striking Clock.
Sliding hood.   Dial with engraved centre.
Oak case, veneered with black-veined walnut.

In the possession of D. A. F. Wetherfield, Esq.

6 ft. 8 ins. high.   Dial 10 ins. square.

Date about 1675-80.

Fig. 79.

Fig. 80.

Enlarged Dial of Fig. 79.

Fig. 79.

THOMAS TOMPION, LONDON.

Eight-day Striking Clock.

Sliding hood, bolt-and-shutter maintaining power.

Oak case veneered with walnut "oysterpieces," and inlaid
with stars of ebony and hornbeam.

In the possession of D. A. F. Wetherfield, Esq.

6 ft. 8 ins. high.   Dial 10 ins. square.

Date about 1675–80.

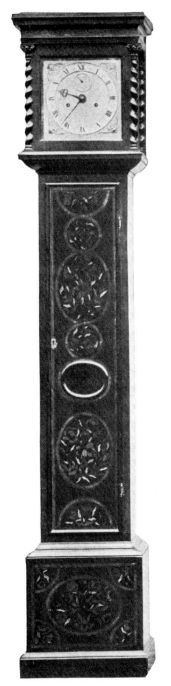

Fig. 81.

Fig. 81.

JOSEPH KNIBB, OXFORD.

Eight-day Striking Clock, oak case
veneered with walnut and inlaid with
marqueterie of various woods in oval
and circular panels,

In the possession of D. A. F. Wetherfield, Esq.

6 ft. 5 ins. high.   9-in. dial.

Date about 1675.

Fig. 82.

JOSEPH KNIBB, LONDON.

Month Striking Clock.   Skeleton dial
with minutes numbered.   Case of oak
veneered with laburnum banded with
olive wood, and inlaid with marqueterie
in oval and circular panels.

In the possession of D. A. F. Wetherfield, Esq.

6 ft. 8 ins. high.   10-in. dial.

Date about 1680.

Fig. 82.

are nearly all 30-hour movements—in fact, one might have stated this as a universal rule, were it not for the remarkable example already illustrated in Fig. 35—and in every instance, with two trains the one placed *behind* the other, the winding being effected by the pulling up of a weight. This method made for simplicity of construction and repair, and, so long as the clock was placed on a bracket, it was free from drawbacks. The weights were adequately supported by plaited cords, which, travelling over pulley-wheels, afforded the necessary driving power in their pull over the wheels as the weights descended. With the advent of the long case, however, it was found to be much more desirable to wind the clock from the face of the dial with a key, and this necessitated the planting of the two trains side by side. The pulley-wheels had also to be replaced by barrels, terminating in winding squares carried through the holes in the dial, and with the weights attached to a looped line of gut, which was coiled round the barrel as the clock was wound up. One occasionally encounters square-dial wall clocks with the two trains placed the one behind the other, arranged to pull up the weights and enclosed in a long case at a later date. Fig. 74 is an example of an early clock of this type. Such specimens are, however, properly wall clocks, made to stand upon a bracket, and either left open or enclosed with a wooden hood, and do not belong to the class of long-case clock, no matter how they may masquerade as such.

The earliest examples of long-case clocks are nearly always 30-hour, but with the two trains planted side by side, and made to be wound with a key. Figs. 75 and 77 are two specimens of this type. The Fromanteel is, perhaps, the very earliest example of a long-case clock which was ever made. The case is of oak, stained black and polished, and panelled out in squares in a manner very suggestive of the Dutch and German cabinets of the period. This form of case was a favourite one with the leading makers until about 1690, and its persistence is probably due to the conservative character which is usually found among the leading exponents of all crafts. It is usually the lesser lights who are the pioneers, the first enjoying a secured position, the second having still one to make. The movement of the Fromanteel clock exhibits many characteristics of very early origin. The escape-wheel, with its anchor, are both very small, the former hardly the size of a shilling—with a very shallow release. The two trains are also planted in a very irregular fashion, and the movement has an hour hand only, of the early open-spade lantern style. The dial is very simple in character, without engraving of any kind, and without attached spandrel corners. The date is approximately about 1670-75.

Fig. 77 is an early example of the work of Thomas Tompion, the "Father of English Clockmaking," a title merited as much by quantity as by quality. The movement here is also a 30-hour, with the hood made to slide upwards in the fashion general with the early long-case clocks. The form of the case, veneered with striped walnut panelled with holly lines, does not mark a progression of the marqueterie cutter's art so much as the beginning of an innovation, an attempt to introduce the gay inlay of marqueterie, which afterwards became so general that the conservative character even of the leading makers had to give way before the tide. One can well understand the spirit of the maker of fine clocks, with all his attention and pride centred on his own productions, rebelling against the idea of making the case overshadow, in decorative appearance, the clock itself. It must have been something like overpowering a simple picture by a ponderous and elaborate frame, the former being stultified by the latter in consequence. The demand for the simple walnut or black panelled cases persisted for a considerable while, and, apart from any jealousy between the makers of clocks and cases respectively, there is no doubt that the simple cases are always refined and appropriate to a clock possessing, above all, a useful function, whereas the elaborate marqueterie cases are frequently gaudy, and often in questionable taste.

Fig. 79 is a good example of the work of Tompion of about 1675–80, in his fully developed and most refined manner. The dial is simple in form, the hour-ring narrow, with the minutes engraved on the outer edge—a usual, but not an infallible sign of an early clock, as the absence of this detail is no necessary indication of later date, as we shall see subsequently. The seconds' dial is large, reaching from the inner edge of the hour circle almost to the hand collet—invariably an early feature—the cherub corners are simple in type, and the hour hand is of the open spade form, finely pierced and chiselled. This clock has the earliest form of "maintaining power," known as the "bolt and shutter," which has already been described in a previous chapter. For the purpose of this book there is very little difference, in result, between an evolution from a simple to an ornate type of case, due in the one instance to a gradual development of the case-maker's art, or, in the other, to the endeavour to "force an alien conception on a reluctant mind." There is especial evidence, in the work of Tompion, to show that he accepted the marqueterie case, in its most ornamental stage, very cautiously. Until the very close of his career we meet with many of his long clocks where the cases are either panelled and ebonised in the simple Dutch manner, or veneered with striped English or black walnut. An example such as Fig. 79, simple although it be in comparison with the more ornate specimens which will be illustrated at a later stage, still shows an elaborate style of case for Tompion himself. One may, with advantage, attempt here a chronological description of marqueterie cases, examples of each kind of which will be found in the following pages. Those which are panelled and ebonised, or others veneered with plain walnut, can be disregarded, as being due to other considerations than an undivided evolution of a particular fashion. We can begin with the case shown in Fig. 79, which is veneered with "oysterpieces,"—*i.e.* veneers cut crosswise from saplings—and decorated with a simple inlay of stars, put together with alternate pieces of ebony and holly to give an effect of relief. In the next stage we have an inlay of jessamine leaves and flowers, usually cut from bone or ivory, either in the natural shade or stained red and green, in a panelled ground of walnut or ebony, the panels being either oval or circular in form. As the development of marqueterie proceeds, the inlay becomes more gay in its colour scheme, until the close of the seventeenth century, when a quieter taste supervenes, and marqueterie is usually cut from yellow woods, sycamore, plane tree, holly or box in a walnut or ebony ground. A double change now appears; in the one instance the tendency is for the marqueterie to become finer until it develops into a mass of meaningless scrolls—or "seaweed" marqueterie as it is frequently termed—either of light woods in a dark ground or vice versa. The various progressions until this ultimate stage is reached will be noticed in subsequent examples. The other development is from the panelled to the "all over" form, and this change will be illustrated in each stage. Thus, as a usual rule, seaweed marqueterie in panels is later than "all over" floral marqueterie. Other modifications will be noticed, later on, when actual examples are considered.

Figs. 81 and 82 are two specimens of the work of Joseph Knibb, the first being one of the very rare examples of the work of this maker signed as from Oxford. Joseph Knibb was one of three brothers of the same trade, Samuel and Peter being admitted to the Clockmakers' Company in 1663 and 1677 respectively. Joseph obtained his "freedom" in 1670, and was working in London some six or seven years later, so that if we disregard the possibility of the name-engraved dial of Fig. 81 being prior to the construction of the clock as a whole—always a probable contingency with renowned makers—this fact establishes a date of about 1675 for this Oxford clock. The second of the two examples is somewhat later in type, and is fitted with a "skeleton" dial—*i.e.* with the silvered hour-ring cut away between each of the Roman numerals, showing the matted ground of the dial underneath—and each of the minute divisions on the outer edge is separately numbered from 1 to 60. Both of these details were favourite conceits with noted makers, and are found on bracket as well as long-case clock dials from about 1680 to 1710. This minute numbering of the hour circle necessitated the placing of the minute divisions in from the outer edge, a separate ring outside being reserved for the Arabic numerals themselves. This detail is worthy of note, as one frequently meets with undeniably early dials where the minute divisions are set in, but with the numbers 5, 10, &c., up to the 60, only in the outer circle. The space reserved for these Arabic figures, in both cases, is very small as compared with the later dials, and it is a reasonable assumption that such dials have either been re-engraved at a later date, when the separate numbering of each minute was dispensed with—a somewhat unlikely contingency—or, what is more probable, that such dials were planned for the minute numbering, the numerals between the 5 and the 10, and so on, to be engraved and waxed subsequently, if the price received for the clock warranted the expenditure. With the early clocks the nature of both these possibilities has to be borne in mind, namely, that of a subsequent alteration at a later date, or a change of plan between the periods when the clock was begun and finished.

Fig. 83 is a typical example of the work of William Clement, a noted maker, who is credited with being the first to apply the anchor escapement of Robert Hooke to long-case clocks. The case is panelled and veneered with ebony, in the Dutch style, with the columns flanking the hood and the centre of the pediment enriched with mountings of gilt brass. The clock strikes the hours and quarters from the one train, and is fitted with a long pendulum with a beat of $1\frac{1}{4}$ seconds' duration. The pendulum is shown by the side of the case in the illustration, photographed to the same scale. The dial has all the early characteristics of the narrow hour-ring, the large seconds' dial—numbered from 5 to 60, but with each division divided into four parts instead of the usual five, each swing of the pendulum carrying the finger across one spare, *i.e.* 48 in one minute—the winding holes low and wide apart, the minute divisions on the extreme edge of the silvered hour circle, the hands simple in type and finely wrought, and the cherub-headed corner-pieces well chased. The side view of the movement, showing the striking work, with the locking-plate high up on the back plate, is given in Fig. 85. These elaborate movements are very rare in long-case clocks of this early date, but this example may be taken as characteristic of the work of William Clement. The name is signed on the base of the dial in Latin in the favourite manner of this period.

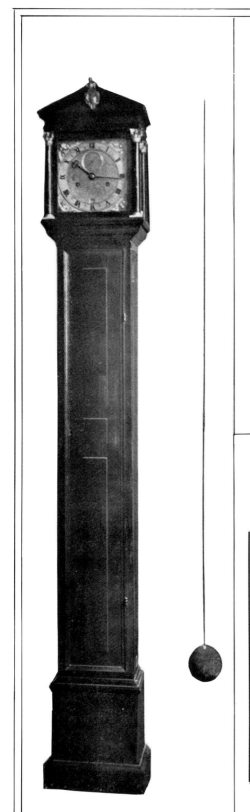

Fig. 83.

Fig. 84.

Enlarged Dial of Fig. 83.

Fig. 83.

"GULIELMUS CLEMENT, LONDINI, FECIT."

Eight-day Quarter-Striking Clock.
Four bells.
$1\frac{1}{4}$ seconds' pendulum (the pendulum is
shown by the side of the case).
Ebony case, ormolu mounted.
Slide-up hood.

6 ft. 2 ins. high × 8½ ins. width of waist
× 5¼ ins. depth of waist.
8 in. dial.   1⅝ in. hour circle.

Date about 1675.

Side view of movement of
Fig. 83, showing the
striking-work.

Fig. 86.

Fig. 87.
Enlarged Dial of Fig. 86.

Fig. 86.
"EDUARDUS EAST, LONDINI, FECIT."

Month Clock with curious ring round hour circle, making one complete revolution in a year.   Short bob pendulum.
Oak case veneered with walnut, and inlaid with stars of holly and ebony.

5 ft. 8¼ ins. high × 7⅝ ins. width × 5⁷⁄₁₆ in. depth of waist.
6¼ in. dial.
In the possession of Sir William Lever, Bart.

Date about 1675.

Fig. 86 is another remarkable clock, a miniature month timepiece by Edward East, from Sir William Lever's collection. The waist of the case is nearly filled by the heavy weight necessitated by the going for this period, and in consequence of the lack of room, the pendulum is of the short "bob" type, reaching from the crutch to the bottom of the back plate only. The irregular planting of the train for such a small clock has resulted in the main-wheel being placed at the bottom with the winding square below the hour circle. The outer ring, outside the Roman numerals, is divided into the days and months of the year, and revolves once in 365 days. The little pointer at the top indicates the day, the circle being merely "friction tight" and adjustable with slight pressure. The case is veneered with walnut and inlaid with stars of holly and ebony. The whole clock is a very rare example of the work of a noted maker, and possesses many points of interest to the collector.

The next example, Fig. 88, furnishes an instance of the change of plan on the part of a maker before referred to. The dial exhibits early characteristics, with the exception of the ringing of the winding holes, which is a detail seldom, if ever, found before about 1700-10. The probability is that when the dial was renovated, at a date when the rings round the winding holes were fashionable, the matting of the dial was found to be scratched or bruised, by careless use of the key in winding, and the turning of the rings was adopted either as the cheaper form of renovation—as the matting of these early dial centres with a single fine punch was a long and costly proceeding—or to conform to the prevailing fashion. Edward Stanton, or Staunton—the old clockmakers frequently allowed their love of variety to influence the spelling of their names as engraved on their dials—was a noted maker. Apprenticed in 1655, he was "free" in 1662 and master in 1696, so that the date here given is probably later rather than earlier than that of the actual making of the clock. The absence of the usual seconds' dial is not significant, as the fashions governing this detail were not very stringent or defined.

Fig. 90 is a Tompion clock in a panelled case, partly of black stained pear-tree and partly veneered with ebony. To the student of furniture, the Dutch character of this case, especially of the moulding details of the hood, hardly needs emphasizing. The hour circle, with the minute divisions set in from the outer edge, supplies a probable instance of the change of plan in the engraving of the dial before alluded to. The hood is devised to slide upwards for winding purposes, in the manner shown in the second illustration—the hoods of cases of this type

Fig. 89.
Enlarged Dial of Fig. 88.

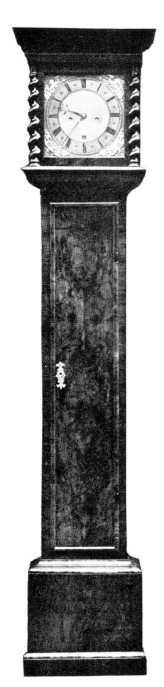

Fig. 88.

Fig. 88.

"EDW. STANTON, LONDON."

Eight-day Striking Clock. Bolt-and-shutter maintaining power.

Day of month in aperture below hands.
Oak case veneered with burr walnut.

6 ft. high. Waist 10½ ins. wide × 6½ ins. deep.
10 in. brass dial. 1½ in. brass hour circle.

Date about 1680–5.

Fig. 90.

Fig. 92.
Enlarged Dial of Fig. 90.

Fig. 90.

THO. TOMPION, LONDINI, FECIT.

Eight-day Striking Clock.
Bolt-and-shutter maintaining power.
Sliding hood.
Finely carved hands and chased corner-
pieces.   Ebonised and ebony veneered case.

7 ft. high × 10¼ ins. width × 6½ ins. depth of waist.
10 in. dial.   1¾ in. hour circle.

Fig. 91.

View showing sliding hood up, and releasing
spring of hood actuated by closing the
bottom door.

Date about 1680–5.

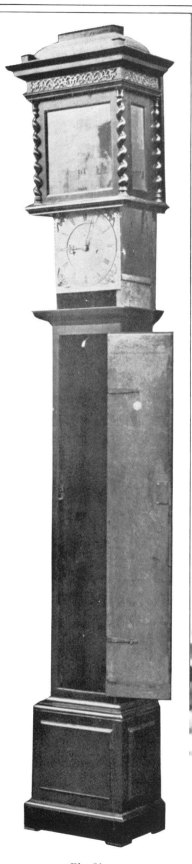

Fig. 91.

being unprovided with doors, although they were frequently fitted at a later date, being also made to slide forward in the later fashion. The spring device under the hood, at the top of the trunk, will be noticed, this being arranged so that when the hood is down the closing of the lower door locks the hood. This ingenious system was probably adopted to prevent the careless habit of winding the clock without opening the lower door, with the consequent jerk of the weight and straining of the gut·line at the last turn of the winding key. Various devices of this nature were adopted by the leading clockmakers to render their clocks, as far as practicable, "fool proof."

Fig. 93 is a graceful clock by Richard Lyons, the dial with a somewhat unusually wide hour circle for this period and an hour hand of the broad open spade form. The case is especially choice, veneered with light coloured figured walnut, the mouldings of delicate section and beautifully worked. A somewhat rare characteristic is the twisted columns surmounted by carved Corinthian capitals. This detail will also be noticed in the Knibb clock already illustrated in Fig. 81. Fig. 95 is another of these early simple clocks of about the same date, unfortunately with the original bolt-and-shutter maintaining power removed.

Fig. 97 is another example of the work of Edward East, perhaps the earliest of the renowned makers of long-case clocks of the later seventeenth century. The hour hand shows the evolution from the lantern clock style, and the minute hand is also of very early type. The marqueterie of the case, an inlay of walnut scrolls in a ground of yellow sycamore, is characteristic of the last quarter of the seventeenth century, but it is unsafe to instance this as a guide, as the fashion for marqueterie of this simple type again recurred on the clock cases of certain makers two or three decades after the date of this specimen. The small size of the case, and the name, " Eduardus East Londini," engraved on the bottom edge of the dial, however, are unmistakable indications of a period before 1700.

The next example, Fig. 99, is exceptional in possessing a $1\frac{1}{4}$ seconds' pendulum, with the seconds' dial divided into multiples of 4 instead of the usual 5—48 in all, instead of 60—in the same manner as in Fig. 83. These long pendulums, reaching to the bottom of the case, were fitted by many of the leading makers to their clocks, and undoubtedly admitted of closer regulation and more exact timekeeping. It is rare to find an original glazed and brass-ringed aperture fitted to these long-pendulum clocks, although they were often added at a later

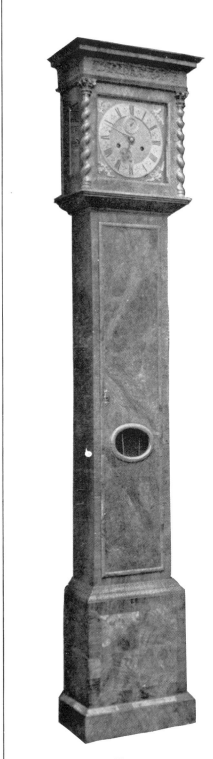

Fig. 93.

Fig. 94.
Enlarged Dial of Fig. 93.

Fig. 93.

RICHARD LYONS, LONDON.

Eight-day Striking Clock.
Oak and deal case veneered with veined English walnut
and banded with the same wood.   Unusual spiral pillars
to hood with carved capitals.

6 ft. $7\frac{1}{4}$ ins. high $\times$ $10\frac{3}{4}$ ins. width, and $6\frac{1}{4}$ ins. depth of waist.
10 in. dial.
In the possession of Bernard Matthews, Esq.

Date about 1685-90.

Fig. 96.

Enlarged Dial of Fig. 95.

Fig. 95.

ANONYMOUS.

Eight-day Striking Clock.
Bolt-and-shutter maintaining power removed.   Outside
locking plate.   Oak case veneered with burr walnut.

6 ft. 8 ins. high.   Waist 10¼ ins. wide × 5¾ ins. deep.
10 in. dial.
In the possession of W. G. Mare, Esq.

Date about 1680–5.

Fig. 97.

Fig. 98.
Enlarged Dial of Fig. 97.

Fig. 97.

"EDUARDUS EAST, LONDINI."

Eight-day Striking Clock.
Bolt-and-shutter maintaining power. Oak case veneered with
walnut and inlaid with walnut marqueterie in panels of
sycamore.

6 ft. 3 ins. high × 10 ins. width × 6½ ins. depth of waist.
10 in. dial. 1¾ in. hour circle.

Date about 1780-5.

Fig. 99.

Fig. 100.

Enlarged Dial of Fig. 99.

Fig. 99.

"THO. JOHNSON, LONDINI, FECIT."

Eight-day Striking Clock.
Bolt-and-shutter maintaining power. $1\frac{1}{4}$ seconds' pendulum.
Oak case veneered with walnut and inlaid with marqueterie
of stained ivory and coloured woods in a panelled ground
of ebony.

6 ft. $5\frac{1}{2}$ ins. high × $10\frac{1}{2}$ ins. width of waist × $6\frac{1}{4}$ ins. depth of waist.
10 in. dial. $1\frac{7}{8}$ in. hour circle.
In the possession of Richard Hoffmann, Esq.

Date about 1680-5.

date. This example has been altered in this way, as it is obvious that the case was not originally planned for the lenticular glazed hole in the base.

Fig. 101 is of similar appearance to the Tompion already illustrated in Fig. 90, and, in comparison, may be described as the "poor man's clock." The movement is an 8-day, single-train timepiece, with the dial centre, round the hand collet, engraved in imitation of the earlier lantern clock with central alarum disc. The graceful proportions of the simple case are worthy of note, also the fretting of the frieze of the hood, some indication that the case was originally planned for a striking clock. The case is probably somewhat earlier than the clock, although the dial of the latter is signed on the bottom, under the hour-ring, in the fashion of 1675–85.

Figs. 103 to 106 illustrate the versatility of the Court horologist to Charles I, Edward East. He was probably the earliest of all the noted makers, being established in Fleet Street in 1635, and probably in Pall Mall at a still earlier date. Mr. F. J. Britten refers to East as "at the Sun outside Temple Bar" in 1690. He died a few years later. Fig. 103 is a choice and ingenious example of his work, a clock devised to show the time by night. East probably made several of this pattern, Mr. J. W. Bourne possessing a bracket clock on the same system also by him. The dial, shown in Fig. 104, has the numerals pierced, so that a lamp placed behind the movement will light up the dial. In Fig. 103 is shown the small shelf upon which the lamp is intended to be placed, and also the small species of pent roof covering the movement, designed to catch any drips of oil or grease and to protect the works. The outer dial has a pierced lunette numbered for the four quarters of the hour, with minute divisions between. The 12 just emerges on the left-hand side at the hour, and in the illustration indicates twelve minutes past. Behind the lunette is a disc pierced with two holes, one containing the hour numeral as shown, the other being immediately opposite, and hidden by the outer engraved dial. Behind this disc are the hour numerals on separate plates, linked together as shown in Fig. 106, where the dial is shown from the back. The ingenious nature of the mechanism is shown by the fact that the disc carries with it five of these plates between the two holes. As the decagonal wheel in the illustration makes one-tenth of a revolution, it picks up one of the numbered plates on the left and drops one on the right. The hole through which the figure 12 shows, for example, holds the plate

Fig. 102.

Enlarged Dial of Fig. 101.

Fig. 101.

Fig. 101.

THOMAS HALL, LONDON.

Eight-day Clock.

Deal case, panelled and ebonised.   Curious engraving
round centre of dial.

6 ft. 4½ ins. high × 10¼ ins. width of waist.

10-in. dial.

Date about 1690-5.

Fig. 103.

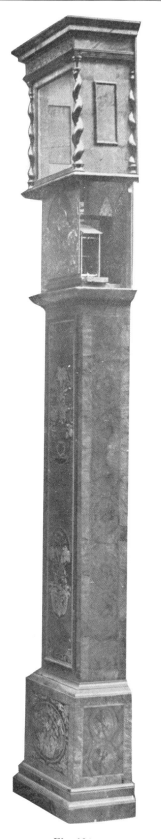

Fig. 104.

Fig. 103.

EDUARDUS EAST, LONDINI.

Eight-day Night Clock.
Sliding hood.   Finely engraved dial.
Oak case veneered with walnut
oysterpieces and inlaid with coloured
marqueterie in panels of ebony.

6 ft. 10 ins. high × 10½ ins. width of
waist × 7 ins. depth of waist.

Date about 1680–5.

Fig. 104.

Side view of Fig. 103, showing the
hood lifted on to its coil-spring catch,
the shelf at the back for the light,
and the gabling of the movement to
catch the grease from a candle.

Fig. 105.

THE DIAL OF THE CLOCK (FIG. 103) ENLARGED.

$10\frac{1}{2}$ ins. wide × $11\frac{1}{2}$ ins. high.

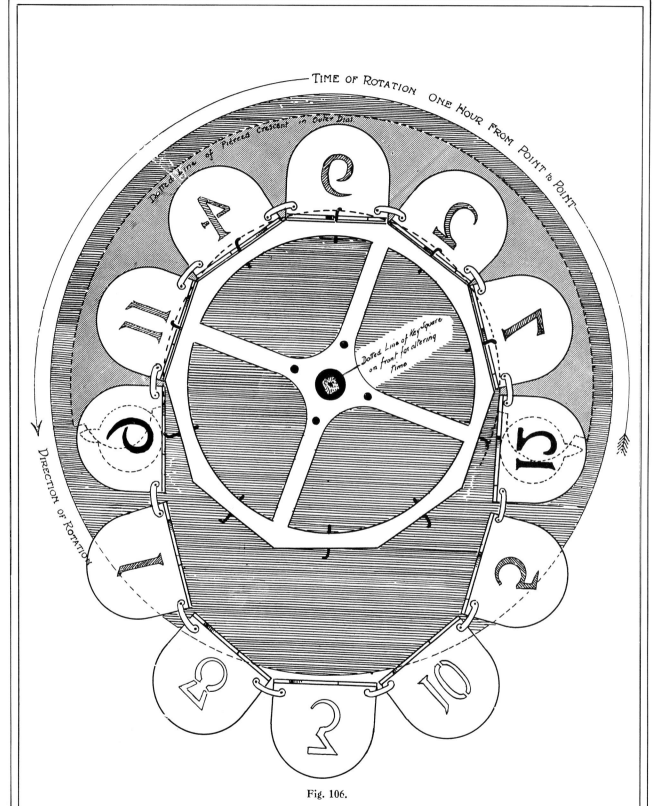

Fig. 106.

THE MOTION-WORK OF THE NIGHT CLOCK (FIG. 103), BACK DISC REMOVED, LOOKING
FROM BACK TO FRONT.

pierced with this number until the wheel has revolved to the opposite position, where the figure 6 is indicated, a revolution which takes, approximately, an hour to accomplish. It carries with it the 7, 2, 9, 4, and 11. These numbered plates are so arranged that the fifth to the left of the visible number (or the right on the reversed view of the dial shown in Fig. 106) is the next hour, the fifth to the right being the one immediately preceding. The whole string of the numbers revolve once in rather more than two hours, although it takes twelve for each to appear, in turn, through the apertures in the revolving disc. Of the two winding squares, the upper one is for the setting of the hour, the lower for the winding of the clock. The system, although simple enough when explained, is exceedingly ingenious, and must have demanded considerable inventive and mechanical ability to devise. Some indication of the pride which Edward East must have experienced in his production is shown by the beautiful and costly engraving of the dial plate.

Fig. 107 is a typical example of a clock and case of about 1685, the marqueterie in panel being very similar to that of the East clock previously illustrated. The simple, but beautifully worked hands are worthy of careful notice. The hood is crested with a carved pediment—a not infrequent detail with the cases of leading makers at this period. The inlay of coloured ivory and stained woods on a ground of ebony surrounded by walnut "oysterpieces" is a good indication of a high-grade clock.

During the latter part of the seventeenth and the first years of the eighteenth centuries a demand existed for long-case clocks of small, and frequently diminutive proportions. A fashion afterwards arose for the opposite extreme, when clocks were made of enormous size, a specimen of which, nearly ten feet high, is in the wardens' room of the Drapers' Company. These miniature clocks often necessitated such radical modifications of prevailing types that they are difficult to classify in order of date without relying, almost entirely, upon the preserved records of the makers themselves. The dials are, of necessity, smaller than the usual fashion of the time, and the seconds' dial is nearly always omitted for similar reasons. The Knibb clock shown in Fig. 109 indicates the commencement of this fashion. The case is nearly of normal height, the dial is 9 inches square, and the trunk unusually narrow. Joseph Knibb adhered to the small escape-wheel with the shallow release for many years, his pendulums having a very narrow arc in consequence. Fig. 109 is an early example of this maker's work, a fact indicated by the square topped bell, the simple cherub corners, and the pierced

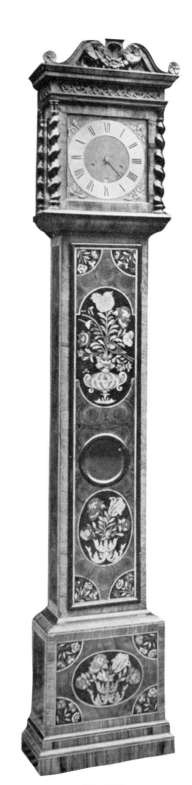

Fig. 107.

Fig. 108.
Enlarged Dial of Fig. 107.

Fig. 107.

"THO. BRADFORD, LONDINI, FECIT."

Eight-day Striking Clock.
Bolt-and-shutter maintaining power.   Oak case veneered
with walnut "oysterpieces" and inlaid with marqueterie
of stained ivory and coloured woods in a panelled
ground of ebony.

6 ft. 6 ins. high (over cresting 6 ft. 10 ins. high).
10½ ins. width × 6½ ins. depth of waist.
Slide-up hood.   10 in. dial.   1¾ in. hour circle.

Date about 1685.

Fig. 110.
Enlarged Dial of Fig. 109.

Fig. 109.

JOSEPH KNIBB, LONDON.

Eight-day Striking Clock.
Case inlaid with floral marqueterie in panels.

In the possession of Percy Webster, Esq.

6 ft. 3½ ins. high × 6 ins. width of waist.   9 in. dial.

Date about 1680.

Fig. 109.

and "carved" hour hand of the open spade type. The character of the case corresponds with that of the clock, being veneered with veined and "feathered" walnut and decorated with coloured floral marqueterie in ebony panels.

Fig. 111 is later than the Knibb clock by some fifteen years, and is illustrated here to show the degree to which the making of these miniature clocks was carried. The proportions of a case as small as this specimen has precluded the use of the usual long pendulum, the waist having an inside width of only 5¼ inches. The clock is exceptional in several ways. The pendulum is of the short "bob," or bracket-clock type, swinging behind the back plate only to the depth of the bottom of the hood. Although fitted with two winding squares, the clock does not strike, but is fitted with a pulling string and repeats the hours and quarters. The left square winds up the going train, that on the right the alarum spring. The small alarum disc with its pointer can be seen in the illustration, and the alarum is set by aligning this pointer with the butt of the hour hand when this points to the desired hour. A late feature of the dial is the ringed winding holes. The case is inlaid with marqueterie in panels in a similar way to the Knibb clock, but the marqueterie itself exhibits the later fashion of meaningless scrolling, in place of the well-designed floral ornament of the earlier examples.

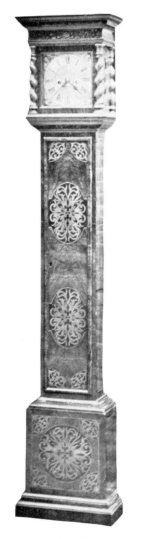

Fig. 111.

"HEN. MASSY, LONDON."

Eight-day Clock.
Pull quarter repeater and alarum.
Oak case veneered with walnut and
inlaid with scroll marqueterie.

5 ft. 2¾ ins. high.   Waist 7 ins. wide
× 5 ins. deep.
6½ in. dial.   1 5⁄16 in. width of hour circle.

Date about 1695.

The fashion for these miniature clocks, although more prevalent at the very close of the seventeenth century, persisted until the last quarter of the eighteenth. As the century grows older, however, examples become more and more rare, the taste being for the opposite extreme. The more renowned makers, however, appear to have vied with each other in the direction of making these miniature clocks as elaborate as possible. Thus, one-month and even year movements have been found in cases no larger than the Massy clock shown here. In other examples the movements are fitted with 8- or 10-bell chimes, and original chiming movements in long-case clocks of any size are always rare. The leading makers appear to have taken a great delight in making these small clocks as complicated as possible, and the added difficulties inherent to the diminutive size would appear to have added to the pleasure of the task.

It is curious to notice how arbitrary must have been the fashions which dictated the general form of these early clock cases. Within certain limits, of

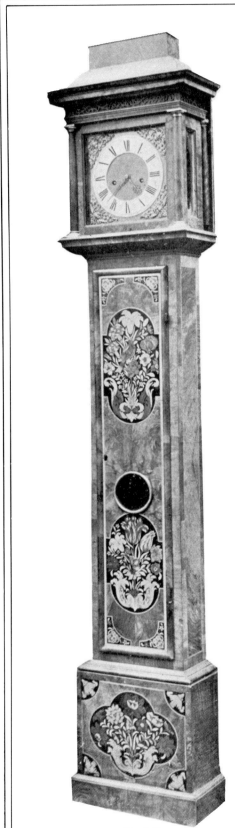

Fig. 112.

Fig. 113.
Enlarged Dial of Fig. 112.

Fig. 112.

JOHN WISE, LONDON.

Eight-day Striking Clock.
Oak case veneered with burr walnut and inlaid with
marqueterie of stained ivory and coloured woods in
a panelled ground of ebony.   Slide-up hood.

7 ft. 2 ins. high × 11 ins. width of waist × 6½ ins. depth
of waist.
10 in. dial.   1¾ in. hour circle.

Date about 1690.

Fig. 115.
Enlarged Dial of Fig. 114.

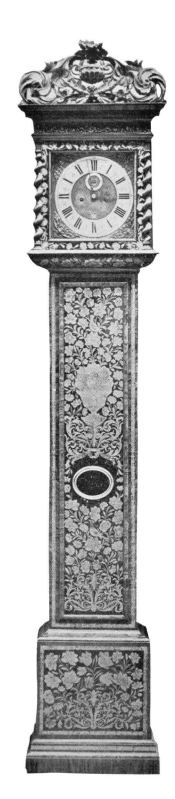

Fig. 114.

Fig. 114.

"THO. STUBBS, LONDON."

Eight-day Striking Clock.
Seconds' dial.   Day of month.
Oak case veneered with walnut and inlaid with floral
marqueterie of holly.
Carving above hood of pear-tree.

6 ft. 11 ins. high.   Waist 8⅞ ins. wide × 6¼ ins. deep.
11 in. dial.

Date about 1695.

course, the scope and purpose of the clock itself must have governed, to a large extent, the shape and proportions of the case, but it will be noticed that in minor details, unaffected by any utilitarian considerations, we find the same endless repetition. This is, in a way, an argument for the foreign origin of these marqueterie cases, as it is difficult to understand trade rivals placing their clocks—which often differed considerably where one would hardly expect variations of type to be practicable—in cases of the same form and ornamentation. Fig. 112 is quite an exceptional specimen in the unusual cresting of the hood. Unfortunately the "bull's-eye," the hands, and the corner-pieces are not original.

Much of the evidence for the dating of examples depends upon details of the movements which cannot be adequately illustrated here. Thus the Stubbs clock shown in Fig. 114 is earlier than the general style of the case or the dial would appear to imply. The movement is of the "outside locking-plate" type already referred to in the chapter on the mechanism of long-case clocks, an infallible sign of early date, as the rack system, once adopted, became general throughout the trade, the liability to derangement of the locking-plate action by the turning of the hands backwards, or without allowing the clock to strike, constituting a grave drawback. Fig. 114 has several late characteristics, such as the pattern of the hands, the ringing of the winding holes, the width of the hour circle and the recessing of the minute divisions, which can probably be accounted for by the theory of later modifications. The case is beautifully decorated with all-over floral marqueterie of holly in a ground of English walnut, well designed and cut. The hood is crested with a carved pediment of pear-tree—an endeavour to relieve the plain square character of the

Fig. 116.
MANSELL BENNETT,
Dial and Three Crowns,
CHARING CROSS.
Eight-day Striking Clock.
In the Victoria and Albert Museum.
7 ins. high × 1 ft. 1½ in. wide.
11 in. dial.
Date about 1695.

135

early hoods, which was adopted, in several instances, by Tompion and Christopher Gould. This feature is possibly the prototype of the later domed hood, which became so fashionable shortly after 1700.

The Mansell Bennett clock from the Victoria and Albert Museum, Fig. 116, shows the usual type of case of this period, although as a specimen of untouched workmanship it is not free from reproach, the base being an obvious addition, and probably much of the cornice also.

From 1695 to 1705 the trade fashions which had formerly governed the choice of small details appear to have been greatly relaxed, and one encounters many puzzling features in the clocks made between these years. They serve to emphasize the necessity, in forming a judgment, of first considering the clock as a whole, secondly, the possibility of the clock being married to a strange case (no unlikely contingency when we remember that these old clocks have only been esteemed during, at most, the last thirty years), and thirdly, the modifications which may have taken place when the clock was restored at various periods. We must not forget that a clock would not persist for more than 200 years without some attention, and one can only hope that this was given by a qualified workman instead of the usual "clock jobber." The likelihood of actual replacements, especially with corner-pieces—which are easily detachable—and hands, which are readily breakable and of perishable material, has also to be considered. When all these points have been duly weighed and debated, however, one frequently encounters specimens where evidences refuse to square with theories. Fig. 117 is an example of this. It is difficult to believe that the maker first engraved the scrolled ring round the hands and then covered a part of it with the circle of the seconds' dial. The hour-ring is also disproportionately large, especially for this period, and has probably been larger, as the hour divisions on the inside have disappeared, although the devices between each of the Roman numerals still remain. The hour-ring may be, and almost certainly is, a replacement; but why? The hour circle would hardly be readily lost, or even damaged beyond repair, although it may have been reversed—a not unusual proceeding. The whole clock is exceptional; the winding hole being low on the face of the dial, and the day-of-the-month aperture very high, almost directly under the hand collet. The case is a better example of the period than the clock, and when placed side by side with that of the Mansell Bennett previously illustrated, serves to show how the Museum specimen has been vandalised in the process of restoration.

Fig. 119 is a late clock with early characteristics. The dial is small for this

Fig. 118.
Enlarged Dial of Fig. 117.

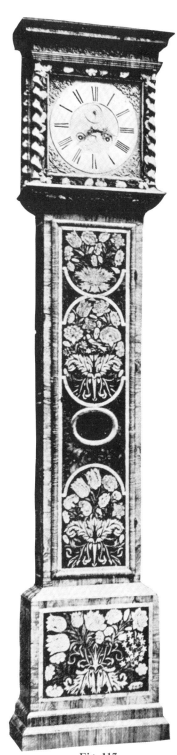

Fig. 117.

Fig. 117.

NATHANIEL BARROW, LONDON.

Month Striking Clock.
In oak case veneered with walnut and inlaid with
floral marqueterie in panels.   Sliding hood.

7 ft. 1 in. high × 12½ ins. width of waist.
11 in. dial.

Date about 1695–1700.

Fig. 120.

Enlarged Dial of Fig. 119.

Fig. 119.

JOHN WISE, LONDON.

Eight-day Striking Clock.
Seconds' dial.   Day of month.
Sliding hood upwards.

Oak case veneered with walnut and inlaid
on front and sides with floral marqueterie of
plane-tree and pear-wood.

7 ft. high.   Waist 11 ins. wide × 6½ ins. deep.
10 in. dial.

Date about 1700–5.

Fig. 119.

Fig. 121.

Side view of Fig. 119.

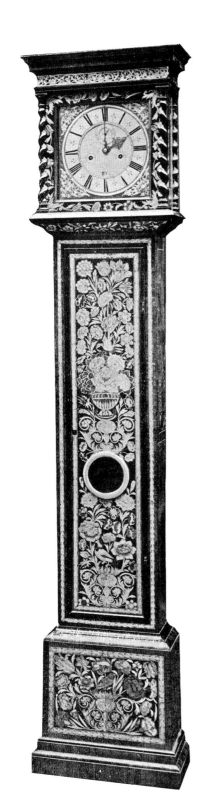

Fig. 122.

Fig. 123.
Enlarged Dial of Fig. 122.

Fig. 122.

SAMUEL MACHAM, LONDON.

Eight-day Striking Clock.
Seconds' dial.   Day of month.
Sliding hood upwards.
Oak case veneered with walnut, banded with rose and
palm woods, and inlaid with coloured floral marqueterie.

6 ft. 10½ ins. high.   Waist 12 ins. wide × 6¾ ins. deep.
11 in. dial.

Date about 1700–5.

Fig. 124.

THOMAS JOHNS, LONDON.

Eight-day Striking Clock. Bolt-and-shutter maintaining power. Oak case veneered with walnut and inlaid with floral marqueterie.

7 ft. 1 in. high. Waist 12 ins. wide × 6½ ins. deep.
11 in. dial.

Date about 1700–5.

Fig. 125.

ALEXANDER IRVING, WESTMINSTER.

Eight-day Striking Clock. Oak case veneered with walnut and inlaid with marqueterie of holly in a ground of ebony.

7 ft. 3½ ins. high × 1 ft. width of waist.
12 in. dial.

Date about 1700–5.

Fig. 124.

Fig. 125.

period—10 inches instead of the usual 11 inches or 12 inches of this date—the hour hand is of the broad pierced spade-headed type much favoured by Dan Quare, the winding holes are nearly level with the centre of the hands, the day-of-the-month aperture is low down, right on the inside edge of the hour circle, and on the silvered ring the minute divisions are on the outer edge and carried through the figure of the Arabic 5 in the fashion of ten or fifteen years previously. The hood is also made to slide upwards in grooves and held in place by a spring when elevated to its fullest extent. Long-clock cases inlaid with marqueterie on the sides as well as the front, as in this example, are exceedingly rare.

Fig. 122 is a true type of the period to which it belongs, the only detail reminiscent of earlier times being the device of the Tudor rose engraved round the centre of the hands in imitation of the lantern clocks with central alarum discs. The glazed hole in the lower door is ringed with a rim of gilded wood in place of the usual brass circle. The walnut-veneered case is edged with bandings of cross-cut rose and palm woods, and inlaid with coloured floral marqueterie. The fret in the frieze of the hood is of stamped brass. The hood is made to slide upwards in the earlier fashion. Fig. 124 is an example of about the same period, with the unusual feature of a third winding hole and square by which the shutters of the holes below are opened and the maintaining power set in operation. The case is a particularly choice specimen of self-coloured, "all-over" floral marqueterie. The Alexander Irving clock shown in the next illustration may be bracketed with it in point of merit, the case being of even finer proportions, although the moulded base is a restoration. Fig. 126 is a provincial rendering of the same fashion, the dial suffering somewhat by the replacing of the original hour hand with one not only of much later fashion but also obviously intended for a much larger dial. The base here is also a somewhat ignorant restoration, but the whole clock is useful as showing the high standard which was maintained, at this period, even in insignificant country villages, Ampthill at this date having a total population of less than 1000 inhabitants.

Had the evolution of the long case been coincident with the development of the marqueterie cutter's art in England, the regular progression of the clocks would have probably synchronised with that of the cases also. It is a piece of negative evidence, although curiously convincing in its way, of the Dutch origin of many of these elaborate clock cases, that if we trace a progressive development by the clocks themselves we are compelled to anticipate fashions or to return to others apparently

Fig. 126.

Fig. 127.
Enlarged Dial of Fig. 126.

Fig. 126.

WILLIAM CARTER, AMPTHILL.

Eight-day Striking Clock.
Curious engraved dial.   Oak case veneered with walnut
and ebony and inlaid with coloured floral marqueterie.

7 ft. 1 in. high × 11 ins. width of waist.
11 in. dial.

Date about 1700.

Fig. 129.
Enlarged Dial of Fig. 128.

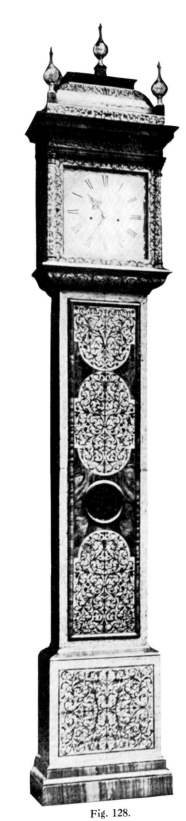

Fig. 128.

Fig. 128.

WILLIAM COOK, LONDON.

Eight-day Striking Clock.
Case inlaid with fine scroll marqueterie of pear-tree and
rosewood in panels of plane-tree in a ground of walnut
veneered on oak.

In the possession of W. Clare Lees, Esq.

7 ft. 5½ ins. high × 11½ ins. width of waist.   10¾ in. dial.

Date about 1695–1700.

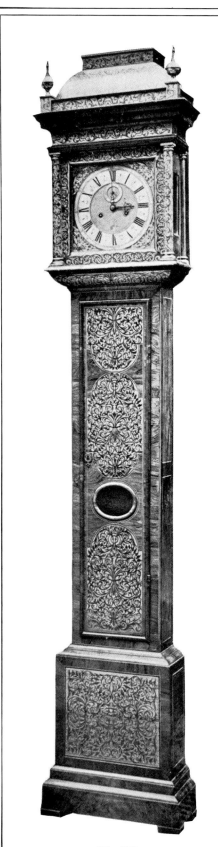

Fig. 130.

Fig. 131.

Enlarged Dial of Fig. 130.

Fig. 130.

E. SPEAKMETT, LONDON.

Eight-day Striking Clock.
Seconds' dial.   Day of month.
Oak case veneered with walnut and inlaid with walnut
scroll marqueterie on a ground of plane-tree, in panels.

7 ft. 11 ins. high.   Waist $11\frac{3}{4}$ ins. wide × $6\frac{1}{4}$ ins. deep.
12. in. dial.

Date about 1700.

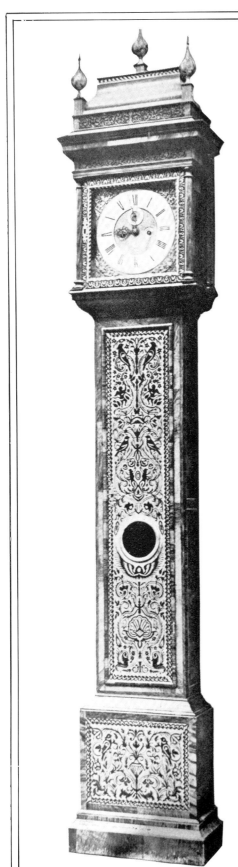

Fig. 132.

Fig. 133.
Enlarged Dial of Fig. 132.

Fig. 132.

THOMAS WHEELER, LONDON.

Eight-day Striking Clock.
Oak case veneered with walnut and inlaid with black
marqueterie of scrolls and birds in a ground of
plane-tree.

7 ft. 10 ins. high × 11¼ ins. width of waist.
11 in. dial.

Date about 1700.

obsolete. Thus the change from gay to sober coloured marqueterie, from natural forms—flowers and leaves—to highly conventionalised ornament or a mass of meaningless scrollwork, from the panelled to the "all-over" form, is true of English-made furniture, but is emphatically not so with these long cases. The possibility of a re-marriage of clock and case will not get over the difficulty, for two reasons. You cannot put a late 12-inch dial into an 11-inch hood, or vice versa, and no theory of changing will account for a poor clock in an elaborate case, although a catastrophe might logically account for the reverse proceeding. We are compelled, therefore, to take clocks with their cases as we find them, as a general rule, and to remember the possibility, especially before 1700, of skilled Dutch and less competent English artisans working in a species of one-sided competition, to supply the clockmaking trade with these long cases. It must also not be forgotten that these marqueterie cases hardly ever agree with the furniture made after the same general patterns, the era of marqueterie in furniture extending, approximately, from 1685–90 to 1700–5, whereas marqueterie clock cases are both earlier and later, from 1675–80 to about 1715.

Figs. 128 and 130 are two unlike examples, both as regards clocks and cases, yet of approximately the same dates. The William Cook appears to be earlier than it actually is, having the broad hour hand, the minute divisions on the outer edge of the hour-ring, and a small dial. The movement, however, is constructed on irregular lines, as, for example, in the day-of-the-month wheel at the top, seen through a ringed aperture, and the absence of the usual seconds' dial. The planting of the trains, the general workmanship, and the record of the maker, all preclude an earlier date than about 1695–1700. The case, on the other hand, is of later style, the fashion for the seaweed marqueterie in panel being nearly the latest of all the marqueterie phases. Fig. 130 is a characteristic example of its period, possessed of an obvious incongruity in the early meagre hour hand, but otherwise quite a good specimen. Fig. 132 has also the drawback of a badly-matched pair of hands, but the case is well proportioned and beautifully decorated with ebony marqueterie of very unusual type in a ground of plane-tree. Fig. 134 shows the last stage of the first branch of case development. It will be noticed that all the clock cases hitherto illustrated have a quarter-round, or "belly moulding" under the hood. This is an almost general indication of an early clock, and in the later stages this moulding is not only veneered, but also inlaid with marqueterie to match the rest of the case. It will also be remarked that in some of the examples already illustrated, the columns of the hood are also inlaid in

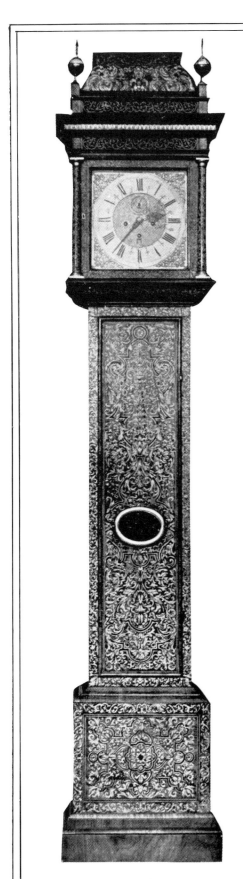

Fig. 134.

Fig. 135.

Enlarged Dial of Fig. 134.

Fig. 134.

RALPH CLOWES, LONDON.

Eight-day Striking and Chiming Clock.
Chiming on 8 and 10 bells.   Oak case veneered with walnut
and inlaid with fine scrolled marqueterie.

In the possession of Richard Hoffmann, Esq.

7 ft. 10 ins. high over all × 12½ ins. width of waist.
12 in. dial.

Date about 1700–5.

Fig. 136.

Fig. 137.
Enlarged Dial of Fig. 136.

Fig. 136.

WILLIAM FULLER, LONDON.

Eight-day Striking Clock.
Day of month through aperture below hands.   Oak case
veneered with walnut and inlaid with floral marqueterie.

7 ft. 6 ins. high × 11½ ins. width × 6½ ins. depth of waist.
10¾ in. dial.   2¼ in. hour circle.

Date about 1695–1700.

like manner. This is a feat of veneering, especially considering the brittle nature of the marqueterie and its liability to "spring" with such sudden bending, which demonstrates a skill emphatically not possessed by the English artisans of this period. Fig. 134 shows a later form of spandrel corner than any of the specimens previously illustrated. The movement has been converted and the chimes added at a later date. Original chiming movements fitted to a grandfather clock of this period are very rare. Fig. 134 may be said to be the final stage of the scroll marqueterie, and Fig. 136 marks the close of the all-over floral kind. The case has the peculiarity that the top or dome of the hood has been fitted on grooves so that it can be removed, together with the carved gilded spires, a concession to some of the low rooms of a later period. The case is of admirable proportions and detail, and the movement of fine quality.

Fig. 138 may be described as an approximation to a chiming clock, being fitted with a spiked barrel, which operates the hammers at the quarters and throws off to strike the hour. The movement is later than the type of the case would appear to indicate, the dial having late corner-pieces and rack-striking motion work. The movement is shown in profile

Fig. 138.

Fig. 138.

D. HAWTHORN, DARLASTON.

Eight-day Striking and Musical Clock.
Seconds' dial. Day of month.
Oak case veneered with walnut and inlaid with walnut
scroll marqueterie in oval panels of holly.

7 ft. 1 in. high.   Waist 12¾ ins. wide × 6½ ins. deep.
12 in. dial.   2½ in. silvered circle.

Date about 1705.

Fig. 140.
Side view of Fig. 138.

Fig. 139.
Enlarged Dial of Fig. 138.

Fig. 141.

Fig. 142.
Enlarged Dial of Fig. 141.

Fig. 141.

C. NICHOLAS, LONDON.

Eight-day Striking Clock.
Oak case veneered with walnut and inlaid with floral
marqueterie of various woods.

7 ft. 3 in. high.   Waist 12¼ ins. wide × 6½ ins. deep.
12 in. dial.   2½ in. silvered circle.

Date about 1700-5.

Fig. 143.

in Fig. 140, where it will be noticed that the barrels are not grooved in the usual way. The case is in the style of fifteen years previously, but commercial considerations may have dictated the ill-assorted union in the original instance. In the matter of current fashions provincial makers are not to be depended upon.

Fig. 141 introduces a new detail, the hollow moulding under the hood in place of the quarter-round before referred to. This fashion appears to have originated between 1700 and 1705, and to have become general with the London makers. The dial of this example is quite typical of the first years of the eighteenth century. There is no doubt that with certain makers the dates of manufacture and of publication (if one may use such a word in this connection) of their clocks do not coincide, often by a long period, and one is frequently puzzled to date accurately a clock which was probably begun years before it was actually finished. It could hardly be expected that with every change of fashion a maker should promptly jettison his stock of parts, and there is ample evidence that the principle of "making things do" was largely followed. So far, however, we have not been confronted with changes of fashion drastic enough to materially alter the form of the long-case clock.

Fig. 143.

THOMAS JOHNSON, LONDON.

Eight-day Striking Clock.
Seconds' dial.   Day of month.
Oak case veneered with walnut and inlaid with floral marqueterie in a panelled ground of ebony.

8 ft. 1 in. high.   Waist 12¼ ins. wide × 6¾ ins. deep.
12 in. dial.

Date about 1705.

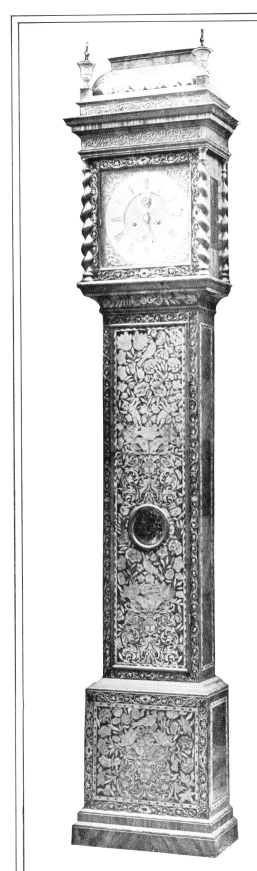

Fig. 145.

Enlarged Dial of Fig. 144.

Fig. 144.

"JOS. DAVIS, RATLEFᵉ HIWAY."

Eight-day Striking Clock.
Day of month through circular aperture below hands.
Oak case veneered with walnut and inlaid with
floral marqueterie.

7 ft. 8 ins. high × 12 ins. width × 7½ ins. depth of waist.
11 in. dial.

Date about 1705.

Fig. 144.

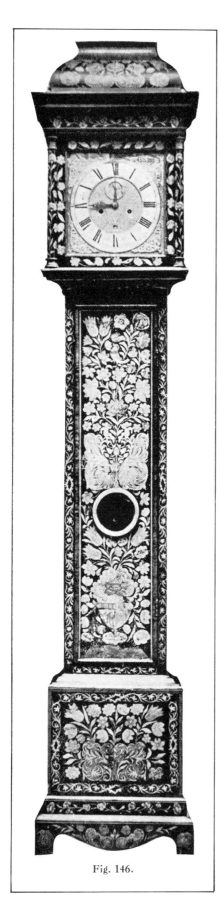

Fig. 146.

In these hollow moulded cases we reach the zenith of the marqueterie cutter's art as far as clock cases are concerned. Fig. 143 has the early floral marqueterie in a panelled ground of ebony. Fig. 144 has the "all-over" marqueterie of close and intricate design, in conjunction with the early spiral turned columns flanking the hood. The gradual broadening of the outer circle on the hour-ring, containing the Arabic numerals, and the increasing height of the cases will be noticed. The taste for the grandiose and lofty apartments of Kent, Ware and Gibbs, had already set in during the first years of the reign of Anne, and probably accounted for the fashion for the lofty hoods and large crowning spires of the later marqueterie cases. It was no uncommon occurrence, when the vogue for lofty apartments declined during the latter half of the eighteenth century, for these domed hoods to be cut down to accord with the less pretentious rooms. Too frequently for the appearance of the clock case this system of amputation sometimes commenced at the wrong end, and the base was mutilated in consequence. Fig. 146 is an instance of an otherwise fine case which has suffered by the loss of the usual lower member of the dome carrying the spires. Occasionally this adaptation to a later environment was anticipated, as in the case already shown in Fig. 136, where the top of the

Fig. 146.

EDWARD FAULKNER, LONDON.

Eight-day Striking Clock.
Oak case veneered with walnut and inlaid with floral marqueterie.

7 ft. 9½ ins. high × 12½ ins. width of waist.
12 in. dial.

Date about 1705–10.

154

Fig. 147.

Fig. 148.
Enlarged Dial of Fig. 147.

Fig. 147.

LANGLEY BRADLEY, LONDON.

Eight-day Striking Clock.
Day of month in aperture below hands.   Oak case
veneered with walnut and inlaid with fine scroll
marqueterie of walnut in a panelled ground of
plane-tree.

8 ft. high over all.   Waist 12 ins. wide × 6½ ins. deep.
11 in. dial.   2¼ in. silvered hour circle.

Date about 1710.

hood has been made to slide off, to accommodate the case to a low room if required.

The necessity for a close examination and comparison of apparently trifling details is well exemplified in the next illustration. At first glance there appears to be a strong resemblance between this clock and the William Cook shown in Fig. 128. A closer inspection will prove, however, that the Langley Bradley is the later of the two, without the necessity of having resource to established records. To consider the clock first; it will be noticed that the hour circle is broad in comparison— $2\frac{1}{4}$ as against $1\frac{7}{8}$ inches—the minute divisions are set well in, the greater prominence being given to the relatively unimportant detail of the Arabic numerals, the hour hand is comparatively insignificant in form, and the movement has the rack-striking device in lieu of the earlier locking-plate. The case also, although superficially resembling that of the Cook clock, has several notable points of difference. It is nearly six inches taller, the moulding of the dome is flatter, that under the hood is concave instead of convex, and the hood, although the dimensions are apparently fixed by the square dial, is more squat in general appearance. In short, the Bradley case lacks the carefully studied lines of that of the Cook, and this in itself is sufficient indication of a late example. Langley Bradley was apprenticed in 1687, obtained his "freedom" in 1695, and became Master of the Company in 1726.

Fig. 149 is approximately of the same date as the previous example, although it is usually wise to allow some margin in the case of a provincial maker. The idiosyncrasy in the spelling of the makers' names, before referred to, extends here, probably to the place of manufacture, "Lavinton" being possibly an engraver's rendering of "Lavendon," a small village in Buckinghamshire. The clock is a remarkably fine specimen of the clockmaker's craft, possessing, as it does, an original chiming movement on eight bells. A slightly later character than the Langley Bradley is indicated (apart from questions of provincial origin) by the larger dial, the broader hour circle, the type of corner-pieces, and the hand collet trenching on the circle of the seconds' dial. The spiral columns flanking the hood suggest the persistence of early characteristics. An apparently insignificant detail is the panelling out of the sides with triple lines—two of holly on either side of an ebony stringing—and this trifling peculiarity is rarely found on any other than a high-grade long case during the marqueterie period.

Another fashion which prevailed to some extent was for marqueterie of Arabesque form, where the ground of yellow sycamore or plahe-tree was inlaid with woods lighter

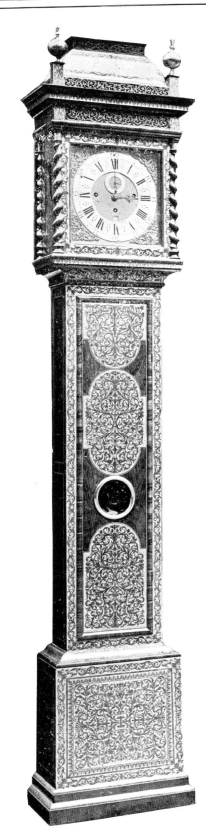

Fig. 149.

Fig. 150.

Enlarged Dial of Fig. 149.

Fig. 149.

JONATHAN BROWNE, "LAVINTON."

Eight-day Striking and Chiming Clock.
Seconds' dial.   Day of month.   Striking on large bell.
Octave chime on eight smaller bells.
Oak case veneered with walnut and inlaid with walnut
scroll marqueterie in panelled ground of plane-tree.

8 ft. 1 in. high.   Waist 12½ ins. wide × 6¾ ins. deep.
12 in. dial.

Date about 1710–15.

Fig. 151.

Fig. 152.
Enlarged Dial and Hood of Fig. 151.

Fig. 151.

BEN COLLYER, LONDON.

Eight-day, two train, Striking Clock.
Case inlaid with fine arabesque marqueterie of
dark wood in a ground of sycamore.

7 ft. 8½ ins. high × 1 ft. 1½ ins. width of waist.
12 in. dial, fine hands.

Date about 1710.

Fig. 153.

HENRY POISSON, LONDON.

Eight-day Striking Clock.
Case inlaid with fine scroll
marqueterie of rosewood and holly
in a ground of plane-tree veneered
on oak.

In the Victoria and Albert Museum.
7 ft. 11½ ins. high × 1 ft. 1½ ins. width
of waist.
12 in. dial.

Date about 1710–15.

Fig. 154.

Clock case inlaid with scroll
marqueterie of rosewood and holly
in a ground of plane-tree veneered
on oak.

In the Victoria and Albert Museum.
7 ft. 9 ins. high × 1 ft. 2 ins. width of case.

Date about 1710–15.

Fig. 154.

Fig. 153.

Fig. 156.

Enlarged Dial of Fig. 155.

Fig. 155.

RICHARD SCRIVENER, LONDON.

Eight-day Striking Clock.

Brass dial and hour circle. Oak case veneered with
plane-tree and walnut inlaid with fine arabesque
marqueterie.

8 ft. high × 12¾ ins. width of waist.

12 in. dial.

Date about 1710.

Fig. 155.

Fig. 157.

Fig. 158.
Enlarged Dial of Fig. 157.

Fig. 157.

"WM. UNDERWOOD, WESTMINSTER."

Eight-day Striking Clock.
Seconds' dial.   Day of month.
Oak case veneered with walnut, panelled with
double herring-boned lines.

6 ft. 8 ins. high.   Waist 12 ins. wide × 6¾ ins. deep.
12 in. dial.   2½ in. silvered circle.

Date about 1720–5.

Fig. 159.

Fig. 160.
Enlarged Dial of Fig. 159.

Fig. 159.

"THOS. TOMPION, LONDINI, FECIT."

Month Striking Clock.
Oak oase veneered with burr walnut inlaid with walnut
bandings and lines.   Pull repeater attached to striking
train, repeating quarters.   Bolt-and-shutter
maintaining power.

7 ft. 1 in. high × 12¾ ins. width × 7 ins. depth of waist.
11¾ in. dial.   2¼ in. hour circle.

Date about 1705–10.

and darker than the ground—generally holly and ebony—thereby producing a very rich effect. The Ben Collyer clock illustrated in Fig. 151 is an early example of this Arabesque inlay. Collyer was a noted maker of the first years of the eighteenth century, and the example shown here is a good specimen of his skill. Figs. 153 and 154—two clock cases from the Victoria and Albert Museum—are somewhat later in character, when the black inlay began to preponderate. The latter of the two examples is an instance of the barbarous custom, before alluded to, of cutting down the base of a clock case to fit a low room. The pillars flanking the hood have also disappeared, together with a dome top, probably at the same period. The Henry Poisson has lost its central spire, and the base is modern; it is otherwise a very good example of the last years of the reign of Anne.

Fig. 155 differs from the Faulkner clock shown in Fig. 146, in exhibiting no indications of spires having been fitted. The hour hand is somewhat poor, but the movement dates from a period when the former close attention to insignificant details was no longer paid. The case is a beautiful speci-men of Arabesque marqueterie of light and dark woods in a ground of plane-tree, the ornament

Fig. 161.

Fig. 161.

SAMUEL MACHAM, LONDON.

Eight-day Striking Clock.
In oak case veneered with walnut and inlaid with
fine scroll marqueterie.

8 ft. high × 1 ft. 1 in. width of waist
12 in. dial.

Date about 1710-15.

being both finely designed and executed. The moulding under the hood, the pillars at the sides, and even the fillet of the cornice, are all inlaid to correspond. The clock is a late production of a very early maker, Richard Scrivener having obtained his C.C. as early as 1639. The example shown here is probably rather the work of his successors in business.

One frequently meets with examples which almost defy classification, the productions of makers working in a bygone fashion. To illustrate a number of instances would merely puzzle the reader, as one is compelled to adhere to established types—in other words, where the one pattern has been repeated frequently enough to establish a fashion. When we have to deal with the work of a couple of centuries before our era, any system of dating, to be even approximately reliable, can only be the classification of types and the assigning of periods when each came into fashion. Had every maker of clocks followed the dictates of his individual fancy without any reference to pre-existing types, either of his own or his fellow-craftsmen, any rule for dating his productions would be sheer absurdity after this lapse of time.

Fig. 157 is one of these irregular examples before referred to, and it is interesting to note the jumble of early and late characteristics. It must be borne in mind that it is the latest feature which establishes the date ; a maker could revert to an antecedent fashion ; he could not anticipate one. In this specimen, although the hour circle is broad, the seconds' dial is unusually small. The hour hand is late in character, and the corner-pieces also, although these latter may be subsequent additions. Apart from the movement, which is the most valuable indication, the case is a better indication of late date than the dial, the squat base being characteristic of the London ciocks of 1725. The ornamentation of the case is also of irregular type ; in short, this specimen may be described as a square dial clock of the arch-dial period. The planting of the train and the general workmanship of the movement fully bear out this assumption.

The fine month clock by Tompion shown in the next illustration is a typical example of this noted maker's work. The general characteristics, especially those of the dial, would appear to warrant a later date than the one given here, but we must remember that, although this clock is a late specimen of the master's work, Tompion died in 1713, and also the arched-dial clock in the Pump Room at Bath (of which more hereafter), was made certainly before 1709. In Fig. 159 the original bolt-and-shutter maintaining power is intact, and the striking train is fitted with a pulling-string, to repeat the hour last struck.

Towards the close of the reign of Anne, the character of the marqueterie in these long clock cases changed considerably, the former ornament of flowers and leaves giving place to a most intricate arrangement of scrolls, nearly always cut from yellow sycamore or holly, and inlaid in a ground of walnut. Occasionally this scheme was reversed, the light wood being used for the ground and the darker for the inlay. The time and labour involved in the double cutting of this intricate marqueterie—as both the ornament and the ground had to be separately cut by the marqueterie saw—must have been considerable, and a time-saving practice was sometimes adopted of cutting panels in pairs, where the waste of the inlay was used for the ground of the second panel, and vice versa. When to this is added the fact that from four to six veneers were cut at the one operation, it is not remarkable that cases are sometimes found with identical inlay.

Fig. 161 is an example of this fine, or "seaweed" marqueterie, which has already been shown in panelled form in Figs. 128 and 130. The Arabesque style of Fig. 155 is an earlier variety of the "seaweed" marqueterie. In Fig. 161 some economy has been effected by the cutting of the ground of the lower panels of the door and the base in two halves at the one operation, the ornament being designed with a central line to permit of the cutting being done in this way. Figs. 162 and 163 are given to show the method of exchanging inlay and ground in two different cases, before referred to. It will be noticed, on examination, that the design of the marqueterie is identical in the two instances, the only difference being that in the one the ornament is of dark wood in a light ground, and the reverse of this in the other. There is no doubt that the marqueterie of the two has been cut from the same pouncing, and this in itself is some evidence that the manufacture of clock cases was not always under the direct control of the clockmaker.

The theory of the Dutch origin of nearly all of these marqueterie cases of the reigns of William III and Anne has already been referred to. As supporting evidence, the following four examples may be instructive. The first two, Figs. 164 and 166, are Dutch clocks in Dutch cases. The dial of Fig. 164 has the early cherub-headed corner-pieces quite in the English style, the triangular aperture above the centre of the hands showing the day of the week—Dingsdag (Tuesday)—and the presiding deity of each day—in this case Ziu; the Teutonic Mars, God of War. This is purely a Dutch conceit, but the engraving of the hour circle and the piercing of the hands are in the English manner, although, notably enough, the hour hand is in the arch-dial style of 1740. The case is light in colour, which suggests a foreign origin; but

Fig. 162.

THOS. WESTT (? WEST), LONDON.

Eight-day Striking Clock.
Case inlaid with mosaic marqueterie in a
ground of plane-tree veneered on oak.

In the possession of Sir Horace Brooks
Marshall.

7 ft. 1½ ins. high × 12¼ ins. width of waist.
11 in. dial, fine corners.

Date about 1710.

Fig. 163.

DAN. ROBINSON, LONDON.

Month Striking Clock.
Case inlaid with fine mosaic marqueterie
of various woods in a ground of walnut
veneered on oak.

7 ft. 6 ins. high × 1 ft. 1 in. width of waist.
12 in. dial.

Date about 1710.

Fig. 162.

Fig. 163.

Fig. 164.

Fig. 165.
Enlarged Dial of Fig. 164.

Fig. 164.

H. SCHOUTEN, AMSTERDAM.

Eight-day Striking Clock.
In oak case veneered with bleached walnut.

In the possession of Percy Webster, Esq.

7 ft. 1 in. high × 11 ins. width of waist.
11 in. dial.

Date ———

Fig. 166.

Fig. 167.
Enlarged Dial of Fig. 166.

Fig. 166.

AHASUERUS (?) FROMANTEEL, AMSTERDAM.

Eight-day three train Striking and Chiming Clock.
Oak case veneered with quartered burr-walnut.

7 ft. 9 ins. high × 1 ft. 1¼ ins. width of waist.
11 in. dial ; exceptionally fine hands and corners.

Date ———

Fig. 169.
Enlarged Dial of Fig. 168.

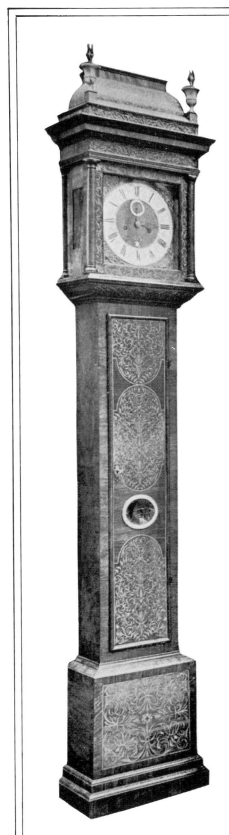

Fig. 168.

Fig. 168.

"JACOBUS HASSANIUS, LONDON."

Eight-day Striking Clock.
Oak case veneered with walnut and inlaid with fine scroll marqueterie.

7 ft. 10 ins. high × 11½ ins. width × 6⅜ ins. depth of waist.
10¾ in. dial.   2⅛ in. hour circle.

Date about 1710.

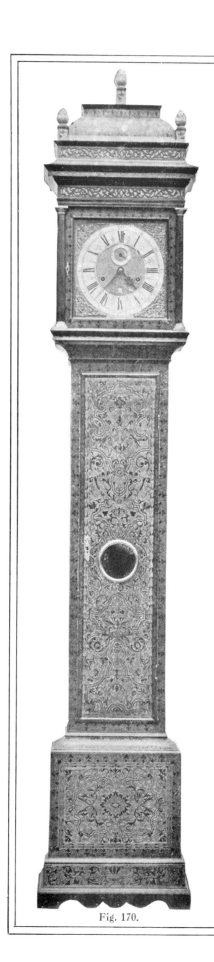

Fig. 170.

Fig. 171.
Enlarged Dial of Fig. 170.

Fig. 170.

ABRAM OOSTERWYK, MIDDELBURGH.

Month Striking Clock (two bells).
Dial signed " Abra. Oosterwyk, Middel[h.]"
Case inlaid with fine arabesque marqueterie of dark
wood on a light ground.

In the possession of D. A. F. Wetherfield, Esq.

8 ft. 2 ins. high.   Dial 12 ins. square.

Date ———

Fig. 172.

Fig. 173.
Enlarged Dial of Fig. 172.

Fig. 172.

JOSHUA WILSON, LONDON.

Eight-day Striking Clock.
Oak case veneered with burr-walnut.

7 ft. 6½ ins. high × 11¾ ins. width of waist.
11 in. dial.

Date about 1710.

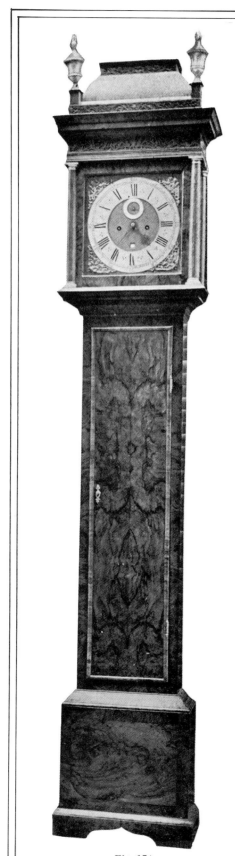

Fig. 174.

Fig. 175.
Enlarged Dial of Fig. 174.

Fig. 174.

DAN^{l.} DELANDER, LONDON.

Eight-day Striking Clock.
Day of month in aperture below hands.
Oak case veneered with burr-walnut.

8 ft. high over all.   Waist 12½ ins. wide × 6½ ins. deep.
Carved and gilded spires.
11 in. dial.   2½ in. silvered hour circle.

Date about 1710.

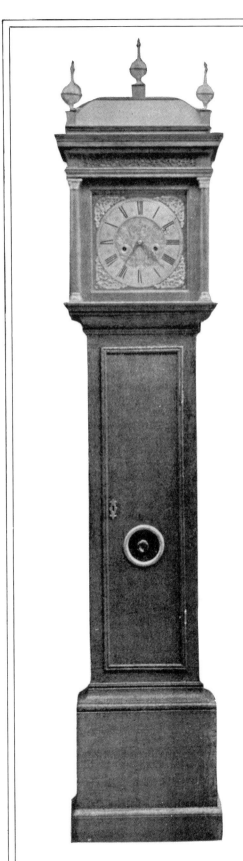

Fig. 176.

Fig. 177.
Enlarged Dial of Fig. 176.

Fig. 176.

"FRAN: BERRY, HITCHIN."

Eight-day Striking Clock.
Day of month in aperture.
Oak case.

7 ft. o$\frac{1}{2}$ in. high (without central spire).   Waist 12$\frac{3}{4}$ ins.
wide × 6$\frac{3}{4}$ ins. deep.
11 in. dial.   2 in. silvered hour circle.

Date about 1705-10.

if stripped of its ball spires and the moulded bracket feet, the Dutch character would not be very apparent in the photograph.

Fig. 166 has the English spires, the similarity to some of the English cases being even more close. Here the broad moulding above and below the base and the turned ball feet give a foreign character to the case, but the long waist and the general design of the hood, with the classical cornice and fretted frieze, the ogee, fillet, and bold hollow under the hood, are quite English in style. The general re-semblance of the dial to that of the Ben Collyer clock, Fig. 151, is very marked, the hands, the hour circle, and the pierced brass corners being of identical pattern. Added to this, although the dial is signed " Fromanteel, Amsterdam," the Froman-teels, Ahasuerus and John, were noted English makers, the former being a maker of steeple clocks at East Smithfield. The family is also credited with the first in-troduction of the pendulum into England, a claim which, if open to dispute at the present day, was accepted at the time, the presumption being that members of the family had opportunities of carefully examining the clock made for the States of Holland by Christian Huygens in 1657. Fig. 166 is probably the work of a member of a collateral branch of the same family established in Amsterdam, and dates from about the same period as the Ben Collyer clock, the dial of which it so closely re-sembles.

Figs. 168 and 170 are both typically English in style, both as regards cases and dials. The first is the work of a Dutchman domiciled in England, the second is the work of a Middelburg maker, the case itself bearing a label to this effect, and the dial being signed in the usual way. With two examples such as these, the evidence in support of the Dutch origin of these marqueterie cases becomes overwhelming, when added to that adduced at the outset of this chapter.

During the vogue of these elaborate marqueterie cases the taste for quieter types, such as Figs. 172 and 174, and the Tompion clock previously illustrated in Fig. 159, shows that the decline of marqueterie had already set in. In furniture, the veneers of richly veined and burred walnut had supplanted inlay of coloured woods, some years before. The difficulties attending the importation of the marqueterie cases from Holland must have been considerable, as England and Holland were keen trade rivals at this period, and the supply must have been found too intermittent and uncertain, in view of the gradually growing demand for these long clocks. Both Figs. 172 and 174 are English-made cases, veneered with home-grown walnut of rich figure. In the former the lower door is overlaid with pieced walnut burrs, and in the latter the effect has been obtained by the vertical jointing of two veneers of identical figure—that is, cut the one immediately under the other from the same log. Fig. 176 is a country-made clock in a case of plain oak, with the dial centre engraved in the earlier fashion. The progression of the corner-pieces of these three clocks will be noticed on examination, although this is an insufficient reason for placing them at different dates, Fig. 176 being, if anything, the earliest, and yet having the latest type of spandrel corners.

The vogue of the arched dial may be said to commence about 1715, but isolated specimens are to be met with some years before. The most notable of these is the Tompion clock in the Pump Room at Bath, before referred to, the date of which (1709) is recorded on a tablet in the same room. The clock is quite an exceptional example of Tompion's later work, and cannot be accepted as a current type, but apart from this there are many reasons why the arched dial should have evolved as a logical necessity rather than a wayward fashion. The desire to add to the functions of the clock, by an equation of time—as in the Tompion specimen at Bath—calendar-work, a strike-silent dial with its pointer, or by any of the other contrivances which were reserved for the embellishment of the arches of the later dials, is a natural one with makers who took the pride in their work which is so evident at this period, and who made constructional difficulties for the sheer pleasure of overcoming them. Many of these devices must have rendered additional space beyond that afforded by the square dial not only desirable, but positively necessary. Even apart from these considerations, a clock so well known as the one in the Pump Room, by the leading maker of the day, and presented in such exceptional circumstances (it was probably the last clock ever made by Tompion), must have been almost sufficient to have inaugurated a style. Tompion occupied the position practically of a dictator of clock fashions at the close of his career. His work is characterised by strong prejudices as well as great originality. Clocks of his make in marqueterie cases are exceedingly rare, although he flourished at the period when the vogue for marqueterie was at its height. If conservative in this particular, however, he was an innovator in others ; he was almost certainly the pioneer of the arched-dial clock, although, as he inaugurated this feature at the close of a long and prosperous career, it is doubtful whether he ever made as many as half a dozen clocks with dials of the arched form.

Fig. 178 is a year timepiece, with the dial signed "Thos. Tompion, London," now in the First Lord's private office at the Admiralty. This clock has been referred to as an example of Tompion's work, and even so acute an observer as Mr. F. J. Britten, while remarking that the style seems late for Tompion, attributes it to

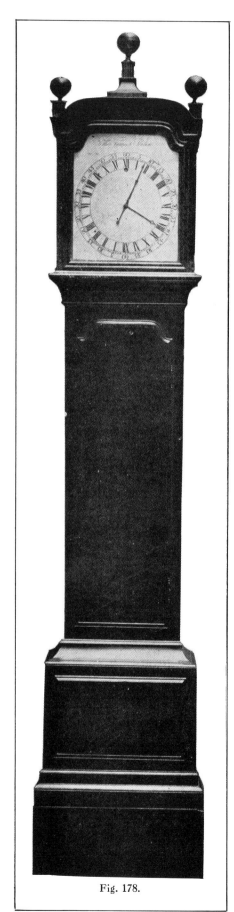

Fig. 178.

Graham, his successor. As a matter of fact, the clock was probably made some eighty years after Tompion's death. The case is veneered with curl mahogany, and is of the fashionable regulator type of 1800. Two examples of almost identical form are given later in Figs. 254 and 255. The cornice of the hood has a brass plate affixed, engraved with the words " Presented by Queen Anne," and the general style of this should have been enough to arouse suspicion, as a clock thus given by royalty would not be acknowledged in this scanty fashion. The full title of the donor, together with that of the recipient and the date and circumstances of the gift, would certainly have been stated had the legend of this brass plate been true. Queen Anne could not possibly have presented a clock case veneered with curl mahogany, as the wood was utterly unknown in England at the date of her death.

There is, however, strong reason to suppose that a clock, and presumably one by Tompion, was presented, and to the Admiralty—the latter for the reason that royal gifts are not readily bartered away. By a curious piece of red tape, the care of the furniture at the Admiralty, including all the clocks, with the exception of one by Grignion, is the province of the Office of Works, and such furniture figures as the property of that body, all repairs being done

Fig. 178.

" THOS. TOMPION, LONDON." (?)

Year Timepiece.
Oak case veneered with curl mahogany.

In the Admiralty Offices, Whitehall.

Date about 1800.

under the supervision of the Office. There is abundant evidence at the Admiralty to show how great must have been the vandalism practised under the guise of restoration by the Office of Works, even up to recent times. For example, an Act of Parliament clock has had its lacquered face removed and a common painted dial substituted, embellished with the Admiralty device and provided with a glazed bezil. A superb long-case clock by Langley Bradley has been robbed of its pierced hands, these having been replaced by a pair of blued steel, of the kind usually found on common kitchen dials. In the private quarters attached to the Admiralty offices is a clock in a common grained deal case, with a square silvered dial of pronounced nineteenth-century type. This is probably the missing Tompion clock, now vandalised almost beyond recognition. Attached to the dial, and over-lapping some of the engraving, are four beautifully chased and water-gilt corner-pieces of the 1700 type, and the striking work is of the outside locking-plate kind, and of the quality which one would have expected from a maker of the rank of Tompion. The movement is an eight-day, and is quite untouched. The signature has vanished with the original dial. Some attempt was probably made, many years ago, to "restore" the clock after it had been neglected for a long period, and the work was evidently done in most ignorant fashion. Later on the circum-stances of the royal gift were remembered, and the clock in question inquired for. The association between the giver and the gift had long before been neglected, and a solution was found in attaching a spurious label and a forged signature to the most remarkable timepiece available, the year clock then in the Council Chamber. The ignorance displayed in fathering a clock of the period of 1800 on a maker of nearly a century before can be understood when the brutal treatment meted out to the original one is noticed. Had the Langley Bradley clock been chosen, with the original signature stoned out and that of Tompion substituted, the forgery might have passed unnoticed, as the Bradley is a month clock of regal form, with a very early form of arched dial enriched with the insignia of the Admiralty. The so-called Tompion has only merited the notice thus accorded to it, as the state of affairs before described is hardly what one would have expected from a Government Department. To render suspicion a certainty, in another room at the Admiralty is the fellow of this "Tompion" clock, by Eardley Norton, probably the original maker of both.

The addition of the arch to the former square dial is such a radical alteration that it can be easily understood how serious the fashion must have been for makers holding a large stock of the older type of dials, and possibly with cases made to

Fig. 179.

Fig. 180.
Enlarged Dial of Fig. 179.

Fig. 179.

WINDMILLS & BENNET, LONDON.

Eight-day Striking Clock.
Bolt-and-shutter maintaining power.
Day of month and day of week in apertures inside
hour circle.
Oak case veneered with burr-walnut.

7 ft. 2 ins. high (without centre spire).   Waist 11¼ ins.
wide × 7½ ins. deep.
Dial 12½ ins. × 9½ ins.

Date about 1720–30.

Fig. 182.
Enlarged Dial of Fig. 181.

Fig. 181.

CHARLES GRETTON, LONDON.

Eight-day Striking Clock.
"Strike-silent" lever on left-hand side of dial.   Dial
signed in three places.   Added arch top.

11 ins. wide × 15⅜ ins. high ; arch 4¼ ins. high.

Oak case veneered with walnut and inlaid with floral
marqueterie of various woods.

In the possession of Richard Hoffmann, Esq.

8 ft. 5½ ins. high over all × 11⅛ ins. width of waist.

Date about 1720–5.

Fig. 181.

Fig. 183.

Fig. 184.

Enlarged Dial of Fig. 183.

Fig. 183.

DAVID HUBERT, LONDON.

Eight-day Striking Clock.
Silvered dial.   Brass corners.
Oak case veneered with burr-walnut.

6 ft. 4½ ins. high.   Waist 11 ins. wide × 6¾ ins. deep.
Dial 14 ins. × 10 ins.

Date about 1730.

match. Hence it is not unusual, and quite natural in the early arched-dial clocks, to find the arch added to an existent square dial, riveted on to the plate from behind. Fig. 179 is a clock of this kind, and it will be noticed that the dial is otherwise of very early form and style of engraving, with the minutes on the outer edge of the circle. A curious feature is the presence of two apertures, above and below the collet of the hands, for the days of the week and the month respectively. The dial is unusually small for the date of the clock itself—another early indication—and the general form of the case does not show any marked departure from the square dial years preceding.

Arched-dial clocks in marqueterie cases are exceedingly rare. The Wetherfield collection has one, by Andrew Davis, and the Charles Gretton clock illustrated in Fig. 181 is another of these exceptional specimens. The arch of the dial has been added, in the same way as with Fig. 179, and apart from this feature, both case and clock are quite of the earlier type, especially as regards the style of the marqueterie and the quarter-round moulding under the hood. A curious point is the signing of the dial in three places, on the bottom, between the V and the VII of the Roman numerals, and in the silvered boss in the arch. The first

Fig. 185.

Fig. 185.

WINDMILLS & WIGHTMAN, LONDON.

Eight-day Striking Clock.
Oak case veneered with burr-walnut.

7 ft. 8 ins. high × 1 ft. 3 ins. width of waist.
Dial 12¾ ins. × 16½ ins. high.

Date about 1725–30.

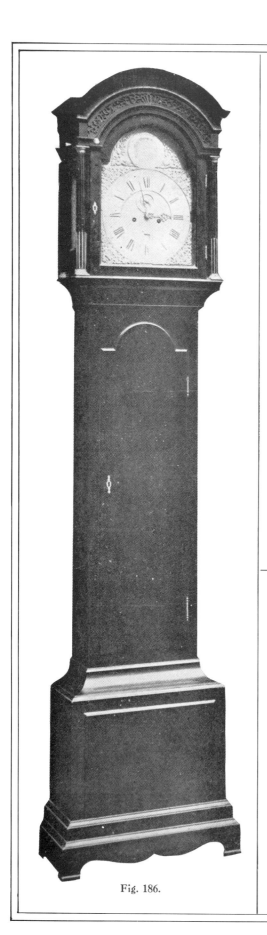

Fig. 186.

Fig. 187.
Enlarged Dial of Fig. 186.

Fig. 186.

JOHN DAVIS, LONDON.

Eight-day Striking Clock.
Seconds' dial, day of month aperture. "Tempus Fugit"
in subsidiary dial in arch.
Walnut case veneered on oak.

8 ft. 6 ins. high × 1 ft. 2 ins. width of waist × 7 ins. depth
of waist.
Dial 17 ins. high × 12 ins. wide.

Date about 1730.

Fig. 188.

Fig. 189.
Enlarged Dial of Fig. 188.

Fig. 188.

THO. BUDGEN, FECIT (CROYDON).

Eight-day Striking Clock.
Curious arrangement of dial, with signs of the Zodiac, &c.
Oak case veneered with veined English walnut.

6 ft. 11 ins. high × 14 ins. width × 6½ ins. depth of waist.
Dial 12 ins. wide × 16 ins. high.

Date about 1730–40.

makers of arched dials appear to have made this addition merely for effect, without any useful purpose being served. The third signature in the arch, therefore, is simply by way of embellishing an otherwise empty space, but the presence of the other two is incomprehensible. The case of this clock is finely proportioned and of beautiful workmanship. It was evidently made for the new form of dial, as although the arch has been added to the dial, the door in the hood is in its original state.

Two details may be noted here, as invariable indications of early arched dials —namely, the hour divisions on the inside of the hour-ring, and the low arch, rarely as much as the half of a circle. The presence of the silvered boss with the maker's name engraved thereon is a usual but not an infallible sign. Fig. 183 is a good type of an early complete arched-dial clock, the case simple in form, veneered with choicely-figured walnut, the hour-ring with the Arabic numerals large and the minute divisions well set in. The corner-pieces of this period will also be noticed, the type having already been illustrated in Chapter VIII. Clock cases of this period are also usually characterised by the squat base, a detail found especially in the later lacquered cases, particularly in those of provincial origin.

Fig. 185 is exceptional in being a typically English case, as compared with those either of Dutch make or modelled after the fashions of Holland. This example has evidently been made by a joiner, to accord with much of the plain walnut furniture of the period of Anne. The veneers used are of a different character to those usually found on clock cases, and this distinction will be noticed if this specimen is compared with the one immediately preceding. The suggestion of the familiar domed or hooded cabinet of the first years of the eighteenth century is also unmistakable. The clock, however, is later than this resemblance would imply, and is a good instance of the truth of the observation made at the outset of this chapter, that the earlier clock cases anticipate subsequent furniture fashions, whereas after 1710 they follow them at a period varying from ten to thirty years.

In this specimen it will be noticed that the arch is used for a subsidiary dial with a "strike-silent" finger. This is an indication of a date approximating to 1730. The dial of Fig. 186 has the same feature, and may be regarded as a typical example of its date in every respect. The broad spade hands tend to become smaller after 1730, although the minute hands become coarser. This tendency is continued until the close of the century, by which time the one becomes merely a smaller copy of the other. The case of Fig. 186 is veneered with straight-grained dark walnut, and is a type which was afterwards extensively copied when mahogany became the fashionable wood—about 1750–60—for clock cases, and nearly thirty years before for furniture—another instance of how the casemaker followed in the train of the joiner at a respectful interval.

Although clocks tend to become depraved in type after the introduction of the arched dial—the former attention to minute details, especially of exterior ornamentation, being no longer bestowed—the workmanship of the movements does not deteriorate when the more elaborate clocks come into vogue. Fig. 188 is a curious and complicated clock of about 1730–40, with a 24-hour dial. In the arch is a rotating globe showing the phases of the moon, with a revolving disc showing its age immediately below. Of the two lunettes on either side of the seconds' dial, above the hand-centre, the one on the left shows the days of the week, each with its astronomical sign, that on the right the name of each month with its zodiacal sign. The dial below the hands has a silvered ring engraved in two circles, on the inside with the signs of the Zodiac, which the pointer headed with a lunar crescent indicates, and on the outside the days of the month, marked by a finger in the usual way. The zodiacal signs for the whole year are set forth on the two segments on either side of the inner edge of the hour-ring. Of the three hands, that tipped with the sun shows the hour of the day, that with the moon the relative time

Fig. 190.

JOS. SHELLY, LONDON.

Eight-day Striking Clock.
Seconds' dial. Day of week and of month.
Oak case veneered with burr-walnut.

8 ft. 6 ins. high (without centre spire). Waist 1 ft. 2 ins. wide
×9½ ins. deep.
Dial 16¾ ins. × 12 ins.

Date about 1720.

Fig. 190.

for the antipodes, or any position to which it is set, as it has the same rate of revolution as the other hand. The third indicates the minutes. The silvered ring is engraved with the Roman numerals from I to XII repeated on the outside, and the minutes, in Arabic figures, from 1 to 60. The minute hand, therefore, revolves twenty-four times as fast as each of the others. The case is veneered with English walnut, highly bleached by the action of light and age, and is probably the work of a cabinetmaker. Thomas Budgen of Croydon was a maker of some repute, considering that he was working in, what was then, a remote village.

Fig. 190 closes the progression of these plain walnut cases which superseded the elaborate marqueterie examples of William III and Anne. The arch of the dial is provided with a segmental aperture through which is shown the day of the week, that of the month appearing in the usual square orifice below the hands. The case is a beautiful specimen, the wood carefully selected and choicely figured. The proportions are also unusually fine for this period.

We have seen that the marqueterie inlaid cases declined in favour after about 1715-20, and were superseded by those veneered with plain walnut. The rarity of the latter, however, coupled with the fact that they represent solely the fashion of 1720-35 as far as long-case clocks are concerned, appears to indicate that the long clock itself declined at this date. It can be readily understood that whereas a "grandfather" case would harmonise well with the modest rooms of the William III and Anne periods, it would be dwarfed by the lofty and grandiose apartments of the early Georgian era, when Kent and Vanbrugh—of Houghton and Blenheim fame respectively—were concerned. The fact that bracket clocks preserve an unbroken chronological order at this period suggests that the small clock took the place of the larger one at this date. The fashion for lacquer decoration, however, extended to clock cases in due time, and again gave the long-case clock a lease of fashionable favour for a while, but the early lacquer cases are also rare, and it may be said that from 1735 to about 1755-60—when mahogany cases came extensively into vogue—the long-case clock was comparatively neglected. The fashion for lacquer-work was always sporadic, and extended right through the eighteenth century. We cannot expect, therefore, to find the same rigid adherence to fashionable types as in the marqueterie cases. Here we find a case of a bygone fashion decorated in the new manner, there we meet an example which conforms to no prevailing manner at all. Lacquer cases are, therefore, entitled to be considered apart, in the usual progression of types, and demand individual attention, which it is the purpose of the following chapter to give.

Chapter X

Lacquered Cases of Long Clocks

WITH the decline of the marqueterie cases, which coincides almost with the introduction of the arched dial, the long case itself appears to have fallen into disfavour, as mentioned in the last chapter. In the years from 1720 to 1740, apart from the plain walnut examples, which merely reproduce, as a general rule, the general forms of the antecedent marqueterie cases, we have only to consider those which were decorated with raised gilded gesso, either monotonous or polychromatic, on a ground of japan, usually known as lacquer-work. The term "lacquer" has only a modern significance in the sense in which it is used here; during the eighteenth century, lacquering, or "lackering," implied a protective coating of varnish designed to protect base metals from the tarnishing effects of the atmosphere. To avoid confusion, however, the use of the modern term, in the present instance, is preferable. In the documents of the time we meet with references to "Bantam-work" (incised lacquer), so called from the name of a Dutch trading station of that name in Java, "Jappan" or "Indian" cabinets—all terms implying some kind of lacquer decoration.

Long-case clocks being in themselves exceptional during the years from 1720 to 1740, specimens are consequently rare, and those decorated with lacquer-work of that date are seldom met with. After 1740 lacquered cases become more plentiful, but the general character of the work is usually so poor in quality, that they cannot be classed with the earlier examples. In these later clocks, not only is the ornament badly drawn, and usually executed in base metal, but also a mere daubing with varnish paint takes the place of the previous carefully prepared ground.

As with the marqueterie, so with the lacquered cases, it must be regretfully confessed that the earliest and finest of the examples containing clocks by noted English makers are usually of Dutch origin. The art of lacquer decoration had reached a high stage of perfection in Holland during the latter half of the seventeenth century, whereas it was utterly unknown in England, or treated as a polite occupation to be taught in young ladies' schools, until the beginning of the reign of Anne. These seventeenth-century clock cases were evidently greatly prized, the

Fig. 191.

Fig. 192.
Enlarged Dial of Fig. 191.

Fig. 191.

CHRISTOPHER GOULD, LONDON.

Eight-day Striking Clock.
Bolt-and-shutter maintaining power ; beautifully pierced
hands.   Each minute on dial numbered.
Black lacquer case.

In the possession of D. A. F. Wetherfield, Esq.

7 ft. 8 ins. high.   12 in. dial.   Very rare and fine example.

Date 1695-1700.

finest movements alone being reserved for them, with dials highly engraved, and corner-pieces chased and water-gilt. Fig. 191 is an exceptional specimen from Mr. Wetherfield's collection. The hour hand, with its central "rose," is beautifully pierced and "carved," the spandrel corners chased and gilt, and every minute on the hour-ring separately numbered. The ground of the lacquered case is hard and brilliant, and of a degree of excellence, both technically and artistically, which was certainly not known in England at that date, if one may judge from such treatises on "lackering" as the folio of Stalker and Parker published in 1688.

Lacquer-work on clock cases, as on furniture, may be divided into three classes. The first includes the early cases of Dutch manufacture and decoration, the second the exceptionally rare examples of English-made cases which were sent in the tea-ships of the East India Company to be lacquered in China or Japan, and the third is the true English lacquer, varying in quality from that of the Dutch examples to mere daubings of black or coloured paints and metals.

The second of the above classes is much rarer even than would have been thought, considering the number of the East India Company's ventures and the facilities these apparently offered. However advantageous such a course may have been in theory, there were many grave drawbacks to it in practice, especially with clock cases. The risks of a voyage to the East were many; the Indiamen were heavily armed, and on more than one occasion had held their own with the frigates, and even the line-of-battle ships of other nations. The loss of one of these vessels on the homeward journey, laden with merchandise from the trading stations of the Far East, was an event of almost national importance. The risks, however, especially on the out-bound journey, were many, and the time which must have elapsed between the sending out of a clock case to the East and its safe return, was a matter of years. This alone, with an industry the fashions of which were constantly changing, was a serious consideration, and must have militated against the adopting of such a course.

It is, unfortunately, impossible to give documentary evidence as to the extent of the practice in the lacquering of furniture, as, apart from the fact that the bills of lading of the East India Company were destroyed wholesale after 1867, when the East India House in Leadenhall Street was demolished, it is more than doubtful whether even these would have thrown any light on the matter, as articles of furniture sent for this purpose would probably have been a private venture of the captain, and would not have figured in the Company's records in any way.

Fig. 193.

Fig. 194.
Enlarged Dial of Fig. 193.

Fig. 193.

WILLIAM WEBSTER, EXCHANGE ALLY.

Eight-day Striking Clock.
Brass dial and hour circle.
Case of oak decorated with lacquer work of Chinese
workmanship, on a ground of the Imperial
lemon-yellow.

In the possession of the Rev. J. O. Stephens.

7 ft. 8 ins. high × 13½ ins. width of waist.
Dial 17¾ ins. high × 13 ins. wide.

Date about 1730.

Fig. 195.

Fig. 196.
Enlarged Dial of Fig. 195.

Fig. 195.

"EDMUND BULLOCK, ELLESMERE. 303."

Eight-day Striking Clock.
Oak case decorated with Chinese figures on a ground
of tortoiseshell lacquer.

In the possession of Colonel Henry Howard, C.B.

8 ft. 8 ins. high (without spires). 1 ft. 4 ins. width of waist
× 7 ins. depth of waist.
Dial 1 ft. 7 ins. high × 1 ft. 1½ ins. wide.

Date about 1740.

Fig. 197.

We have, therefore, to fall back on the plan of judging the extent of the custom by the Oriental lacquer on English-made pieces which have survived; an obviously imperfect criterion. Fig. 193 is an authentic specimen of an English-made case decorated with Chinese lacquer, containing a clock by William Webster. The case is of English oak, the ornament polychromatic on a lacquered ground of the Chinese Imperial yellow. The case is tall and graceful, the decoration beautifully executed and of astonishing minuteness. The sides are ornamented in similar fashion to the front. The clock itself, although of good quality, is hardly worthy of its splendid case. The dial and hour circle are both of polished brass, evidently kept in the one tone of yellow to accord with the colour scheme of the case. There is some evidence to show that the arch of the dial has been added, hence the name of the maker on the two brass plates fixed so as to cover the join. It is possible that the case was sent to China about 1720; the arched door to the hood precludes a much earlier date. It was probably received in England some ten years later, which accords with the period of the dial and its maker.

Fig. 195 is a clock which was either made to the order of the East India Company or for one of its officers. The tradition says that it was, at one

Fig. 197.

"HY. RICHARDSON, LONDON."

Eight-day Striking and Chiming Clock.
Black lacquer case.

7 ft. 5 ins. high × 11 ins. width × 6¾ ins. depth of waist.
11 in. dial.   2¼ in. hour circle.

Date about 1700.

Fig. 199.
Enlarged Dial of Fig. 198.

Fig. 198.

Fig. 198.

GEORGE ALLETT, LONDON.

Eight-day Striking Clock.
Seconds' dial.   Day of month.
Bolt-and-shutter maintaining power.
Oak case decorated with gilded and polychromatic gesso
ornament on a ground of blue lacquer.   Silvered
spires, capitals, hinges, and ring round pendulum boss.

7 ft. 5 ins. high (without centre spire).   Waist 12 ins. × 6⅝ ins. deep.
11 in. dial.

Date about 1700–5.

Fig. 200.

Fig. 201.

Enlarged Dial of Fig. 200.

Fig. 200.

JOHN HOCKER, READING.

Eight-day Striking Clock.
Oak case decorated with gilded gesso on a ground of
tortoiseshell lacquer.

In the possession of Messrs. Law, Foulsham & Cole.

7 ft. 10½ ins. high × 12¾ ins. width of waist.
12 in. dial.

Date about 1735.

Fig. 202.

**WINDMILLS & ELKINS,
LONDON.**

Eight-day Striking Clock.
Brass dial, silvered hour circle.
Days of the month in arch, seconds'
dial below.
Oak case decorated with raised gilded
gesso on a green lacquered ground.

9 ft. high × 1 ft. 1½ ins. width of waist.
Dial 17 ins. × 12½ ins.

Date about 1730–5.

Fig. 203.

JOHN PYKE, LONDON.

Eight-day Striking Clock.
Brass dial, silvered hour circle.
Seconds' dia!. Day of month in
aperture below hands.
Oak case decorated with raised gilded
gesso on a green lacquered ground.

In the possession of Lord Ashby St. Legers.

8 ft. 1 in. high (8 ft. 11 ins. to top of
central spire).
Dial 16 ins. × 12 ins.

Date about 1730–5.

Fig. 202.

Fig. 203.

period, in India, the property of Hugh Howard, an ancestor of Colonel Henry Howard, C.B., the present owner. As against this may be set the fact that the date of the clock cannot be earlier than 1735, the broad waist of the case and the whole character of the dial pointing to an even later period, whereas Colonel Howard's ancestor died in 1739. The circle in the arch, with the full-rigged Indiaman painted thereon, suggests some association with John Company or its officers—there is an "Act of Parliament" clock decorated with a similar device at the India Office—but the plate must have been applied subsequent to the making of the clock, as the name "Edmund Bullock, Ellesmere" (Shropshire), appears underneath, together with the number 303. Had the painted disc been original, the maker would certainly have selected another place upon which to engrave his name—between the Roman VII and V, for example. The case is decorated with Chinese figures and scenes, on a tortoiseshell lacquered ground, the whole having the appearance of Dutch workmanship. The drawing of the ornament is unusually crisp and fine—some indication of an early date.

Figs. 197 and 198 are two lacquered clocks of early date. The first is a three-train striking and chiming clock on six bells, and is undoubtedly early, the striking work being of the outside locking-plate kind. The hands are later in character than the dial,

Fig. 204.

Fig. 204.

AYLMER STOPPES, LONDON.

Eight-day Striking Clock.
Phases of the moon in arch.
Case decorated with gilt gesso on a ground of green lacquer.

8 ft. 1 in. high × 1 ft. 2 ins. width of waist.

Date about 1735.

but these are obvious replacements. The case is decorated with black lacquer, the ornament well drawn but much tarnished. Both in this and the next illustration, as in the Christopher Gould clock previously shown, the rounded moulding under the hood (an almost infallible sign of an early case) will be noticed. Fig. 198 is a remarkable clock by George Allett, one of the apprentices of Thomas Tompion, an 8-day rack-striker with the original bolt-and-shutter maintaining power intact. The hour-hand is well pierced and carved, the hour-ring silvered, and the corner-pieces of early and exceptional type. The movement has six pillars between the plates, and is quite in Tompion's manner, and the unusual signature on the oval cartouche below the hands suggests an early example. The case is well proportioned, and is decorated with silver and coloured Chinese ornament on a lacquered ground of a beautiful powdered blue. The caps and bases of the columns and the spires are also silvered to correspond. A curious feature is the action of the shutters of the winding holes, which are opened by depressing the small lever in the segment at the outside edge of the dial on the right. This appears to have been a usual device with Allett, another clock with a similar dial having the same action.

The third variety of these lacquered cases, before referred to, is the true English lacquer, which, contrary to the usual development of handicrafts, is high in quality in the earlier specimens and very poor after about 1750. At this period, however, the general character of the long-case clock began to become depraved, especially in the hands of provincial makers of the Midland Counties. The period of English lacquer on clock cases may be said to coincide with that of mahogany in furniture, approximately from 1735 to 1760. Walnut cases were sparingly made during the same period, and towards the end of the first half of the eighteenth century mahogany began to be used, finally becoming almost the exclusive fashion during the remainder of the century. We can, therefore, place the evolution of long-case clocks up to 1750 in tabular form, something like the following :—

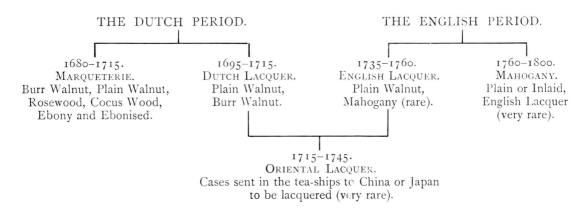

THE DUTCH PERIOD.   THE ENGLISH PERIOD.

1680–1715.   1695–1715.   1735–1760.   1760–1800.
MARQUETERIE.   DUTCH LACQUER.   ENGLISH LACQUER.   MAHOGANY.
Burr Walnut, Plain Walnut,   Plain Walnut,   Plain Walnut,   Plain or Inlaid,
Rosewood, Cocus Wood,   Burr Walnut.   Mahogany (rare).   English Lacquer
Ebony and Ebonised.   (very rare).

1715–1745.
ORIENTAL LACQUER.
Cases sent in the tea-ships to China or Japan
to be lacquered (very rare).

Fig. 205.

Fig. 205.

JOSEPH KIRK,
NOTTINGHAM.

Eight-day Striking Clock.
Brass dial and corners, silvered
hour circle.
Red lacquer case.

7 ft. 9½ ins. high × 1 ft. 1½ ins. width
of waist.
Dial 13 ins. × 16½ ins.

Date about 1740.

Fig. 206.

D. WENHAM, DEREHAM.

Eight-day Striking Clock.
Brass dial and corners, silvered
hour circle.
Silvered convex boss in arch
inscribed "Tempus Fugit."
Red lacquer case.

7 ft. 5½ ins. high × 1 ft. 1½ ins. width
of waist.
Dial 12½ ins. × 17 ins.

Date about 1750.

Fig. 206.

Fig. 200 is the first example of true English lacquer. The case is peculiar in many ways. The general form, with the square dial and rectangular lower door, is of the early fashion of 1705–10, but the workmanship of the movement and the name of its maker indicate a date fully twenty-five years later. The clock has been made for its case, and is evidently the work of its maker shortly after his apprenticeship had expired. John Hocker was the apprentice of Edward Joselin in 1728, and this example must date from some years after, as an apprentice would not be allowed to sign a dial with his own name. There is nothing beyond the dictates of an arbitrary fashion to prevent a maker of this date from reverting to the patterns of twenty or thirty years before, and Hocker's master must have been educated in the older square-dial school, he being apprenticed to James Woolverton in 1690. The case of Fig. 200 is similar in form to that of Fig. 161, and by a coincidence both specimens are in the same hands. The ornament is traced in gold with very slight relief, the ground being of tortoiseshell lacquer. It is very rare to find lacquered clock cases with the grounds of other colours than red or black ; occasionally a green or brown shade was attempted, but considerable difficulty seems to have been experienced in keeping the colours bright, green lacquer being usually almost

Fig. 207.

MARKWICK MARKHAM, LONDON.

Eight-day Striking Clock.
Oak case decorated with gilded gesso on a blue lacquered ground.

7 ft. 6½ ins. high × 13¾ ins. width of waist.
Dial 17½ ins. high × 13 ins. wide.

Date about 1750.

Fig. 207.

Fig. 208.

black, and brown a very dingy hue. In this example no attempt has been made at copying Oriental forms, with the exception of the palisading in the middle of the lower door. Figures of men on horseback and dogs are very familiar objects in lacquer decoration of this period. The dial, hands, and corner-pieces, the small square aperture surrounded by engraving and the turned rings round the winding holes are of the fashion of 1700. The available records of the Clockmakers' Company are useful in this instance, in distinguishing between the work of an early maker and a later one with old-fashioned ideas.

Fig. 202 is a tall clock case of about the same period as the preceding, quite in the fashion of the time, and of beautiful proportions and workmanship. The ornament is raised and gilded on a lacquered ground of dark green, the design of Chinese figures, palisading, palms and birds being well drawn and modelled. An unusual feature of the case is the two double-scrolled trusses supporting the hood. The pinnacles above are of wood, carved and gilded.

Fig. 203 is not so lofty as the preceding, but is of exceptional quality, a rare example of a fine green lacquered ground. The ornament is beautifully executed, and in pure gold leaf and powder. The carved and gilt wood pinnacles on this and Fig. 202 were the

---

Fig. 208.

WILLIAM CLAY, LONDON.

Eight-day Striking Clock.
Phases of the moon in arch.
Red lacquer case.

8 ft. 1½ ins. high × 1 ft. 1½ ins. width of waist.
Dial 13 ins. × 17½ ins.

Date about 1750.

usual fashion for elaborate cases, particularly those decorated with lacquer-work of high quality.

Fig. 204 is another green lacquered clock case of later date, the waist broader and shorter, and the general proportions not so fine as in Fig. 202. The cornice and frieze moulding, both arched to follow the line of the dial, appear to have been a fashion of about 1730–40, alternating with another pattern where both cornice and frieze mouldings were arched, but without superstructure. The ornament of the case of Fig. 204 strongly resembles that of Fig. 202 both in design and execution.

Fig. 205 is in the earlier fashion of Fig. 204, but being of provincial manufacture is probably somewhat later in date. The ground of this case is of the " Common Red," as it is styled in the text-books of the period.

Fig. 206 is later and of inferior quality, robbed also of much of its dignity by the absence of the spires above the cornice. It is exceedingly rare to find red lacquer of high quality on clock cases of this period, possibly owing to the difficulty of obtaining a ground of the necessary brilliancy and purity of colour.

Figs. 207 and 208 are of nearly the same period. Fig. 207 is a notable specimen of fine English lacquer, the ground of a beautiful blue. Markwick Markham

Fig. 209.

JOHN CHRISTIAN, AYLSHAM.

Eight-day Striking Clock.
Oak case decorated with black lacquer.

8 ft. 4½ ins. high × 1 ft. 1½ ins. width of waist.

Date about 1745.

Fig. 209.

had evidently considerable business connections in Turkey, judging by the number of his dials where Turkish hour numerals are substituted for the Roman. His place of business was behind the Royal Exchange, where a whole colony of famous clock-makers formerly assembled.

Fig. 208, although of similar form to the Markwick Markham clock, is of much inferior quality. It has a plain enamelled dial with incised hour circle, a fashion which began about 1760. The ornament is in the Chinese manner, in very low relief, on a red ground.

Fig. 209 is somewhat earlier, the case tall and graceful, the ornament also in very low relief, the fine mesh-work and circular paterae merely etched with gold.

It will be noticed that these clock cases become broader and less graceful towards the latter half of the eighteenth century, and the clocks themselves bear witness that the former intelligent interest taken in minute details of form and suitability of purpose was now rapidly on the wane.

Mahogany appears to have attained a firm popularity by about 1760, the later cases being almost exclusively veneered with this wood. The early specimens repeat many of the forms of the earlier walnut cases from 1720 to 1740, although the latter were made too sparingly to have established a fashion.

After about 1755, however, the grandfather type of clock again came into fashion, with mahogany, either plain, carved or inlaid, as the exclusive wood. The walnut and lacquered cases cannot be regarded other than as sporadic specimens, establishing no defined type. With the mahogany cases the vogue for the long-case clock was again resumed, and it is possible in these examples to trace the further development of the long-case until the period of its final degradation, in the hands of provincial makers, at the close of the eighteenth century.

Chapter XI

Long-case clocks from 1760 to 1800

THE introduction of mahogany into England, as the fashionable wood for furniture, occurred about 1720-25, but it was not until nearly forty years after that it came to be extensively used for the veneering of the cases of grandfather clocks. Mahogany (from the Indian name—mohagoni) is the timber of *Swietenia Mahogani*, of the family of the Cedrelaceæ. The tree is lofty and branching, with flowers like the false sycamore, and fruit the size of a turkey's egg. It is found in many parts of Central America, Cuba, Jamaica, Honduras and the Bahamas. This latter is generally known as Madeira-wood, and is inferior to the true American mahogany. During the last thirty years other kinds have been imported from the Gold Coast, but American mahogany is more valued for furniture than that of African growth.

The usual type of English grandfather case of the eighteenth century was nearly always veneered with mahogany on oak; the solid wood was very seldom, if ever, employed. One variety only of American mahogany, that from Cuba, was always used, generally of the kind known as curl-figure. At a later date the doors of the hood and trunk were sometimes made from Honduras mahogany, veneered with the finer wood from San Domingo. Inlay was very sparingly used, and only during the last few years of the eighteenth century, but carving was often lavished on the more elaborate examples. As a general rule, however, mouldings and applied frets were relied upon for ornamentation, and one noticeable peculiarity which distinguishes these mahogany cases, almost without exception, is that they bear signs of having been made by the general cabinetmaker rather than the specialised maker of clock cases, as was almost the general rule with the examples before about 1725. The profession of the clockmaker was no longer the close preserve which it had been at the commencement of the century. The standard of craftsmanship, from its artistic side, was much lower after 1740 than it had been before. The former fine traditions of the trade had become depraved and dissipated, and, as a necessary consequence, the general forms of these later clock cases became more heterogeneous, each maker suiting his own individual fancy. London-made clocks still followed defined fashions, however, until the end of the first half of the nineteenth century, and it is in these that we can trace the development of the long-case clock, whereas, in those of provincial, and especially of Midland

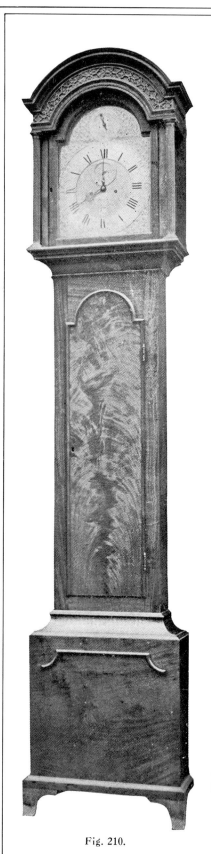

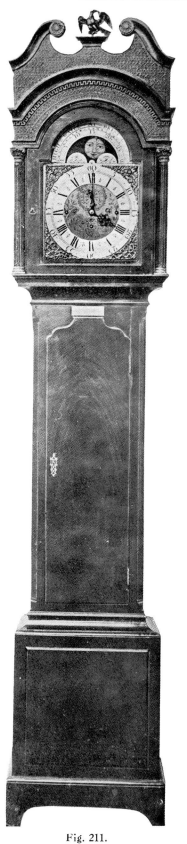

Fig. 210.

JAMES SCHOLEFIELD, LONDON.

Eight-day Striking Clock.
Strike-silent hand in subsidiary
dial in arch.
Mahogany case.

7 ft. 8½ ins. high × 13½ ins. width
of waist.
Dial 16½ ins. high × 11¾ ins. wide

Date about 1760.

Fig. 211.

SAMUEL WHITCHURCH, KING'S WOOD.

Eight-day Striking and Chiming
Clock.
Engraved centre to dial.
Phases of the moon in arch.
Mahogany case.

In the possession of His Majesty the
King of Norway.

8 ft. 5 ins. high × 14½ ins. width
of waist.
Dial 17 ins. high × 12½ ins. wide.

Date about 1765.

Fig. 210.

Fig. 211.

origin, the decline of the grandfather case, culminating in the gigantic and ugly Yorkshire clocks, can be witnessed.

Fig. 210 is a good example of the high quality of London clocks of 1760, the case veneered with choice curl-figure mahogany, the cornice of the hood arched to follow the line of the dial and its enclosing door, and the head of the lower door arched to correspond. The strike-silent dial in the arch is an earlier fashion, but the absence of the hour-divisions on the inside of the silvered circle show that the dial is contemporary with its case. Fig. 211 is of similar form, with the exception of the fretted pediment, with its taurus surmounted by a brass eagle, which alters the general appearance very considerably. The fretting of the frieze above the hood-door, the dentil-course and the pediment suggest the influence of Thomas Chippendale and his school, as far as the clock case-making industry was ever affected thereby. In the clock the phases of the moon are shown in the arch—an indication of a date after 1760—and in the semicircle above is engraved " High Water at Bristol Channel." King's Wood—or to give its modern spelling, Kingswood—is a town in Gloucestershire of some 11,000 inhabitants. The clock illustrated here was presented to His Majesty King Haakon of Norway by the Corporation of the City of London, and was purchased from Messrs. Gill and Reigate.

These arch-headed clock cases of the early mahogany period have their prototypes in the burr-walnut veneered cases of 1735 to 1750, referred to in a previous chapter. The use of solid oak in lieu of walnut or mahogany veneers was not exceptional at this date, even for clocks of high quality—some evidence that the making of the cases had become the province of the furniture joiner

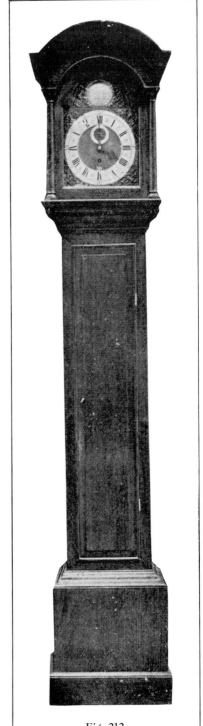

Fig. 212.
ROBERT HARRIS, LONDON.

Eight-day Clock.
Oak case.

7 ft. 1 in. high × 11 ins. wide
× 6¾ ins. deep.
Dial 10 ins. × 14 ins.

Date about 1745-50.

Fig. 213.

Fig. 214.
Enlarged Dial of Fig. 213.

Fig. 213.

RICHARD GANTHONY, LONDON.

Eight-day Striking and Chiming Clock.
"Chime-silent" dial in arch.   Seconds' dial in circle.
Silvered dial, engraved centre.   Brass corner-pieces.
Mahogany case.

8 ft. high.   Waist 15 ins. wide × 7 ins. deep.
Dial 16½ ins. × 12 ins.

Date about 1810–15.

rather than the work of a distinct trade. Fig. 212 is a good clock in an oak case of this kind, which, although of somewhat earlier date than the two examples already illustrated, fully explains the genesis of form of the first mahogany cases. It is a good indication of a dial of before 1750, when the arch is low and squat, considerably less than the half of a circle, and ornamented with a boss surrounded by an engraved band, as in this example.

One frequently encounters specimens, after about 1760, which present a curious jumble of characteristics rendering accurate classification almost an impossibility. Fig. 213 is an instance of this. Richard Ganthony was a well-known maker of the early nineteenth century. He was Master C.C. in 1828-9. The date of this clock cannot be earlier than 1810, yet it possesses many of the characteristics of 1770, especially in the design of the case and the variety of the veneer used for the lower door. There is a possibility, which must always be considered, of the clock having been made for an older case. In general style of the shaping of the waist door and the raised panel of the base, in furniture, would be referred to the influence of Batty Langley, and a date of about 1750. Allowing thirty years for the maker of clock cases to assimilate the furniture fashions of the time, it is probable that the case dates from about 1780, and the movement from 1810, the latter following many of the characteristics of the period of the case, such as the chime-silent dial in the arch and the pattern of the hour and minute hands.

Long clocks from 1770 to 1780 may usually be distinguished by the arches of the dials being provided with calendar work—phases of the moon and the like—or with moving ships or figures, attached to, and oscillating with, the pendulum. The latter devices are more usual with West Country clocks. Fig. 215 is a London clock in a Lancashire type of case—unusual in being veneered with walnut instead of mahogany—with a rigged ship attached to the pendulum arbor, which approaches, but never reaches, a battlemented castle flying the Union Jack. The case is somewhat coarse, in the provincial style, but with the scrolled pediment and the moulded bracket feet of the 1770 period.

These scrolled pedimented cases are usually referred to as "Chippendale," and they certainly do exhibit some influence of the great cabinetmaker's style, although at a subsequent period. Chippendale's vogue may be said to extend from the publication of the 1st edition of the *Gentleman and Cabinetmakers' Director* in 1754 to his death in 1779, but his Gothic and fretted period—the most character-

Fig. 215.

Fig. 216.
Enlarged Dial of Fig. 215.

Fig. 215.

THOS. BLINKER, LONDON.

Eight-day Striking Clock.
Seconds' dial.   Day of month.   Moving ship in
arch of dial.
Oak case veneered with walnut.

7 ft. 10 ins. high.   Waist 14½ ins. wide × 8 ins. deep.
Dial 17 ins. high × 12 ins. wide.

Date about 1770.

istic and that which was most imitated, as being decorative and rational, compared with his Chinese extravagancies—is from 1756 to 1765. What Chippendale might have done with the long-case clock is shown by the designs in three editions of the *Director*, which will be illustrated and described in a later chapter. Chippendale was too versatile a designer, and too much of a pioneer to have allowed himself to be fettered by the general form of the grandfather case—the result of tradition as much as of utility—and although the details of his style were sparingly adopted by the makers of these long cases, a really typical Chippendale case is not only unknown, but impossible.

Fig. 217 is a fine example of a so-called Chippendale case by a Lancashire maker. The fretted pediment centres in a carved and valanced taurus, originally surmounted by a wooden spire to match those on either side. The frieze below the hood is enriched with an applied fret, and the door of the trunk is flanked by triple turned columns in the Gothic manner. The base is chamfered on the corners, and edged with quoins of mahogany carved from the solid wood. The case rests on the usual moulded bracket feet in the manner of the period. The clock itself is of

Fig. 217.

Fig. 217.

ARCHIBALD (?) COATS, WIGAN.

Eight-day Striking Clock.
Phases of the moon in arch.
Mahogany case, carved and fretted.

8 ft. 1 in. high × 1 ft. 4 ins. width of waist.
Dial 18½ ins. high × 13 ins. wide.

Date about 1780–5.

Fig. 218.

Fig. 219.
Enlarged Dial of Fig. 218.

Fig. 218.

NATHANIEL BROWN, MANCHESTER.

Eight-day Striking Clock with alarum.
Engraved centre to dial.
Phases of the moon in arch.
Carved mahogany case.

In the possession of W. Clare-Lees, Esq.

7 ft. 8 ins. high × 15 ins. width of waist.
Dial 18 ins. high × 13 ins. wide.

Date about 1780–5.

Fig. 220.

Fig. 221.
Enlarged Dial of Fig. 220.

Fig. 220.

BENJAMIN BARLOW, OLDHAM.

Eight-day Striking Clock.
Centre-seconds.   Phases of the moon in arch.
Mahogany veneered case.

7 ft. 7 ins. high × 1 ft. 4½ ins. width of waist.

Date about 1780-5.

rather inferior quality as compared with the elaborate case with its carefully selected veneers, now bleached to a fine golden brown by the action of time and sunlight. Another clock, very similar in form and detail to this, realised a large sum at the Dean sale at Christie's in June 1909.

Figs. 218 and 220 are further examples of the Lancashire clocks of this period, distinguished rather for their cases than for the clocks themselves. The first exhibits many of the characteristics of the Sheraton school—which, incidentally, is older than the arrival in London of the last of the great furniture designers—in the "pear drop" cornice under the hood, the influence of Robert Adam in the flute-and-patera frieze and the carved mouldings of the base, and of Chippendale in the panelling of the lower door and the fretting of the canted corners of the base. An unusual feature is the roped moulding of the frieze below the hood, prolonged down the sides of the waist and finishing in carved tassels. The central alarum disc of the dial is general in the Lancashire clocks, although very rare in those of London make. Fig. 220 is also from the same quarter, and has a very exceptional form of dial centre, the two arches being of pierced metal with a painted landscape between. The small centre-seconds' hand, of the fashion shown here, and the seconds engraved on the inside of the hour circle are also unusual features. The phases of the moon are shown in the arch in the usual way. The case is of figured mahogany carved and fretted, and it is possible that this and that of the Manchester clock just illustrated are from the hands of the same cabinetmaker, as the frets on the chamfered corners of the bases of each are identical, evidently cut from the same "rubbing." In the pediment of the Oldham case is inlaid a globe with the cardinal points of the compass. The columns flanking the hood are reeded, with brass capitals and bases. The moulding of the framing in the doors of the hoods is a familiar feature in these Lancashire clocks. The subsidiary cornice under the hood has a small dentil course, the frieze is enriched with an applied fret, and the small bead under is carved in a roped pattern. The quarter-columns on either side of the waist are reeded with brass capitals and bases to match the hood. The bracket feet are moulded and shaped as in the four examples previously illustrated.

Fig. 222 is a less ornate type from the same locality, but of inferior quality—the case simple and the dial painted white. The spires surmounting the pediment are missing.

If the influence of Chippendale be suggested by the employment of pierced or

Fig. 222.

FLETCHER, CHESTER.

Eight-day Striking Clock.
Painted dial, decorated corners.
Phases of the moon in arch.
Subsidiary seconds' dial.
Mahogany case.

7 ft. 9 ins. high × 1 ft. 4 ins. wide.
Dial 12½ ins. × 17 ins. high.

Date about 1785.

Fig. 223.

WILLIAM PAINE, TROWBRIDGE.

Eight-day Striking Clock.
Phases of the moon in arch.
Mahogany veneered case inlaid
with shells of satin-wood.

7 ft. 9 ins. high × 1 ft. 3 ins.
width of waist.
Dial 17 ins. high × 12 ins. wide.

Date about 1785.

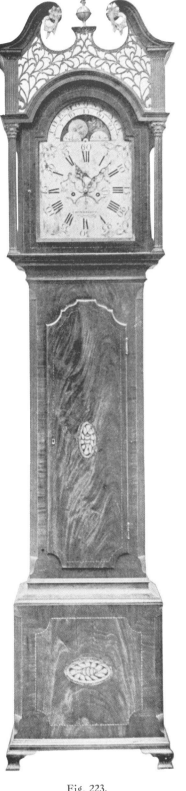

Fig. 222.

Fig. 223.

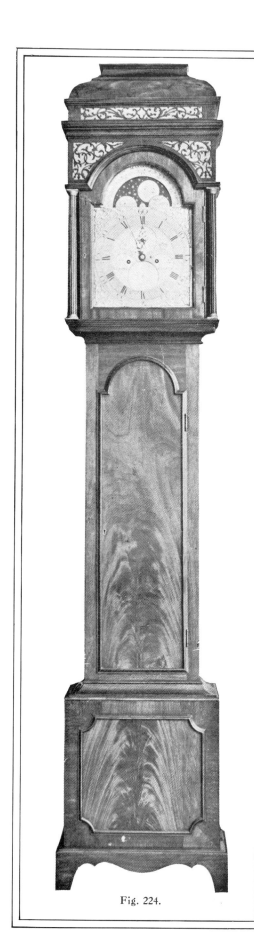

Fig. 224.

Fig. 225.
Enlarged Dial of Fig. 224.

Fig. 224.

JOSEPH QUARMAN, TEMPLE CLOUD.

Eight-day Striking Clock.
Arched dial.   Phases of the moon in arch.
Subsidiary dials for days of the month and seconds.
Oak case veneered with curl mahogany.

7 ft. 10 ins. high × 1 ft. 1½ ins. width of waist.
Dial 13½ ins. × 18½ ins.

Date about 1780.

Fig. 226.

Fig. 227.
Enlarged Dial of Fig. 226.

Fig. 226.

"Jsʰ· ISREALS, LONDON."

Eight-day Striking Clock.
Silvered and brass dial.   "Strike-silent" dial in arch.
Seconds' dial and day of month in circle.
Oak case veneered with mahogany.

8 ft. 1 in. high (without centre spire).   Waist 13¾ ins. wide
× 6¾ ins. deep.
Dial 17 ins. × 12½ ins.

Date about 1775.

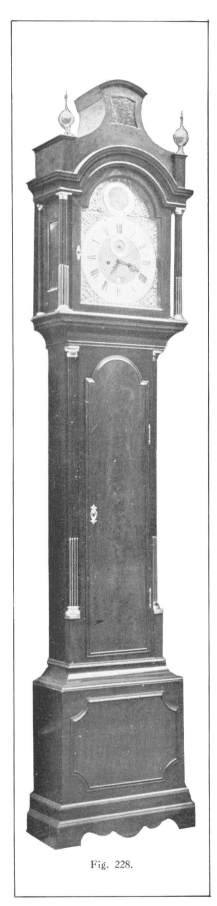

Fig. 228.

applied frets, that of Heppelwhite and Sheraton is indicated, as in the next example, by the sand-shaded shells inlaid in the lower door and the base. The piercing of the pediment is a later addition, the original having, probably, an inlay of holly lines in solid wood. West Country clocks are always difficult to classify, as they follow the usual fashions of the London specimens very sporadically.

Fig. 224 properly belongs to the period of Fig. 222, which it closely resembles, but the alteration of the dome above the arching of the dial has mutilated its style and robbed it of much of its original character. The dial is a fine example of the 1780 period in original condition. The earlier type of hour and minute hands was usually retained for high-class clocks until the close of the eighteenth century.

The next development in the fashion of grandfather cases was the hollowed pediment of the type shown in the next eight illustrations. Although the form of these cases is late—from 1775 to about 1810 —it is not unusual to find them fitted with dials of the fashion from 1730 to 1750, as in Figs. 226, 228, and 229, with the hour divisions engraved on the inside of the hour-ring, and the "strike-silent" subsidiary dial in the arch. Fig. 231 shows the type of its period, with the centre of the dial silvered and finely engraved,

Fig. 228.

JOHN CARTER, LONDON.

Eight-day Striking Clock.
Day of month. "Strike-silent" dial in arch.
Mahogany case.

8 ft. 0½ in. high × 14 ins. width × 7¾ ins. depth of waist.
Dial 17 ins. × 12 ins.   2½ in. hour circle.

Date about 1775.

Fig. 229.

Fig. 230.
Enlarged Dial of Fig. 229.

Fig. 229.

JOHN CARTER, LONDON.

Eight-day Striking Clock.
Day of month ; moon's phases in arch.
Mahogany case.

8 ft. 4½ ins. high × 14½ ins. width × 8 ins. depth of waist.
Dial 17 ins. × 12 ins.   2½ in. hour circle.

Date about 1775.

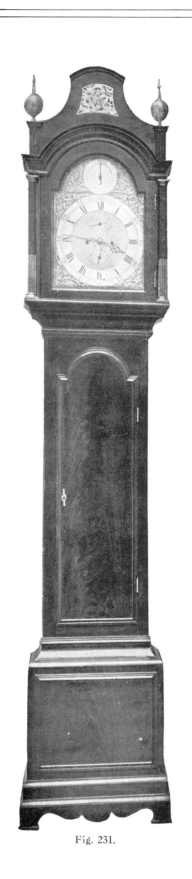

Fig. 231.

Fig. 232.
Enlarged Dial of Fig. 231.

Fig. 231.

── PUCKRIDGE, LONDON.

Eight-day Striking Clock.
"Strike-silent" dial in arch.   Seconds' and day of
month dials inside circle.   Silvered dials.   Brass corners.
Oak case veneered with mahogany.

7 ft. 10 ins. high.   Waist 14 ins. wide × 6¾ ins. deep.
Dial 17 ins. × 12 ins.

Date about 1775–80.

Fig. 233.

Fig. 234.
Enlarged Dial of Fig. 233.

Fig. 233.

RICH^d. WILLS, TRURO.

Eight-day Striking Clock.
Silvered dial; day of month; windmill and
moving figures in arch.
Mahogany case.

7 ft. 8 ins. high × 1 ft. 1½ ins. width × 7 ins. depth of waist.

Date about 1780-5.

Fig. 235.

Fig. 236.
Enlarged Dial of Fig. 235.

Fig. 235.

EDMUND MARTIN, LONDON.

Eight-day Striking and Musical Clock in mahogany case.
Silvered and painted dial.
Movable figures representing Adam and Eve in
aperture of arch.
Subsidiary dials for "strike-silent" and for seven tunes
as follows :
"Over the Water to Charlie." "Lady Coventry's Minuet."
"Tweeside." "March in Scipio."
"Last time I came o'er the Moor."
"Hundredth Psalm." "The Harvest Home."

In the possession of Percy Webster, Esq.

8 ft. 6 ins. high × 15 ins. width of waist.
Dial 17¾ ins. high × 12½ ins. wide.

Date about 1790.

Fig. 237.

Fig. 238.
Enlarged Dial of Fig. 237.

Fig. 237.

SAM^{l.} RAVEN, LONDON.

Eight-day Striking Clock.
Silvered dial. "Strike-silent" dial in arch.
Seconds' dial and day of month inside circle.
Oak case veneered with mahogany.

8 ft. high (without centre spire). Waist 17 ins. wide
× 14 ins. deep.
Dial 17 ins. × 12 ins.

Date about 1795.

Fig. 239.

two subsidiary dials being provided inside the hour-ring for the seconds and the day of the month respectively. Fig. 233 is a West Country clock case of the same form, with the later type of movement, the dial silvered, the corners engraved, and the flamboyant type of minute hand. The arch has a windmill and moving figures attached to and moving with the pendulum.

Fig. 235 is an elaborate musical clock of London make, playing seven tunes. Fig. 237 has the plain silvered dial of the close of the eighteenth century, and Fig. 239 shows this type of case persisting into the nineteenth century.

So far the influence, in an extremely modified form, of both Chippendale and Sheraton, has been noticed in the examples illustrated in this chapter. As already pointed out, clock-case makers following a fashion were usually some twenty years later than the same style with the cabinetmaker. Here and there we meet with examples of clocks made for a specific purpose and location, which are quite in the furniture manner of their period. Such specimens are, however, too rare and exceptional in their origin to fall into line with the usual development of the long-case clocks of the eighteenth century, although they usually possess both an historical and a technical interest.

Figs. 240 and 241 are a pair of remarkable clocks

Fig. 239.

BENJAMIN CROOKE, CHURCH STREET, HACKNEY.

Eight-day Striking Clock.
Silvered dial.   Oak case.

7 ft. 8 ins. high × 1 ft. 1¼ ins. width of waist.

Date about 1805.

Fig. 240.

"AYNS^{th.} (AYNSWORTH) THWAITES, CLERKENWELL, LONDON."

**Eight-day (?) timepiece.
Brass case and supporting frets.
Trunk veneered with amboyna and mahogany,
carved and inlaid.**

This clock, together with its companion, is in the Finance Committee Room (196) at the India Office, and was removed from the Company's establishment in Leadenhall Street in 1867.

Date about 1760–5.

Fig. 241.

"AYNS^{th.} THWAITES, CLERKENWELL, LONDON."

Companion clock to the above, and now in the same room.

When the Company's establishment was abolished in 1867 this clock was sold or given away. It was found on the Continent by Mr. Bertram W. Currie (Member of the Council of India 1880–95, and Chairman of the Finance Committee 1885–95), purchased by him, and presented to the Office.

Date about 1760–5.

Fig. 240.

Fig. 241.

Fig. 242.

HENRY JENKINS, LONDON.

Astronomical Clock with dial
showing various time all over
the world.
Mahogany case.
Compensation of pendulum on
lunette in lower door.

7 ft. 4 ins. high × 11½ ins. width
× 7½ ins. depth of waist.

Date about 1770–5.

Fig. 243.

**THOMAS MUDGE,
WILLIAM DUTTON,
LONDON.**

Eight-day Striking Clock.
"Strike-silent" finger in arch.
Silvered dial.
Mahogany case.

7 ft. 7 ins. high × 12¼ ins. width
× 7¾ ins. depth of waist.
Dial 17 ins. high × 12 ins. wide.

Date about 1785.

Fig. 242.

Fig. 243.

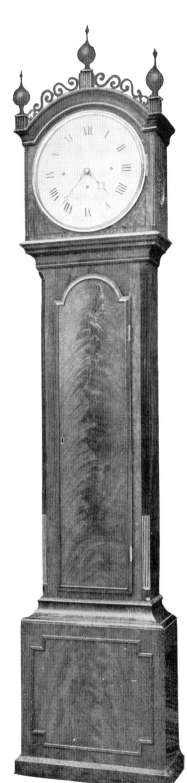

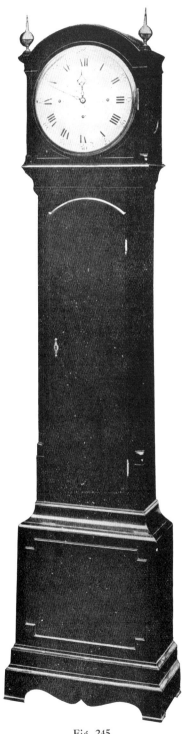

Fig. 244.

**"J. SMITH,
FLEET STREET."**

Eight-day Striking and Chiming
Clock.
Chiming on four and eight bells.
Mahogany case.

7 ft. 8 ins. high.   Waist 14 ins.
wide × 7¼ ins. deep.
13 in. painted convex dial.

Date about 1780.

Fig. 245.

**"JOHN LANE,
FETTER LANE."**

Eight-day Striking and Chiming
Clock.
Chiming on four and eight bells.
Mahogany case.

6 ft. 8 ins. high.   Waist 13¼ ins.
wide × 7 ins. deep.
12 in. painted dial.

Date about 1785.

Fig. 244.

Fig. 245.

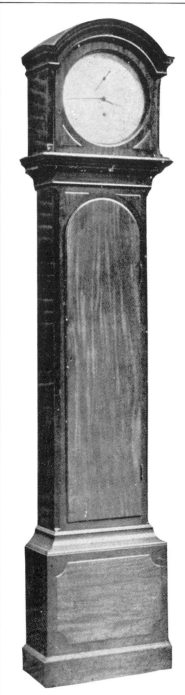

Fig. 246.
**JEFFERYS & JONES,
LONDON.**

Regulator Clock.
Mahogany case.
Counterpoised minute hand.
Wood rod pendulum.

6 ft. 1 in. high.   Waist 11¾ ins. × 6¾ ins.
10 in. dial.

Date about 1800.

by Aynsworth Thwaites of Clerkenwell, made for the East India Company about 1760–5, and now in the Finance Committee Room at the India Office at Whitehall, standing on either side of one of the marble mantelpieces which were removed from the Company's former offices in Leadenhall Street in 1867. The two clocks are *en suite*, both having the movements enclosed in brass drums, with pierced doors on the sides. The drums are connected to the wooden trunks by brass chased frets on the fronts, and behind these are engraved back-plates hiding the pendulums, which extend about half-way down the tapered cases. These trunks are veneered with amboyna in the panels, banded with mahogany and bordered with small carved "strap" mouldings of the same wood. The carving of the friezes is also in mahogany, applied on amboyna veneer, but portions have become detached and are now missing. The general form of the cases and the design of the carving indicate the influence of Robert Adam, whose style was paramount at the date when the clocks were made. The one on the left is a timepiece, and as far as could be ascertained, an eight-day. The one on the right of the fireplace, Fig. 241, is no longer in its complete state. In the centre is a revolving disc, coloured dark blue, and decorated with stars, pierced with a hole, through which the moon, on a separate disc, is seen. The quarters of the moon are indicated by the position of the disc during revolution. Above and on the sides of this are three segmental apertures, the one on the left indicating the month of the year, on the right the day of the month, and above, the day of the week. Immediately round the dark-coloured lunar disc, the white enamelled dial is engraved in two circles, the inner one with the Roman figures from I to XII repeated twice, showing the hours of the day and night by a small pointer, now

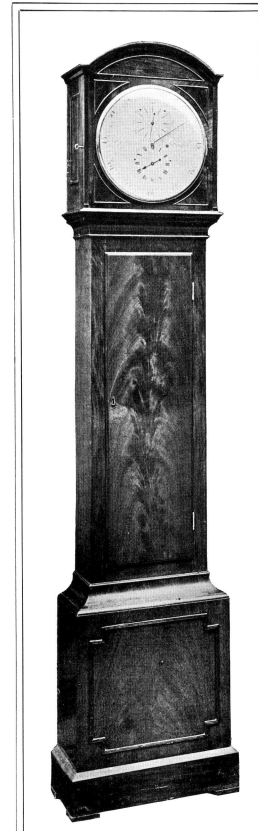

Fig. 247.

Fig. 248.
Enlarged Dial of Fig. 247.

Fig. 247.

T. J. UPJOHN, LONDON.

Eight-day Regulator Clock.

Subsidiary dials for hours and seconds.
Centre minute hand.
Oak case veneered with mahogany panelled with
mouldings and cock beads.

6 ft. 8½ ins. high.   Waist 1 ft. 1½ ins. wide × 7 ins. deep.
Enamelled dial 12½ ins. diameter.

Date about 1805-10.

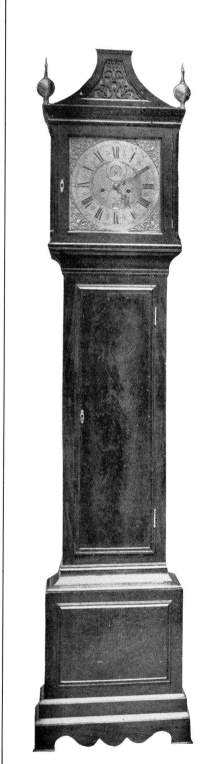

Fig. 249.

Fig. 250.
Enlarged Dial of Fig. 249.

Fig. 249.

JOHN PURDEN, LONDON.

Eight-day Striking Clock.
Seconds' dial.   Day of month.
Oak case veneered with mahogany.

7 ft. 3 ins. high.   Waist 1 ft. 1 in. wide × 6¾ ins. deep.
12 in. brass dial.

Date about 1795.

broken away, and the outer one divided from 1 to
29 (the lunar month), and in the top centre of this
ring "12 hours, 45 minutes." The age of the
lunar month is shown by a pointer attached to the
lunar disc.   On the outside edge of the dial the
cardinal points of the compass are engraved, and
when this clock was in Leadenhall Street the long
pointer was directly connected with a weather vane
on the roof of the East India House, and marked
the direction of the wind.   This action, however, is
no longer operative, and when it was disconnected
in 1867, the clock was evidently regarded as useless, and it disappeared.   It was found on the
Continent afterwards, purchased and presented to
the India Office by Mr. Bertram W. Currie, the
fact being recorded on a silver plate attached to
the right-hand side of the brass drum.   The pair
of clocks are exceedingly interesting, and the workmanship throughout is of the highest class.   Being
made, however, expressly for the East India
Company, they follow none of the recognised traditions of the time, and cannot be regarded as examples of the progression of long-case clocks of
this period.

From 1780 to 1800 many elaborate clocks were
made, apparently as "test-pieces," by the more
renowned makers of the time.   Fig. 242 is a complicated astronomical clock by Henry Jenkins, who
specialised in this class of work, from 1756 to 1774
at 46 Cheapside, and until about 1782 at 68 Aldersgate Street, City.   Another example of Jenkins'
work will be illustrated in a later chapter on
"Bracket Clocks."   In this clock the dial inside
the hour-ring is divided into the 120 degrees of
longitude, and revolves together with the hour
pointer.   If this hour hand be placed at zero (0°),

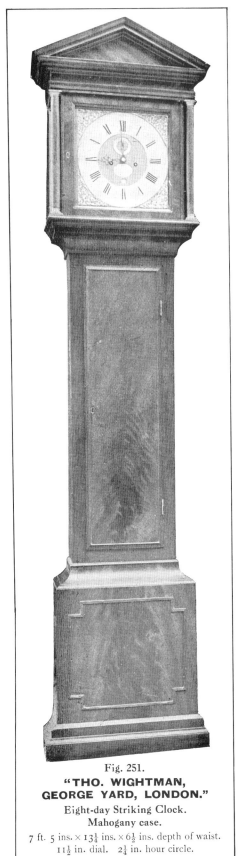

Fig. 251.
**"THO. WIGHTMAN,
GEORGE YARD, LONDON."**
Eight-day Striking Clock.
Mahogany case.
7 ft. 5 ins. × 13¼ ins. × 6½ ins. depth of waist.
11½ in. dial.   2¼ in. hour circle.
Date about 1800.

Fig. 253.
Enlarged Dial of Fig. 252.

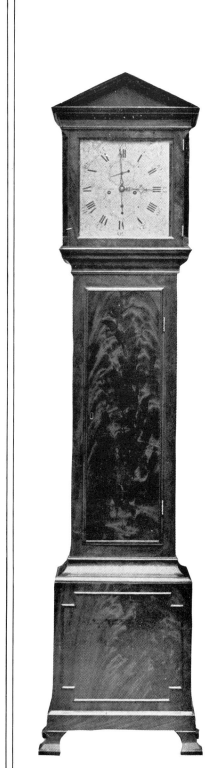

Fig. 252.

Fig. 252.

— MOGINIE, PIMLICO (LONDON).

Eight-day Striking Clock.
Engraved silvered dial.   Subsidiary dials for seconds
(above), day of month (below).
Mahogany case.

7 ft. 1 in. high.   Waist 1 ft. 1½ ins. wide × 6½ ins. deep.
12 in. dial.

Date about 1825.

it will give the hour of the day or night (the hour-ring is numbered from 1 to 24) of all places on the earth in those longitudes. If the clock be taken to another country, the hour hand must be set to the degree of that place, and the revolving dial will mark the time at all places on the earth's surface. The meridian is shown by a bent bar of steel placed vertically across the dial. Horizontally is another curved bar, representing the horizon; and if the upper XII be taken as noon, then the curved horizon (which rises and falls by the action of the clock) will be at its highest on December 21st, and at its lowest on June 21st. It will be a straight line on March 21st and September 21st. The small central disc is marked with the cardinal points. The clock is thus designed to show the time all over the world simultaneously, and, by means of the curved horizon, the time of sunrise and sunset during all periods of the year. The lunette in the lower door contains a barometrical device for the automatic regulation of the pendulum. The clock has the drawback of requiring very nice adjustment before it will function properly, and when once set going must not be allowed to stop, or it will be thrown out of gear, and require readjustment. The hour hand is friction-tight on the disc, and has to be set to the right time and the disc moved round independently until the correct meridian is aligned with the hand. There are four subsidiary dials in the arch: on the left the day of the month; above this the bolt-and-shutter maintaining power; in the centre the minutes and seconds are shown with two hands from the one centre; and on the right the day of the month.

Fig. 243 is a clock of the regulator type, by Mudge & Dutton—an association of two renowned makers at 148 Fleet Street, London, E.C., which

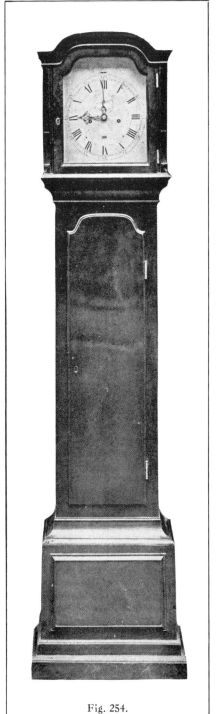

Fig. 254.
BAYLEY & UPJOHN, LONDON.
Eight-day Striking Clock.
Seconds' dial. Day of month.
"Gridiron" pendulum.
Mahogany case.
6 ft. 0½ in. high. Waist 12¼ ins. wide
× 6¾ ins. deep.
Date about 1800.

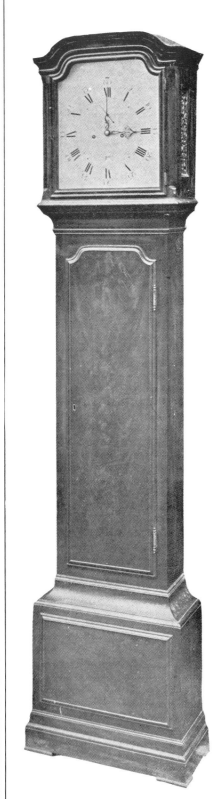

Fig. 255.

Fig. 256

Enlarged Dial of Fig. 255.

Fig. 255.

WILLIAM DUTTON & SONS.

Eight-day Striking Clock.
Seconds' dial.   Day of month.
Oak case veneered with mahogany.

6 ft. 7½ ins. high.   Waist 1 ft. 1½ ins. wide × 7⅜ ins. deep.
Enamelled dial 14 ins. high × 12 ins. wide.

Date about 1805–10.

persisted from 1755 to about 1788. Thomas Mudge was born at Exeter in 1715, and was highly esteemed as a maker of complicated clocks and watches. He was apprenticed to George Graham, and upon his master's death in 1751 succeeded to the business. He made an elaborate watch for Ferdinand VI of Spain at a cost of 480 guineas. He is credited with the invention of the lever escapement. He entered into partnership with his fellow-apprentice, William Dutton, in 1755, but from 1771 to his death in 1794 he appears to have devoted his attention to chronometer work, receiving a reward from the Government of £3000 for his work in this branch of horology. The clocks produced by the firm appear to have been due to Dutton rather than to Mudge, and are invariably of high quality. The case of Fig. 243 is a fine example of careful workmanship.

From 1785 until well into the nineteenth century we get three types of long-case clocks, with the circular, the square, and the serpentine arched tops respectively. All three merge into the regulator clocks, where greater precision of time-keeping is attained by the dead-beat escapement and one of the various forms of the compensated pendulums described in an earlier chapter. The circular-dial clocks are usually three-train, striking and chiming on nests of bells. Two examples are shown in Figs. 244 and 245, both being of high-class workmanship. Fig. 246 shows the development of this style of case into the regulator clocks of 1800 onwards. This clock has a counterpoised minute hand and a wood rod pendulum. Fig. 247 is another typical regulator clock of the first years of the nineteenth century, with a dead-beat escapement and a compensated pendulum.

The usual type of regulator dial has a central minute hand geared to the motion work and marking the seconds on the outside edge, with a separate seconds' finger, attached to the pendulum arbor, on one subsidiary dial above the collet and an hour dial with a single hand below. The escapement of clocks of this kind, as in Figs. 246 and 247, is invariably of the Graham dead-beat kind. These clocks appear to have been made for the use of makers, for the adjustment of clocks and watches, but the casework is invariably of high quality, veneered with choice mahogany curls of exceptional figure.

Towards the end of the eighteenth century we get a revival of the old square-dial clock. Fig. 249 has the hollowed pediment of the Sheraton examples previously illustrated. Fig. 251 shows the gabled hood case—another revival of an older fashion —and in Fig. 252 we approach the regulator clock again.

Fig. 254 shows the style of case of the spurious Tompion year-clock at the Admiralty, already illustrated in Fig. 178, and this was the usual form adopted for high-class regulators. This clock is fitted with the Harrison type of "gridiron" pendulum. The Dutton clock, Fig. 255, closes this series. The similarity of this example to the Admiralty "Tompion" hardly needs emphasizing.

We have, so far, traced the orderly progression of high-grade long-case clocks well into the nineteenth century. It only remains to illustrate and describe those specimens, usually of provincial make, which, in ignoring both fashion and trade tradition, tended to finally degrade the long-case clock, the only types surviving which preserve the former high standard of English clock and casemaking until the middle of the nineteenth century being those of the regulator kind.

Chapter XII

The Decline of the Long-case Clock

THE making of long-case clocks was an important industry throughout the eighteenth century, but during the latter half the sphere of influence of the Clockmakers' Company was narrowed considerably, and with the former attention to minute details of design no longer given, the taste became depraved in consequence. With the cases much of this no doubt was due to the extinction of the specialised industry of the clock-case maker, which was merged in that of the joiner or cabinetmaker. It must also be remembered that, as a rule, only the important makers made both long-case and bracket clocks. In the Company's records certain names figure repeatedly as makers of long-case clocks, and it is doubtful whether their sphere of operations ever extended beyond the weight-driven clock. As the long clocks fell into disrepute, so the standard of these makers was sensibly lowered, and it is instructive to note that the bracket clock suffers no period of degradation, as is the case with the "grandfather."

In the later specimens which exhibit this decline we find a curious jumble of characteristics and qualities. Sometimes the casework is respectable, but often—especially from the point of view of the designer—beneath contempt. Some traditions must have still persisted ; it is impossible otherwise to account for the strong similarity of specimens such as Figs. 257 and 258, as far removed in origin as Portsmouth and Ixworth in Suffolk. A London apprenticeship is no solution, as neither of these cases follow any London fashion. The Portsmouth clock is of good quality, with a well-made case, veneered with choice mahogany. The movement of Fig. 258, however, is very poor in comparison. Fig. 259 may be described as the last stage in the decline of this particular type, which might be instanced as the provincial form if any standard of design or quality had been followed. Clocks of this kind were probably made for servants' quarters, as the workmanship is as common as the general style. Fig. 260 is of good quality—a reversion to the dial fashions of forty years previously, in a case veneered with rich mahogany with "scratched" mouldings on the door and the base.

The Yorkshire clocks stand in a class by themselves. The cases, hardly without exception, are gigantic—almost elephantine—and although often veneered with choice

Fig. 257.

Fig. 257.

EMANUEL HILTON, PORTSMOUTH.

Eight-day Striking Clock.
Silvered dial, "strike-silent" hand
in subsidiary dial in arch.
Seconds and days of the month
in dials below.
Mahogany case.

7 ft. 9½ ins. high × 1 ft. 4 ins.
width of waist.

Date about 1775.

Fig. 258.

—— BARTHROP, IXWORTH.

Eight-day Striking Clock.
Chime-silent hand in subsidiary
dial in arch.
Seconds' dial below and days of
the month in lunette.
Mahogany case.

7 ft. 2 ins. high × 1 ft. 2½ ins.
width of waist.

Date about 1770.

Fig. 258.

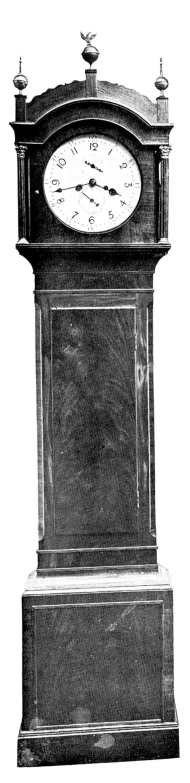

Fig. 259.

ANONYMOUS.

Eight-day Striking Clock.
Unusual dial with Arabic figures
in place of Roman numerals.
Subsidiary dials for seconds and
days of the month.
Mahogany case.

7 ft. 1 in. high × 1 ft. 3½ ins. wide.

Date ———

Fig. 260.

**JOHN CLERKE,
BRENTWOOD.**

Eight-day Striking Clock.
Name engraved on silvered boss
in arch.
Mahogany case.

7 ft. 8 ins. high × 1 ft. 4 ins. wide.

Date about 1780.

Fig. 259.

Fig. 260.

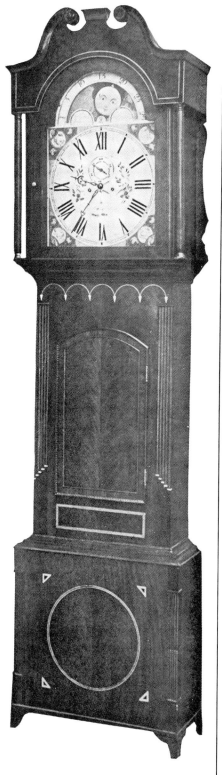

Fig. 261.

T. LEES, BURY.

Striking Clock.
Painted dial, corners in
vitreous colours.
Movable ship in arch.
Brass hands.
Mahogany case.

7 ft. 8½ ins. high × 1 ft. 6 ins.
width of waist.

Date about 1790.

Fig. 262.

**JOHN PILLING,
BOOTHFOLD.**

Striking Clock.
Painted dial. Corners in
vitreous colours. Phases
of the moon in arch.
Brass hands.
Mahogany case inlaid with
ivory.

7 ft. 9 ins. high × 1 ft. 7½ ins.
width of waist.

Date about 1800.

Fig. 261.

Fig. 262.

curl mahogany and inlaid with satin-wood or
ivory, they can only commend themselves to
those who prefer quantity to quality. The dials
are nearly always painted, the arch reserved for
the phases of the moon.

Figs. 261 and 262 exhibit the traces of the
Gothic manner of Chippendale in the heading
of the lower doors, and the pediment of Fig. 263
is curiously reminiscent of the Wigan clock,
Fig. 217. Fig. 262 is enriched with inlaid lines
of holly and ivory. All three examples are
supported on absurdly small bracket feet.

It is curious that the fashion of these
clumsy Yorkshire clocks should have been
adopted as a favourite pattern in the modern
tube-chiming long clocks of many of the leading
London makers of the present day. The cases
of these are usually still further vulgarised by
an elaborate inlay of marqueterie, a taste for
which was very prevalent from 1880 to 1895.

It would be useful if it were possible to
have established a fashion for the hoods of long-
case clocks throughout the eighteenth century,
but any rule is subject to such large exception as
to be almost non-existent. Generally speaking,

Fig. 263.

— BARR, BOLTON.

Eight-day Striking Clock.
Painted dial. Phases of the moon in arch.
Days of the month in segmental dial below hands.
Subsidiary seconds' dial. Arabic figures.
Mahogany case inlaid with satin-wood panels and lines.

8 ft. 1 in. high × 1 ft. 4½ ins. width of waist.

Date about 1790.

Fig. 263.

however, the early long clocks with square dials are either square headed or with moulded dome tops. This system of a moulded dome in two or three terraces is followed in the early arched-dial examples, but with the later specimens the designs of the hoods follow no fixed rule. We can only judge of the fixity of a type by the large or small number of specimens available for classification, and the two which appear to have been most popular are the scrolled "Chippendale" pediment and the double-hollowed cresting, examples of each of which have been already illustrated. Clock cases of these two kinds are nearly always veneered with mahogany, and inlay of any kind is very exceptional. In judging the period of a clock, however, it must always be borne in mind that the size of the hoods of the later examples was nearly always standardised, and the possibility of the divorcing of a clock from its original case is one which the method of placing the movement on a seat-board, without any further fixing, renders exceptionally easy.

One phase of our subject yet remains to be considered, the clock case designs of Chippendale and Sheraton, and we can then devote attention to the bracket clock, which will be found to exhibit a different course of development to that of the "grandfather," for reasons which will be set forth in succeeding chapters.

Chapter XIII

Chippendale and Sheraton Clock Cases

URING the space of a century and a half the names of Chippendale and Sheraton, the two illustrious cabinetmakers of the eighteenth century, have ceased to bear their original application as indicating actual work made either by their hands, in their workshops, from their designs or under their supervision, but have, through custom, come to be regarded as expressing work executed in accordance with the general principles of their designs, and this only in the broadest possible sense. So completely has the identity of the numerous minor craftsmen been merged in that of the two famous makers, that their names are used to indicate cabinet-work often quite foreign in character to their known and published designs. Chippendale was by no means even the pioneer of the applied and open fret, nor Sheraton the originator of floral or fan marqueterie, or the banding of mahogany with satin-wood, or of satin-wood with rose-wood, king-wood or tulip. The terms "Chippendale" or "Sheraton" are often used, however, in the loosest possible manner to indicate cabinet-work embellished after these fashions.

An important point arises here, one which has often been raised, but never satisfactorily settled. Were grandfather or bracket clocks made to the designs of either Chippendale or Sheraton? If so, are any examples known, and if not, why? It is only possible to theorise on this subject, but it is exceedingly improbable if any such examples were ever made, and to those acquainted with the status of the eighteenth-century clockmaker and cabinetmaker respectively, the reason is easily understood. The former craft was by far the most important. The Clock-makers' Company was exceedingly powerful, and possessed important privileges. The clockmaker dictated the designs of his cases, these being regulated by two factors: (1) the size and shape of his dials—for it must be remembered that, at any rate during the latter half of the eighteenth century, the cases were made to fit the clocks, the reverse proceeding being one never adopted except by very unimportant provincial makers; and (2) either the dictates of furniture fashions, or more probably the innate conservatism of the craft itself. It is only necessary to select 100 examples of long-case clocks from 1760 to 1800, quite at random, and from makers scattered haphazard throughout the United Kingdom, and to compare them together, to be struck with the generic resemblance of them all. The same arch-headed upper and lower doors, the cornices straight or following

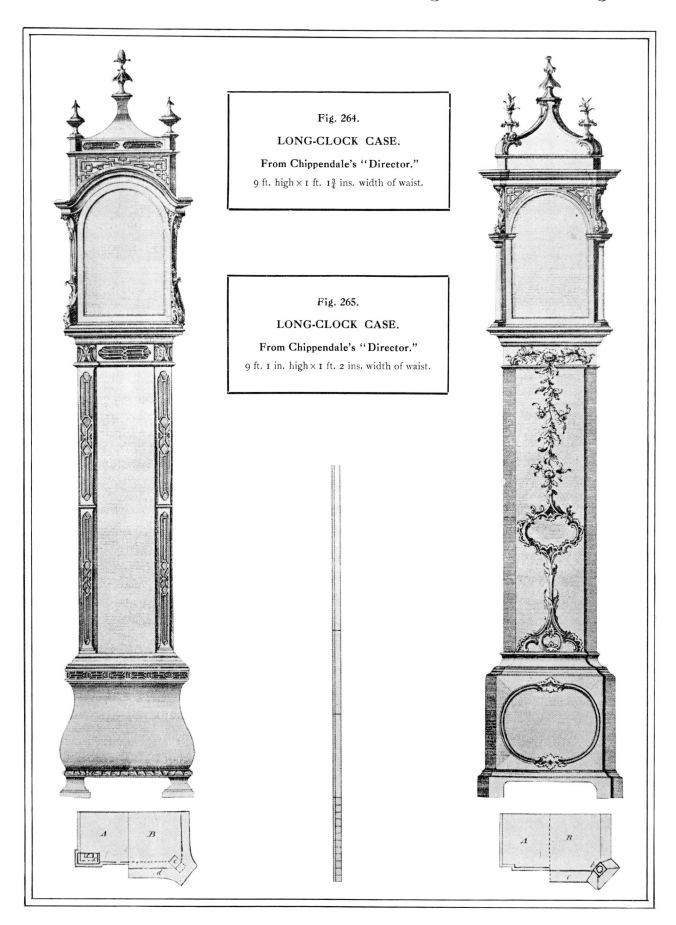

Fig. 264.

LONG-CLOCK CASE.

From Chippendale's "Director."

9 ft. high × 1 ft. 1¾ ins. width of waist.

Fig. 265.

LONG-CLOCK CASE.

From Chippendale's "Director."

9 ft. 1 in. high × 1 ft. 2 ins. width of waist.

Fig. 266.

LONG-CLOCK CASE.

From Chippendale's "Director."

8 ft. 4 ins. high × 1 ft. 2 ins. width of waist.

Fig. 267.

LONG-CLOCK CASE.

From Chippendale's "Director."

8 ft. 9 ins. high × 12 ins. width of waist
in narrowest part.

these arches, the shaped pediments either scrolled or hollowed, with two or three pinnacles of brass in the centre and the corners, the moulded base and cut-out plinths, are details which will be found in nearly all. Only a highly conservative craft would be satisfied with such endless repetition of stereotyped patterns. Out of 500 mahogany grandfather clocks from 1765 to 1810, chosen at random, how many would be found with the fluted or reeded columns with brass caps and bases on either side of the hood? Certainly 99 per cent. Parallel instances to this can be given in other trades. It is only during the last twenty years that the form of the upright piano has undergone any modification. The designs vary, some are inlaid, some carved, others moulded or quite plain, but the general outline remains the same. The iron frame restricts this to a certain extent, but the conservative character of the trade of the piano maker to a far greater degree. Why is this? Simply because the piano manufacturer only makes pianos—an instru-

Fig. 268.   Fig. 269.

BRACKET-CLOCK CASES from Chippendale's "Director."

ment to perform a certain definite function. To accomplish this in the best possible fashion, the maker will improve or alter the action, the "set-off" of the hammers, the mechanism of the dampers or the stringing, but he will decline to remodel the case, probably arguing, with considerable force, that the piano is bought for the flexibility of its touch, and the power, sonority, and sweetness of its tone, not for the design of its case. The craft of the clockmaker is similarly circumstanced. He produces a clock which keeps exact time, indicates the seconds, strikes, chimes, shows the phases of the moon and the days of the year, and probably plays half a dozen tunes. He has now to sell this clock. With the stereotyped form of case, either plain or ornamented with frets, carving, inlay or lacquer according to the value of the clock itself, he is quite safe. To place his valuable clock in a case designed on quite novel lines is to endanger the chances of a sale. It may assist the dis-

Fig. 270.   Fig. 271.

BRACKET-CLOCK CASES from Chippendale's "Director."

posal, but there is a risk, and the clockmaker knowing that with the ordinary type of case he is quite secure, wisely determines not to incur it. He shows a lack of originality, but exhibits strong business caution. The way of the pioneer in all trades is exceedingly hard. With the cabinetmaker circumstances are otherwise. His trade is exceedingly heterogeneous: he makes cabinets, bookcases, bedsteads, tables, settees, chairs, sofas, sideboards, and a hundred other pieces of furniture, and each of these is further sub-divided according to the room in which it is to be placed. Thus we have drawing-room, dining-room, library, bedroom, hall or kitchen chairs, and we expect each to differ. We do not, however, look for a different pattern of castor, or a different make of webbing or hessian in each. The chair must alter, but its component parts may remain the same. Thus it is with clocks. The furniture maker looks for changes in the form of the case, the clock maker—the responsible person concerned—makes his changes in the clock itself and ignores the case almost entirely.

Figs. 264 to 271 illustrate the published designs of long-case and bracket clocks from Chippendale's *Director*. To consider the four grandfather cases first: Figs. 264 and 265 have the upper doors without steps to the arch, thereby necessitating a departure from the usual form of dial—a formidable offence; all four do not seem to provide for a door in the waist; that of Fig. 266, if hinged, would grind on the corner columns when opened. Figs. 264, 265, and 267 have an enormous superstructure, necessitating quite 12 or 14 inches beyond the usual height of the grandfather case, and in Chippendale's time these were already gigantic enough. All four designs are exceedingly costly to make, both by reason of the expensive details and the special character of each part. The pinnacles of Figs. 264, 265, and 267, evidently designed for execution in wood, are dangerously fragile. It is doubtful whether an ordinary 60-beat pendulum could swing in the narrow waist of Fig. 267, especially as the outside width, according to Chippendale's scale of measurement, is only 12 inches, which would leave only 9 inches inside. These are all drawbacks from the clockmaker's point of view, and we can easily imagine a wealthy maker, possibly a liveryman of a powerful City Company, and in all probability exceedingly hidebound in his ideas, rejecting these designs as those of an amateur ill-acquainted with the requirements of his trade. Chippendale's bracket clock designs, or, as he correctly styles them, " Table Clock Cases," are equally unsuitable. They require special dials, and in no instance leave sufficient room in the base for a pendulum of the usual length. The carved pinnacles are sheer absurdities, more so in a bracket case than in a long clock, owing to the increased risk of breakage. The element lacking in all these designs is practicability. Had Chippendale designed a kitchen poker, it would, no doubt, have been a very ornamental affair, but would probably have been quite useless for

Fig. 272.

LONG-CLOCK CASE.

From Sheraton's "Cabinet Maker's and Upholsterer's Drawing Book."

6 ft. 10½ ins. high × 10¾ ins. width of waist.

Fig. 273.

LONG-CLOCK CASE.

From Sheraton's "Cabinet Maker's and Upholsterer's Drawing Book."

6 ft. 10 ins. high × 11¼ ins. width of waist.

its chief purpose, to poke the kitchen fire. Even at the present day some pokers can be found, particularly in front parlours, which fall into this category.

The two designs of Sheraton, given in Figs. 272 and 273, can be dismissed even more summarily. Both have square dials, a long-expired fashion at this period, and apart from the absurdity of the movements illustrated in the designs, neither are practical. The space between the outside edge of the dial and the hood is insufficient, and in Fig. 273 there is hardly room for the striking bell on the top. Fig. 272 is not intended to strike, and Fig. 273 is apparently not made to be wound with a key! A further absurdity is that if we take Sheraton's own scale of measurement as divided into spaces of 1 foot each, these cases measure 13 feet 8 inches high. If, on the other hand, they are only 6-inch divisions—the last one is spaced into six parts—then the waists only measure $10\frac{3}{4}$ inches and $11\frac{1}{4}$ inches respectively in width *outside the cases*, or $8\frac{1}{4}$ inches and $8\frac{3}{4}$ inches wide inside. As Sheraton's other designs are drawn accurately to scale, this is presumably quite intentional; at all events, to alter these designs to practicable dimensions would involve a corresponding alteration in their proportions, unless the cases were made of a preposterous height. Certain writers have commented on the curious wings on either side of the waist of Fig. 273, as evidences of Sheraton's practical ability in designing a case with a narrow waist and yet leaving room for the pendulum-bob to describe its arc. To a designer, however, it is fairly evident that Sheraton could claim no such merit; he was simply striving to modify the straight lines of the ordinary type of case. He obtained a curve in the waist with these wing-pieces, and in the hood and the base with bulged columns. With the exception of the hood, there is not a single vertical external straight line anywhere in the design. As specimens of cabinet-work the models of both of the famous cabinet-makers would be successful, but as clock cases, to contain movements and dials of the form of their period, they are emphatically failures. It would be easy to design a very beautiful and symmetrical grand piano case, if the rigid lines of the iron frame or the principle of the instrument could be modified at will without any loss of tone or mechanical value. The back leg, for instance, could line with the pedal-lyre, producing a balanced case, if the key-board could be altered so as to have the bass notes in the middle and the treble notes on either side. It is to be feared that such a design would be received rather derisively by the majority of piano firms.

Chippendale and Sheraton both knew the principles of cabinet construction thoroughly. This is evident by the designs, particularly those of the latter. It is equally evident that both knew very little about clocks or their manufacture, and this is obvious from a practical examination of the ten designs illustrated in these pages.

Chapter XIV

Bracket Clocks from 1670 to 1800

HE history of the development of bracket clocks differs from that of grandfather cases in several important particulars. It is hardly correct to say that the various models evolve the one from the other, although this is partially true. Unlike the long-case clocks, however, the older models are not extinguished in the later ones, but persist side by side with them for many years. For example, although the brass lantern clocks are undoubtedly the progenitors of those with wooden cases, the former are found throughout the eighteenth century, in country districts, made after the old models, sometimes even with an hour-hand only, and with the two trains placed one behind the other, in exactly the same fashion as the early clocks of the reign of Charles II. In others, again, although the brass lantern form is retained, the subsequent improvements in mechanism are adopted, or more frequently superimposed on or adapted to the old clocks. Thus we find these so-called "Cromwellian" lantern clocks with barrel and fusee, with an anchor escapement and a short pendulum, evidently made long after the fashion for the brass clock had been superseded. It is, therefore, only possible to indicate the commencement of the vogue for each particular form of the bracket clock throughout the eighteenth century, and it must not be forgotten that the models agglomerate rather than evolve, although the tendency with each new form is towards the gradual extinction of the preceding one. The process is, however, exceedingly gradual, and if we consider the productions of remote country makers, it is hardly safe to state any date when a particular pattern becomes finally obsolete.

Disregarding the brass lantern clocks, as the original types have already been considered at an earlier stage of our inquiry, and those made during the eighteenth century being only depraved copies, we can devote our attention to the wood-cased bracket clock from the date of its inception onwards. In the following eight pages diagrams of the entire range of the fashionable models, during the latter part of the seventeenth and the whole of the eighteenth centuries, are illustrated. Nineteenth-century bracket clocks will be considered later on, but the fact that they nearly always reproduce the case models of the eighteenth is a sufficient excuse for ignoring them in the account of the progression of types.

Nos. 1 and 2 are examples of bracket clock cases of about 1670—before any definite fashion could be said to exist. For this reason they are highly exceptional, as not only are these very early clocks exceedingly rare, but the cases vary considerably with each specimen. Both the examples shown here may be described as Dutch in inspiration, if not in actual workmanship; but as they will be more fully considered at a later stage, they can be dismissed for the present as specimens of the very first types of wood-cased bracket clocks.

With the "basket top" in its various forms, Nos. 3 to 9, we reach a fixed fashion, and one which had a very extensive vogue from about 1675–80 to 1700. The earlier *type* is the wood basket, as No. 3, either plain or mounted with brass, as Nos. 4 and 5, but these overlap the brass basket to such an extent that no definite rule can be postulated. The metal baskets (they were occasionally made from silver in lieu of brass) were usually fitted with elaborate lifting handles, as in No. 8 for example, and the various forms are shown in Nos. 6, 7, 8, and 9. The inverted bell cases date from the reign of Anne and persist into that of George II. Cases decorated with lacquer-work are nearly always of this form. Nos. 10, 11, and 12 are the pure types, either plain or brass mounted, and 13 and 14 are elaborated, and subsequent variations. The true bell-top is a later variety, from about 1750 to 1800, and is co-incidental with the remainder of the patterns illustrated here. The broken arch-top begins about 1765, and may be described as the Heppelwhite type, approximating somewhat to the general feeling of his designs, and being usually enriched with inlay of lines or bandings. The arch-top is the Sheraton style of case, from 1785 onwards, alternating with the balloon in its various forms. The lancet is the latest of all the eighteenth-century patterns—seldom found before 1790; and the Chamfer-top and the Gadroon-top are nineteenth- rather than eighteenth-century patterns—seldom found before 1800, and persisting from then to about 1860, as a very usual form. Side by side with these various types, those of the earlier kind persist, especially the bell-top and inverted bell, which were extensively duplicated during the nineteenth century. There are certain details of the dial, such as the silvered hour-ring on a matted brass ground, and the cherub corner-pieces, which are seldom found in conjunction however, and nineteenth-century clocks are usually evident to a mere cursory inspection. Other distinguishing peculiarities will be noticed as the actual examples in the following pages are separately considered.

No. 1.—Early Architectural Case.

No. 2.—Case of similar form to "Grandfather" Hood.

No. 3.—Plain Wood Basket-top.

No. 4.—Wood Basket-top, brass mounted.

THE PROGRESSION OF BRACKET CLOCK CASES.

No. 5.—Wood Basket-top, brass mounted, decorated
front door.

No. 6.—Brass Basket-top, plain case.

No. 7.—Brass Basket-top, highly decorated front door.

No. 8.—Bell Basket-top.

THE PROGRESSION OF BRACKET CLOCK CASES.

No. 9.—"Double Basket Top."

No. 10.—Plain "Inverted Bell-top."

No. 11.—"Inverted Bell-top," brass mounted.

No. 12.—"Inverted Bell-top," corner-mounted in the French style.

THE PROGRESSION OF BRACKET CLOCK CASES.

No. 13.—"Inverted Bell-top," elaborated type.

No. 14. — "Inverted Bell-top," elaborated type.

No. 15.—Plain "Bell-top."

No. 16.—"Bell-top," brass mounted.

THE PROGRESSION OF BRACKET CLOCK CASES.

No. 17.—Bell-top, elaborated.

No. 18.—Deep Broken-arch Top.

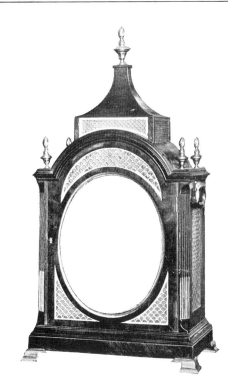

No. 19.—Deep Broken-arch Top, elaborated.

No. 20.—Shallow Broken-arch Top.

THE PROGRESSION OF BRACKET CLOCK CASES.

No. 21.—Shallow Broken-arch Top, elaborated.

No. 22.—Arch-top.

No. 23.—Arch-top, elaborated.

No. 24.—Balloon Case.

THE PROGRESSION OF BRACKET CLOCK CASES.

No. 25.—Elaborated Balloon Case.

No. 26.—Hybrid Arch and Balloon Case.

No. 27.—Lancet-top.

No. 28.—Lancet-top, elaborated.

THE PROGRESSION OF BRACKET CLOCK CASES.

No. 29.—"Chamfer-top."   No. 30.—"Gadroon-top."

THE PROGRESSION OF BRACKET CLOCK CASES.

Fig. 274 is an example of the earliest pendulum timepiece, introduced into England by Ahasuerus Fromanteel in 1658. The Fromanteels were a noted family of Dutch clockmakers, both in Amsterdam and London. Ahasuerus the father was a freeman of the Blacksmiths' Company in 1630 (the Clockmakers were not chartered until late in the following year); and although afterwards elected to the latter body, he appears to have been a somewhat turbulent member, being fined on several occasions for infringing the rules as to the taking of apprentices, etc. Another Fromanteel of the same Christian name, probably a son, was free of the Company in 1655, and a third in 1663. John and Abraham were others of the family who figure in the records, the former being the maker of the two long clocks, now sadly "restored" and mutilated, in the vestry of the Dutch church in Austin Friars. A long-case clock by Fromanteel of Amsterdam has already been illustrated in Fig. 166.

The Fromanteels were certainly the first to introduce the pendulum of Christian Huygens into England in its application as a controller of clocks, and although this innovation has been claimed for Richard Harris and Dr. Hooke, there is very little doubt that the pendulum was first applied to a domestic clock made in England by

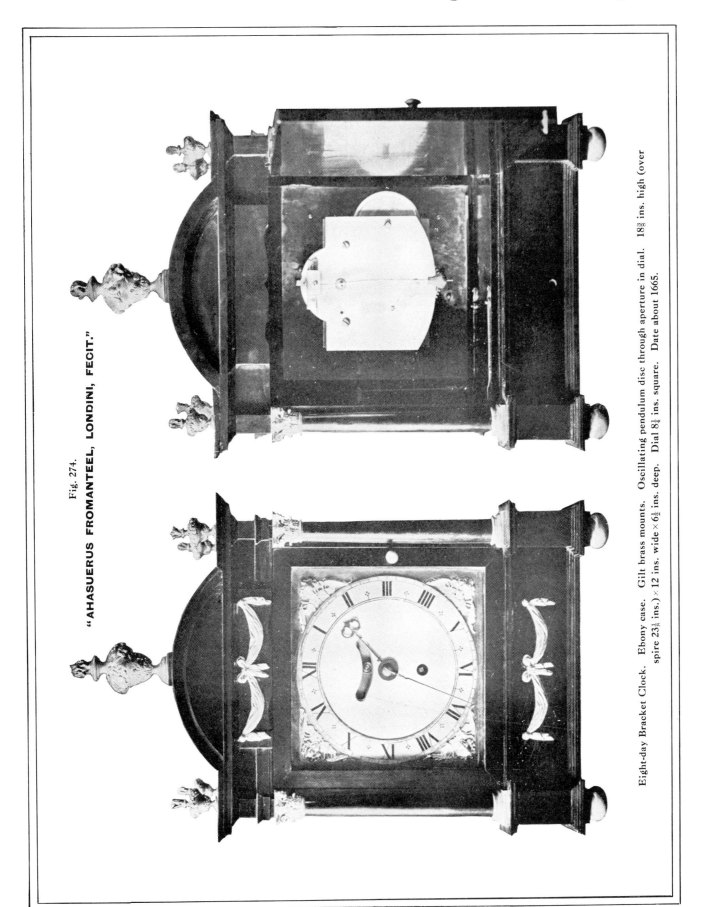

Fig. 274.

"AHASUERUS FROMANTEEL, LONDINI, FECIT."

Eight-day Bracket Clock. Ebony case. Gilt brass mounts. Oscillating pendulum disc through aperture in dial. 18¾ ins. high (over spire 23¼ ins.) × 12 ins. wide × 6½ ins. deep. Dial 8¼ ins. square. Date about 1665.

Ahasuerus Fromanteel. Huygens and Fromanteel were associated together, as a reference in John Evelyn's diary of 1661 conclusively proves.

The case of Fig. 274 is veneered with ebony, and, considering its date, must be pronounced as of both Dutch character and origin. In the base is a drawer for the winding key, etc., the front embellished with the brass double swag of drapery. The doors at the sides and the back are opened by releasing concealed springs, those at the side being operated from under the opened drawer in front. The clock is a timepiece with a train of four (an eight-day) with a crown-wheel escapement and a direct bob pendulum. The hands are especially delicate and finely wrought.

Fig. 275.

WILLIAM KNOTTESFORD, LONDON.

Eight-day Striking Clock. Bolt-and-shutter maintaining power.
Walnut case, black pillars.

19 ins. high × 14 ins. wide × 7¼ ins. deep. 9 in. dial. 1 in. silvered hour circle.

Date about 1675.

Fig. 276.

EXAMPLES OF ENGRAVED BACK PLATES OF BRACKET CLOCKS.

Fig. 275 is another early bracket clock of pronounced Dutch type. The movement is an eight-day striker, of the outside locking-plate type, and has a seconds' dial with a short pendulum and a day-of-the-month wheel. Maintaining power of the bolt-and-shutter kind is provided—a very rare feature in bracket clocks of this date. The hands are exceptionally fine, the dial nicely proportioned and matted, and the cherub-headed corner-piece especially choice. The case is of black-veined walnut, with ebonised spiral pillars, and in the dome is a sliding-lid box to hold the winding key. The back plate is plain, and the frames at the sides and the door at the back are

Fig. 277.

"JOHANNES FROMANTEEL, LONDINI, FECIT."

Ebony, Brass Basket, Eight-day, Quarter Striking, Bracket Clock.

Verge escapement, with curious movement, divided into two sections. Subsidiary dial for day of month.

"Strike-silent" lever. Shutters to winding holes without bolt attachment. Unique angel-head corner-pieces.

In the possession of Richard Hoffmann, Esq.

12 ins. high (over handle 14 ins.) × 7¾ ins. wide × 5 ins. deep. Dial 6 ins. Circle 1⅛ ins. wide.

Date about 1680.

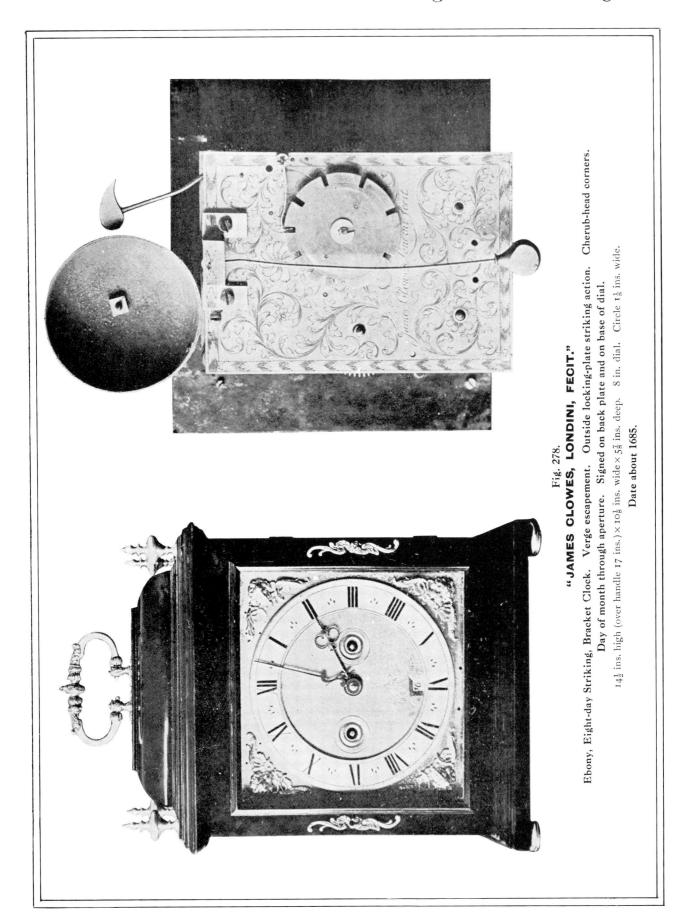

Fig. 278.

"JAMES CLOWES, LONDINI, FECIT."

Ebony, Eight-day Striking, Bracket Clock. Verge escapement. Outside locking-plate striking action. Cherub-head corners.
Day of month through aperture. Signed on back plate and on base of dial.
14½ ins. high (over handle 17 ins.) × 10⅜ ins. wide × 5⅞ ins. deep. 8 in. dial. Circle 1⅛ ins. wide.
Date about 1685.

glazed. The model of the case is an obvious copy from the hood of a long-case clock of this period.

Defined types do not occur in the bracket clock cases until about 1680. Before that date there is little or no uniformity, each maker apparently consulting his own individual fancy in the design of his case. The probability is that it is not until 1680 that the smaller clocks were made in such numbers as to warrant a specialised industry in the making of their cases, and it is only when this specialisation does take place that we get a uniform type. We have already seen that the same circumstances occur with the long case, although this early diversity of form tends to recur when the industry becomes widespread and its ranks are more or less over-crowded in consequence. After about 1685, however, we find a definite style of case well established, a square dial enclosed by a framed door, a small moulded plinth under, and a moulded top of quarter-round section or "basket," either of wood with brass mounts on the corners, or entirely of brass, often beautifully pierced and chased. In exceptional instances these basket tops are water-gilt, and Mr. Wetherfield possesses a splendid example, by Richard Jarratt, with the basket of silver. The corners of the flat moulded tops of these early cases are frequently further embellished with turned brass finials, and the basket itself is generally crowned with a hinged handle. The metal basket tops are either of single or double form. Examples of these types will be referred to later.

The defined fashions which obtain with the dials of the early grandfathers do not prevail with the bracket clocks of the same date, at any rate to the same extent. The minute divisions are either on the extreme outside of the silvered hour-ring, or set inside with the Arabic numerals outside in a separate circle, no rule appearing to regulate this. When we consider that the productions of these early clockmakers were always dictated by considerations of use-value, it is comparatively easy to surmise why this rule should prevail in the grandfather dials and not necessarily in those of bracket clocks. The latter being placed on a shelf or bracket, usually at about the height of the eye, each minute division can be noticed with ease, and the course of the minute hand inspected to a nicety. The position of grandfather dials is regulated by the height of the case, and whether high or low, the position is fixed. The Arabic numerals are of little moment, the minute divisions all-important. In the early long-case clocks, therefore, where the work was carefully studied in every trifling detail, the minute divisions are large and on the extreme outer edge of the hour circle. The Arabic figures, being merely an embellishment with very little practical use, are kept small and in the same ring as the minute markings. Later on, when patterns become more and more stereotyped, the Arabic numerals are engraved in a separate circle, which gradually becomes larger, with the minute divisions correspondingly smaller, after 1700–5.

That this theory of the carefully-studied purpose of each detail of the early clocks, and the absence of this attention in the later specimens, is no mere surmise, is demonstrated by a comparison of the early and late clock hands. The striking difference between the hour and minute hands in the early examples has already been pointed out in a previous chapter, and there is no doubt that this distinction was purposely made. In the later clocks, from 1760 onwards, the two hands tend towards a greater resemblance, until after 1800 the difference is frequently one of length only. With a tall clock, the dial possibly six feet from the floor, this is a positive defect, all the more reprehensible because it should have been appreciated and could have been avoided.

The early spandrel corners, as in the long-case clocks, are usually simple cherub-headed, but this type persists for a longer period in the bracket than in the grand-father clock dial. The quality of the bracket clock, on the average, is higher than that of the long-case, as the former, from its greater portability, could be more readily inspected, and if placed in front of a mirror (a very unusual occurrence, however, as early as at the beginning of the eighteenth century) the back was almost as noticeable as the front. Circumstances such as these no doubt dictated the elaborate back plates and the careful attention which was bestowed on the back of the clock, for mere decorative purposes. Four typical back plates of early clocks are shown in Fig. 276.

Fig. 277 is a very early example of a true basket-top bracket clock, by John Fromanteel, the maker of the two long-case clocks in the Dutch church at Austin Friars. There are several exceptional peculiarities which are worthy of notice. The winding holes are fitted with shutters without maintaining power, and are opened by the small trigger under the VI of the dial. The small circle under the hands indicates the days of the calendar month. The hands are delicate, of the early type of Figs. 274 and 275. Bracket clocks of this period are rarely strikers in the true sense of the word, having no locking-plate. The train is set free by the pulling of a string, and the last hour, and in this example the quarters, are struck on the bells. The left-hand winding square and its spring barrel provide the requisite power. The case of Fig. 277 is veneered with ebony surmounted by a finely chased brass basket and handle. The trains are curiously planted, in two distinct sections. The escapement is the usual type of crown-wheel or verge.

Fig. 278 is a clock by James Clowes of somewhat later date, with the usual locking-plate striking action of the period. The seat-board is slotted to permit the pendulum to swing, and the faces of the bob are flattened for the same purpose. The planting and calculation of the train has involved a pendulum longer than the depth of the back plate, hence this contrivance. The cherub heads of the corner-pieces are in very bold relief—an indication of an early date, and it was usual, in these early clocks, in the desire to get a bell as large as possible, to bolt it vertically to the bell-stand, as the movements were usually shallow, and an overhanging bell would have been in the way of the back door. The ringing of the winding holes is probably a later restoration to a damaged dial. Fig. 278 is still early, shown by

Fig. 279.

JOSEPH KNIBB, LONDON.

Eight-day Ting-tang Quarter-striking Clock. Ebony case. Brass mounts. Skeleton dial with minutes numbered. Gilt corner-pieces.

11¼ ins. high (without handle) × 8¼ ins. wide × 4¾ ins. deep.

Date about 1685.

the simple hands, the narrow hour circle, and the signing of the dial on the bottom edge in addition to the usual place on the back plate.

Fig. 279 is a clock by Joseph Knibb of about the same date as Fig. 278, with a skeleton dial (*i.e.* the spaces between the Roman numerals cut away, the brass matting showing through) and each of the minute divisions separately numbered. This device was only adopted on high-class clocks, and was probably the cause of the later fashion of setting the minute divisions in from the edge of the ring, with the

Arabic numerals in a separate circle outside. Fig. 279 is a ting-tang quarter-striking clock in a case veneered with ebony. The brass fret on the top-rail of the door is missing, otherwise the clock is in original condition. The refined character of the work of Joseph Knibb will be observed in every detail both of the case and the clock.

Fig. 280 is a clock by Lowndes of Pall Mall, similar in appearance, but later in date, to the Fromanteel, Fig. 277. The hour circle is unusually wide for this period, but the same fashions were not preserved in this respect as in the case of the long-case clocks of the same date. The movement has been converted from the direct crown-wheel to the disc pendulum and crutch, with a loss in originality but a gain in accuracy of time-keeping. The bob pendulum permitted of very slight regulation, and being light in weight

Fig. 280.

JONATHAN LOWNDES, LONDON.

Eight-day Striking Clock.
Ebony case. Brass basket-top.

In the possession of Bernard Matthews, Esq.

13½ ins. high (except handle) × 8¾ ins. wide × 5½ ins. deep.

Date about 1685.

Fig. 282.
Back view of Fig. 281.

Fig. 281.

Fig. 281.

THOMAS HARRIS IN Y^e STRAND.

Eight-day Striking Clock.

Minute-numbered dial.

Ebonised case.

16 ins. high × 10½ ins. wide × 5¼ ins. deep.

Date of clock about 1685.

Date of case about 1770.

Fig. 284.

Back plate of Fig. 283.

Fig. 283.

Fig. 283.

JOSEPH WINDMILLS, LONDON.

Eight-day Clock.

Pull repeater, chiming on five bells.

Walnut case.

In the possession of Percival D Griffiths, E sq.

14 ins. high × 9 ins. wide × $5\frac{1}{2}$ ins. deep.

Date about 1690.

Fig. 286.
Enlarged Back Plate of Fig. 285.

Fig. 285.

Fig. 285.

JONATHAN LOWNDES, LONDON.

"Lowndes in Pall Mall Court."

Ebonised, Brass Basket, Bracket Clock.
Pull repeater, quarter chime.

1 ft. 3 ins. high (without handle) × 9¾ ins. wide
× 5¾ ins. deep.

Date about 1695.

was exceedingly liable to derangement by jarring or moving of the clock. The later form was usually substituted shortly after it was introduced, and the crown-wheel escapement was usually converted to the anchor for the same reason and to diminish the arc of swing so as to render possible the enclosure of the larger disc pendulum in the same case.

Fig. 281 is an early type of movement, of the outside locking-plate striking action, and with a minute-numbered dial, which has lost its original case. The

Fig. 287.

NATHANIEL HODGES, IN WINE OFFICE COURT IN FLEETE STREETE.

Eight-day Striking Clock.   Ebonised case, brass mounted.   Brass basket.

In the possession of Miss Bell.

11½ ins. high × 8 ins. wide × 5 ins. deep.

Date about 1695.

Fig. 288.

Fig. 289.
Back of Fig. 288.

Fig. 288.

JAMES BEVERLEY, LONDON.

Ebony Eight-day Bracket Clock.

Brass mounted.

Pull repeater, chiming on six bells.

In the possession of Percival D. Griffiths, Esq.

16 ins. high × 9¾ ins. wide × 5¾ ins. deep.

Date about 1695.

fashion of bracketing the back plate to the sides of the case, although frequently found, is also a later alteration, clocks of this period being always screwed to the seat board through the two bottom pillars of the movement. The cherub corners of this Harris clock are particularly choice, well chased and water-gilt. The case is, of course, nearly a century later than the clock, although the original door has been preserved.

Fig. 283 is an exceptional example of the work of Joseph Windmills, Master C.C. in 1702. The case is in original condition, excepting for the turned feet, which are later additions. The movement is a pull repeater chiming on five bells, the pulling string of which was originally taken through the side of the case, but to diminish the consequent friction it has since been threaded through a hole

Fig. 290.
"HEN. MASSY, LONDON."
Eight-day Clock. Pull repeater, striking hours and quarters on two bells.
Ebony case. Brass mounts.
13 ins. high (without handle) × 8 ins. wide × 5 ins. deep.
Date about 1700.

in the bottom, hence the need for the turned feet of the case. The "cock" over the pendulum suspension is beautifully pierced and engraved, and the back plate is elaborately ornamented in the same way. The bracket-pieces on the top right and the bottom left of the plate somewhat mar an otherwise magnificent clock. The movement is signed in two places: on the back plate, and in the aperture above the hand behind the oscillating disc attached to the arbor of the pendulum. The day of the month is shown through the aperture below, and the chime-silent trigger is at the top centre of the dial. The case is veneered with walnut of fine mottled figure, now bleached to a pale golden brown.

Fig. 285 is another clock by Jonathan Lowndes, signed "Lowndes in Pall Mall Court." The movement is a pull repeater and a quarter-chiming clock, the unusual arrangement of the bells being shown on the top illustration. The pendulum has unfortunately been converted, now hanging outside the pierced cock over the suspension, with the original direct pendulum acting as its crutch.

Fig. 287 is a quarter-striking clock of about the end of the seventeenth century, in an ebonised case with a pierced brass basket. The hour circle is evidently a later replacement, the wide ring containing the Arabic numerals, and the absence of the hour divisions on the inside being a fashion of fifty years later. In the illustration the large bell is removed, although the two striking hammers can be seen. The back plate and the pierced cock are both well engraved, the former having the quaint signature "Nathaniel Hodges in Wine Office Court in Fleete Streete."

Fig. 288 is a rare specimen of about the same date, in a case veneered with ebony and with the mounts richly chased and gilt. The bell-basket form is exceptional, and the beautifully designed and chased handle is worthy of careful examination. The movement is a pull repeater, chiming on six bells and striking on a seventh. The pendulum has been converted and the back plate disfigured by the attached "jaws" for the locking screw and the two braces fastening the movement to the sides of the case.

The revocation of the Edict of Nantes in 1685 by Louis Quatorze, and the persecution of the Huguenots which immediately followed, exiled many of the French clockmakers, and one frequently encounters many names engraved on back plates or dials which betray the French origin of their makers. Henry Massy, the maker of the clock shown in Fig. 290, was the son of one of these refugees, but there is little or

Fig. 292.
Back of Fig. 291.

Fig. 291.

Fig. 291.

HENRY NEVE (NEUE?),

in yᵉ Strand.

Ebonised Eight-day Striking Bracket
Clock with brass double-basket top.

In the possession of Miss Bell.

17 ins. high × 9¼ ins. wide × 4½ ins. deep.

Date about 1700–5.

Fig. 295.
Engraved Back Plate of Fig. 294.

Fig. 293.
"LOWNDES IN PALL MALL COURT."

Eight-day Striking and Pull-repeating Clock.
Case veneered with tortoiseshell.
Water-gilt mounts and dial.   Silvered hour-ring.

13 ins. high (without handle) × 9 ins. wide × 5½ ins. deep.
7 in. dial.

Date about 1700.

Fig. 294.
CHARLES GRETTON, LONDON.

Eight-day Striking and Repeating Clock.
Ebony case.   Brass mounted.

13½ ins. high (without handle) × 9⅛ ins. wide × 5½ ins. deep.
7 in. dial.

Date about 1700.

nothing about his work which is foreign in style. Apart from the dainty character of the entire piece, this clock is notable by the "up-and-down" regulation attachment to the suspension of the pendulum, which is quite original, in spite of the fact that the direct bob pendulum has been converted to the crutch form. This clock is a pull quarter repeater, striking on two bells.

Henry Neve (or Neue), the maker of the next example, was another of the Huguenot refugees. The clock is signed "Neve" on the back plate and "Neue" on the lunette on the dial in which the pendulum disc swings, so the precise spelling is obscure, but it is not infrequent to find the same maker engraving his name in half-a-dozen different ways on as many examples. The case is of the rare

double-basket form, the brasswork finely pierced and chased, but the split balusters on either side of the front door give the whole a decidedly foreign appearance. The corner-pieces, however, are quite in the English style.

Fig. 293 is another clock by Lowndes of Pall Mall Court, of the usual type, but rare on account of the case, which is overlaid with tortoiseshell. The brass mountings and the dial are all finely chased and water-gilt. The movement is a strike and pull repeater, and the feet of the case are of gilded brass, of the somewhat unusual ball-and-claw pattern.

Fig. 294 is a striking and repeating clock by Charles Gretton, with a finely-wrought cock over the pendulum suspension. The ratchets and "clicks" of the fusees are on the outside of the back plate, a method evidently designed for orna-

Fig. 296.
PETER GARON, LONDON.
Eight-day Striking Clock.
Marqueterie case.
In the possession of C. H. F. Kindermann, Esq.
14 ins. high × 9¼ ins. wide × 5¾ ins. deep.
Date about 1700.

Fig. 298.

Back of Fig. 297.

Fig. 297.

Fig. 297.

THO. TOMPION, LONDINI, FECIT.

Ebony Eight-day Bracket Clock.
Pull repeater.   Brass mounted.

In the possession of Miss Bell.

12 ins. high × 8 ins. wide × 5 ins. deep.

Date about 1700–5.

Fig. 300.
Back Plate of Fig. 299.

Fig. 299.
SIMON DE CHARMES.
Eight-day Pull Quarter-repeating Clock.
Red lacquer case.
17½ ins. high (over handle) × 9¼ ins. wide × 5½ ins. deep.
6¾ in. dial. 1¾ in. hour circle.
Date about 1710.

Fig. 301.

ROBERT SADLER,
" Red Lyon Fields."

Ebony Bracket Clock.

Pull repeater, striking hours and quarters
on two bells.

Case veneered with ebony and mounted
with brass.

1 ft. 2½ ins. high (without handle) × 9¼ ins. wide
× 5¼ ins. deep.

Date about 1725.

Fig. 302.
Back Plate of Fig. 301.

mentation, and to balance the pierced pendulum cock above. The pulling string for the repeating action is shown in both illustrations.

It is very rare to find these basket-top cases inlaid with marqueterie, as the fashions of the long cases did not extend to the bracket clocks in this particular. Fig. 296 is an example, unfortunately in anything but an original state, as, in addition to an almost entirely remodelled movement, the lifting handle, the hour circle, and the corner-pieces are all later "restorations."

Fig. 297 is a good example of Thomas Tompion's work, with a curious form of repeating device, and the back plate cut out for the bell. The case is of simple type, well made, and veneered with ebony. The pivoted vertical arm shown on the back view of the clock is for the working of two pulling strings, one on either side of the case. Mr. Wetherfield has in his collection practically the facsimile of this clock, and by the same maker.

Fig. 303.
RICHARD ROOKER, LONDON.
Eight-day Clock.
Tortoiseshell lacquer case.
In the possession of Edwyn H. Beresford, Esq.
14 ins. high × 9½ ins. wide × 6 ins. deep.
Date about 1730.

Simon de Charmes was another of the more notable of the Huguenot exiles. Fig. 299 is a rare example of his work, the case ornamented with painting of flowers and leaves on a ground of red lacquer. The entire case, front, back, and sides, is decorated in the same manner, the work executed with the utmost care and precision. The movement is of the usual type, a pull-quarter repeater on two bells. The dome of the case marks a transition from the true basket to

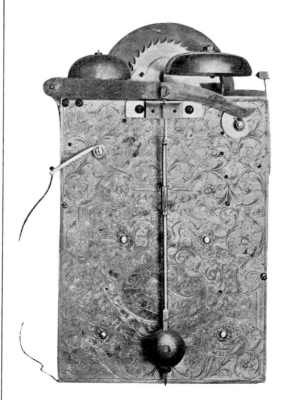

Fig. 305.
Engraved Back Plate of Fig. 304.

Fig. 304.

Fig. 304.

DAN. QUARE, LONDON (94).

Ebony Eight-day Striking Bracket Clock.
Brass mounted, pull repeater, striking hours
and quarters on two bells.
Dial in arch day of month.
Small dials, left, for regulation work,
right, "strike-silent."

1 ft. 3 ins. high × 9 ins. wide × 5 ins. deep.
Brass dial, silvered circle, 9½ ins. × 6½ ins.

Date about 1715–20.

the inverted-bell top, the type which superseded that of the basket early in the eighteenth century.

The basket-top may be regarded as the late seventeenth-century type of case, examples of much later date than about 1705–10 being exceptional. Fig. 300 is one of these late clocks, chiefly remarkable for the unusual corner-pieces, which are a significant indication of a late copy of an early case. The power for the striking is obtained from the coiling of a spring generated by the pulling of the cord shown on the back plate. There are several late characteristics noticeable on the dial and the back plate, which will be apparent on a close examination, such as the style of the engraving, the heart-shaped pendulum cock, and the pattern of the hands and corner-pieces.

Fig. 303 is another late copy of an early style, the case ornamented with tortoiseshell lacquer on the front and sides. The corner-pieces are late in character, and the hour hand is a subsequent and incongruous replacement.

The fashion for the basket-top bracket clock may be said to extend approximately from 1680 to 1705. The type which succeeded it, the "inverted-bell top," had an even longer vogue, persisting, in modi-

Fig. 306.

**"DANˡ· & THOS. GRIGNION,
from the late Mr. Quare, London."**

Eight-day Striking and Repeating Quarter-striking Clock. On six bells. Ebony case. "Strike-silent" dial in arch. Day of month below hands. Visible pendulum disc. Engraved back plate.

1 ft. 6 ins. high (without handle) × 9¾ ins. wide × 5½ ins. deep. Brass and silvered dial 9½ ins. × 6¾ ins. 1½ in. hour circle.

Date about 1730.

Fig. 308.
THOMAS TOMPION & EDWARD BANGER, LONDON.
Eight-day Striking Clock.
Oak case veneered with ebony.
16½ ins. high (without handle) × 9¼ ins. wide × 5¾ ins. deep.
Date about 1720.

Fig. 307
GEO. GRAHAM, LONDON.
Eight-day Striking and Repeating Clock.
Oak case veneered with ebony.
16 ins. high (without handle) × 9½ ins. wide × 5¼ ins. deep.
Date about 1720

Fig. 309.

Fig 310.
Back view of Fig. 309.

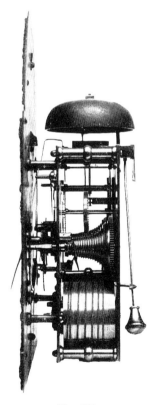

Fig. 311.
Side view of movement of Fig. 309 showing
the crown-wheel escapement.

Fig. 309.

THOMAS HUGHES, LONDON.

Green lacquer Eight-day Striking Bracket Clock.

Brass fretted mesh in front and sides.

In the possession of Henry Van Koert, Esq.

21 ins. high × 11¾ ins. wide × 5¾ ins. deep.

Date about 1730.

fied forms, until about 1770, and during the first thirty years of the period enjoyed an almost exclusive favour. After 1740, however, the patterns of bracket clock cases tend to agglomerate rather than to succeed each other, and with the exception of the basket-top, which is a restricted fashion, more or less, the other forms exist side by side, each new one being added to, rather than extinguishing those which have gone before. This fact will necessitate frequent retracings in our examination of each kind, but this course is preferable to placing the examples strictly in order of date, as in the later clocks periods have little or no significance.

Fig. 312.

"JNO. CRUCIFIX, LONDON."

Eight-day Striking Clock.
Bob pendulum. Engraved back plate. "Strike-silent"; phase of moon in arch. Dial engraved with Turkish numerals.
Red lacquer case.

20 ins. high over handle × 10½ ins. wide × 6 ins. deep.
Dial 10½ ins. × 7½ ins. wide.

Date about 1730.

Fig. 313.

JAMES DE FONTAYNE, LONDON.

Eight-day Quarter Clock.
Striking and chiming on seven bells. Walnut case.
Day of month and moon's phases in arch.

17 ins. high (without handle) × 9½ ins. wide × 5¾ ins. deep.
Dial 10¼ ins. high × 7¼ ins. wide.

Date about 1735.

The inverted-bell top is the earliest form of the bracket clock case with the arched dial, and is rarely found in conjunction with the square type, in contra-distinction to the basket-top, which is essentially the square-dial case. The introduction of the arch to the bracket-clock dial practically coincides, in point of date, with the same addition to the long-case clock, commencing about 1720 and remaining as the fashionable form of dial throughout the eighteenth century. In the same way as with the long-case regulator clocks, we find a return to the older square dial at the very close of the century, but only in exceptional instances, the usual alternative form being the circular dial, which, as we have seen, is another variation of the regulator dial of the same period.

Fig. 304 is an example of the bracket-clock work of Dan Quare, one of the leading horologists of the late seventeenth and the early eighteenth century. He is reputed to have been the inventor of the repeating watch, an honour which has been disputed in favour of the Rev. Edward Barlow, the originator of the rack-striking mechanism for clocks. Quare's movements appear to be fully equal to those of Tompion, and he does not seem to have despised elaborate cases, such as the example illustrated

Fig. 314.

JOHN ELLICOTT, LONDON.

Eight-day Striking Clock.
Red lacquer case.

19 ins. high × 10 ins. wide × 6 ins. deep.

Date about 1735-40.

Fig. 316.

Back Plate of Fig. 315.

Fig. 315.

JOHN ELLICOTT, LONDON.

Walnut Eight-day Striking Bracket Clock.
Verge escapement, bob pendulum. "Strike-silent"
dial in arch. Day of month in aperture.

Case 1 ft. 5½ ins. high × 10 ins. wide × 5½ ins. deep.
Dial 9½ ins. high × 6¾ ins. wide.

Date about 1740.

here. The clock is an eight-day striking and pull repeater, sounding hours and quarters on the two bells shown in the back view. The dial in the arch shows the day of the month, the one in the right-hand corner is the "strike silent," and in the left for the regulation. This "up-and-down" work, as it is termed, is operated by a small cam—shown on the right-hand top corner of the back plate, lifting the arm above it, which shortens the pendulum from its suspension.

This latter, with its flexible spring, is quite original, the up-and-down regulation work demanding a suspended crutch pendulum in lieu of the direct verge, for obvious reasons. The dial is exceptional, with unusual corner-pieces, and is both signed and numbered. The case is veneered with ebony, with embossed and chased brass mounts, the door framed round a brass moulding of ogee section, the corner frets moulded and pierced, and the top mounted on front, sides, and back. The back plate is beautifully engraved, and the pendulum is fitted with a milled screw, so that the clock can be regulated either from the front or the back.

Quare died in 1724, and the curious form of signature on the dial of the next example—" Dan¹ and Thomas Grignion, from the late Mr. Quare, London " — suggests two things: viz. the esteem in which this maker was held at the time, and that Fig. 306 was made not long after his death, as Quare's business was continued under the style of Quare & Horseman, the latter having

Fig. 317.

— **SMALLWOOD, LICHFIELD.**

Bleached Walnut Eight-day Bracket Clock.

In the possession of Basil Dighton, Esq.

16 ins. high × 9 ins. wide × 5½ ins. deep.

Date about 1740.

been his apprentice, admitted to partnership towards the close of his career. The brothers Grignion appear to have been finishers to Quare, and upon his death evidently saw an opportunity of acquiring some of his custom. The association was evidently thought worthy of advertisement in this fashion, as several of the early dials by Daniel and Thomas Grignion are signed in this way. The announcement would only have had a business value for a few years after Quare's death, so we can assume a date not later than 1730 for the example illustrated here. The general form and many of the details of this clock are similar to the Quare, but the quality is inferior. The case has probably been made by the same maker, as this was evidently a separate industry, the general resemblance of the two, and the identity of the profiles of the mouldings being impossible to account for by any other hypothesis. The making of clock hands as a specialised craft is also suggested, as in these bracket clocks they are often of identical design and size, cut and filed from the same template.

In Figs. 307 and 308 we have a close connection of Thomas Tompion's favourite apprentice, George Graham, who succeeded him in business, and his nephew, who was associated in partnership with Edward Banger at about the same date. A comparison of the two clocks will show how close must have been the business association—or rivalry—between the two makers. In both examples the movements strongly resemble each other, the types of the cases are similar, the lifting handles, the hands, the arrangement of the dials, and the mounting of the doors are identical. The pattern of the feet and the spires of the Tompion and Banger clock are the only real points of difference beyond the trifling one of size. In both clocks the two subsidiary dials are for "up-and-down" regulation (left) and strike-silent (right) respectively. The corner-pieces are also identical in pattern in both examples.

Fig. 318.

THOS. UPJOHN, EXETER.

Green lacquer Eight-day Striking Bracket Clock.

21 ins. high × 11½ ins. wide × 6½ ins. deep.

Date about 1760.

Fig. 320.
Back of Fig. 319.

Fig. 319.

WILLIAM WEBSTER,
CHANGE ALLEY.

Walnut Brass-mounted Eight-day Striking Bracket Clock.

In the possession of Messrs. Gill & Reigate.

$16\frac{1}{2}$ ins. high × $9\frac{5}{8}$ ins. wide × $5\frac{5}{8}$ ins. deep.

Date about 1755-60.

Fig. 319.

The lacquering of the cases of bracket clocks was a very general practice, and the workmanship is usually minute and carefully executed. Fig. 309 is a green lacquer case, in original state excepting for the hollow member of the top, which has been removed and the brass spindle-gallery substituted. The movement is in quite

Fig. 321.

"ELLICOTT" (JOHN ELLICOTT), LONDON.

Ebony Eight-day Striking Clock on Bracket.
Brass mounted, and gilt.

19½ ins. high × 9¾ ins. wide × 6 ins. deep.
6¼ in. enamelled dial.

Date about 1760.

an untouched condition, and the side view shows the parts very clearly, such as the attachment of the disc to the pendulum seen through the aperture above the hands, the barrels and fusees, the month-wheel under the dial, and the contrate-wheel of the verge. The method of fixing the clock to its seat-board by screws through the holes in the bulbs of the bottom pillars between the plates —a detail before referred to—can also be understood from this illustration. The rack-striking was nearly always the mechanism adopted in clocks of this period.

During the first half of the eighteenth century an extensive business in English clocks appears to have been done with Turkey and Spain. Markwick Markham exported many clocks specifically made for the Turkish market, the dials engraved with the devices and numerals of the Orient. The clock by John Crucifix, Fig. 312, although of mediocre quality, is interesting in having the Turkish numerals engraved on the hour circle. The phases of the moon are shown in the arch, in the same fashion as with the later long-clocks. The case is

Fig. 323.

JOHN WOODMAN, LONDON.

Eight-day Timepiece and Alarum.
Walnut case.

In the possession of W. G. Mare, Esq.

13½ ins. high (without handle) × 7½ ins. wide × 4¾ ins. deep.

Date about 1760.

Fig. 322.

WILLIAM BULL, STRATFORD.

Mahogany Brass-mounted Eight-day Striking and
Chiming Bracket Clock.
Movable figures in arch of dial.

In the possession of C. H. F. Kindermann, Esq.

23 ins. high × 11 ins. wide × 7¼ ins. deep.

Date about 1770.

decorated with ornament in gold, on a ground of red lacquer, but the painting is inferior to that usually found on cases made for the home market. Of clocks made for Spain we shall have more to say later on.

Fig. 313 is a very good clock of about 1735, the case corresponding to the furniture fashions of twenty to

Fig. 324.

ALEX^{r.} CUMMING, LONDON.

Eight-day Alarum Clock.
Ebony case.

21 ins. high over handle × 9½ ins. wide × 6 ins. deep.
Dial 10 ins. × 7 ins.

Date about 1790.

Fig. 325.

THOS. HUGHES, Junior, LONDON.

Eight-day Alarum Clock.
Walnut case.

16 ins. high over handle × 7 ins. wide × 5 ins. deep.
Dial 6½ ins. × 4 ins. wide.

Date about 1790.

twenty-five years previously. The hour hand is of almost identical form to that on the Grignion clock, Fig. 306. The dial in the arch is divided into 29 spaces, for the days of the lunar month, the pointer being moved forward one space each day by a pin on the day-of-the-month wheel geared to the motion work. This pointer is merely friction-tight on its pipe, and although held by the pin between 11 o'clock and 1, is free during the remaining 21 hours of the day. Attached to this pointer, and moving with it, is the disc at the back, with the painted moon, which revolves into the field of the hole above the centre once in each month. The clock is a quarter strike and octave chime on seven bells, the hour bell supplying the last note of the scale. The case is veneered and faced with choice figured walnut in the fashion of the walnut furniture of the reign of Anne. It has already been pointed out, however, that furniture and clocks never synchronise during the eighteenth century, the clockmaker being usually from twenty to thirty years behind the times.

Fig. 314 is a somewhat inferior clock by a noted maker, in a case of red lacquer. The dial is peculiar in having the early type of cherub-headed corner-pieces. The case has lost its original handle and spires, and suffers considerably in general appearance in consequence.

Fig. 315 is a much better specimen of John Ellicott's workmanship, the case very similar in style to that of the De Fontayne clock previously illustrated in Fig. 313. The movement is an hour striker, with a strike-silent dial in the arch and the usual day-of-the-month wheel below the hands. The corner-pieces are of unusual design. The name of Ellicott is quite a noted one in connection with horology throughout the eighteenth century, the first John, of London Wall (1696-1733), the second John —the maker of this clock—of Sweeting's Alley, Cornhill (born 1706, died 1772), John Ellicott & Sons, of Sweeting's Rents (1769-1788), Ellicott and Taylor (successors of the second John Ellicott, at the same address, 1811-30), and others of the same

Fig. 326.
EDWARD WICKSTED, LONDON.

Eight-day Striking, Chiming, and Musical Clock, playing five tunes on twelve bells from spiked drum.

Mahogany case brass mounted.

"Chime-silent" and tune dials in arch.

2 ft. 3 ins. high over all × 12 ins. wide × 8 ins. deep.

Date about 1790.

name and family, who all figure in the records of the Clockmakers' Company. Other examples of the work of the Ellicott family will be illustrated later on.

Fig. 317 is a provincial version of the London fashion of the inverted-bell top clock case.   The case is of highly-bleached walnut, clumsy in details and proportions, but it is curious to note how the corner-pieces follow the prevailing patterns of the metropolis exactly.   There is little doubt that it was customary for provincial makers to pay periodical visits to London to lay in a stock of parts, such as corners and hands, these being the productions of specialised industries at this period.

Fig. 327.

Fig. 327.

HIGGS & EVANS, ROYAL EXCHANGE.

Eight-day Striking, Chiming, and Musical Clock.
Arch of dial with figures which move every quarter of an hour.
Subsidiary dials for change of tune and day of month.
"Strike-silent" lever under arch.
Verge escapement.   Flat pendulum.
Plays the following tunes on eight bells :

(1) Sicilian Air.
(2) English Air.
(3) Scotch Air.
(4) Whittington Chimes.

Engraved back plate.
Mahogany case, richly ormolu mounted.

2 ft. 8 ins. high over all × 1 ft. 1½ ins. wide × 9 ins. deep.
Centre dial 7½ ins. diameter.
Dial 12¾ ins. high × 8½ ins. wide.

Date about 1795.

Fig. 328.

Fig. 329.

Fig. 328.

RICHARD GRANT, LONDON.

Mahogany Striking Bracket Clock.
Phases of the moon in arch.
Days of the month through aperture below hands.

In the possession of Percival D. Griffiths, Esq.

18 ins. high × 9½ ins. wide × 6 ins. deep.

Date about 1765.

Fig. 329.

JAMES SMITH, LONDON.

Mahogany Brass-mounted Bracket Clock.
Quarter-strike and chime.
Pull repeater, musical, playing on eight bells.
Phases of the moon in arch.

In the possession of Basil Dighton, Esq.

19 ins. high × 10¾ ins. wide × 6 ins. deep.

Date about 1775.

Fig. 318 is a well-made clock in a case of green lacquer, the base of which is reminiscent of the style of Chippendale. The general type is late, indicated by the fretting of the plinth and the pattern of the corner-pieces. The ground colour and the ornament of the lacquer-work are both good, and the case has considerable style for an Exeter maker of this period.

The Webster clock, Fig. 319, is another example with a converted pendulum, the engraved back plate disfigured by the locking-screw and its flange. The bottom of the case has been cut away to allow of the swing of the larger disc. The case is exceptional for this date in being ormolu mounted, but both the mountings and the corner-pieces are coarse and unfinished. The Websters were almost as numerous a family in the eighteenth-century horological world as the Ellicotts, and there were at least three of the same Christian name; the first of Exchange Alley, an apprentice of Tompion and the maker of the long-case clock Fig. 193,

Fig. 330.

Fig. 330.

"JNO. HARRISON, NEWCASTLE."

Eight-day Striking and Chiming Clock.
Pull repeater.   Eight bells.
Ebonised case, ormolu mounts.
Silvered dial, gilt corners.

2 ft. 1 in. total height × 12½ ins. wide × 8 ins. deep.
Dial 8 ins. wide.   Circle 1⅞ ins.

Date about 1780.

Fig. 331.

**JOHN SMITH,
143 HOUNDSDITCH, E.C.**

Mahogany Bracket Clock.

19 ins. high.

Date about 1770.

Fig. 332.

THOMAS REID, LONDON.

Mahogany Bracket Clock.

19½ ins. high.

Date about 1780.

Fig. 333.

**THOMAS CLEMENTS,
LIVERPOOL.**

Rosewood Bracket Clock.

20 ins. high.

Date about 1790.

died 1735; the second of Change Alley, the maker of this clock, was free in 1734, and master in 1755; and the third, William, who obtained his C.C. in 1763. An example of the work of the last member of the family will be illustrated at a later stage.

Fig. 321 is an ebony-cased striking clock on its original bracket by the same John Ellicott as Fig. 315. The chased mounts are in the French fashion of this period, and the circular dial is another concession to the same taste. The movement is in its original condition, and of high quality, the pendulum with a small engraved disc fitted with a central regulating screw, and the back plate finely engraved. The clock has a verge escapement with the horizontal crown-wheel, this being not unusual until the close of the eighteenth century.

Fig. 322 is an Essex clock of good quality, in a mahogany case of the elaborated inverted-bell type, and mounted with ormolu in the French manner. The serpentine and arched form of door, as in this example, was a favourite type after 1760, when mahogany became fashionable for the cases of bracket clocks. The movement is a three-train, strike and chime, and in the arch are two moving figures with a ball between which oscillates with the pendulum, and has the appearance of being batted to and fro. The subsidiary dials are for "strike-silent" and "chime-silent" respectively.

Fig. 323 is a late copy of the early walnut bracket clocks of 1730–40, with an alarum dial in the arch, the pointer of which is missing, and the alaruming work has also been partly removed. The pattern of the corner-pieces and the hands are in themselves sufficient indications of late date, and a comparison of the details of the case with that of the De Fontayne clock, Fig. 313, will show others to which it is not necessary to refer here, but which are immediately apparent to the eye trained to observe eighteenth-century clock cases.

The inverted-bell top was a favourite pattern for the cases of high-class clocks

Fig. 334.

— WEBSTER, LONDON.

Ebonised Eight-day Striking and Chiming Bracket Clock.
Brass mounted.

23½ ins. high × 12½ ins. wide × 6½ ins. deep.

Date about 1780.

during the whole of the eighteenth century. Fig. 324 is an example of the work of a renowned maker during the last decade. The fashion of the dial is of this period, although there is very little to differentiate the case from the patterns of 1730–40 beyond the substitution of ebony for walnut in the veneering. The clock is an eight-day alarum, the dial in the arch, with its pointer, being for fine regulation. Alexander Cumming was chiefly notable as the maker of an exceptional clock for George III, for which he was paid £2000 (equivalent to £5000 of our present-day money). His finest clock work dates from the nineteenth rather than the eighteenth century.

Fig. 325, although of the same date as the preceding specimen, is a reversion to a very early type, the escapement being of the crown-wheel kind, with a direct bob pendulum. Behind the hand collet is the usual alarum disc of the end of the eighteenth century, and certain crudities of proportion, more easily illustrated than described, betray the late specimen. The spandrel corners are of very unusual type.

The inverted-bell top in an elaborated form was the pattern of case usually selected to contain the elaborate musical clocks of this period, of which a good many were made for foreign markets, English horology enjoying a very high esteem at this period on the Continent. Fig. 326 plays five tunes, and chimes hours and quarters. The case is veneered with rich mahogany, mounted with ormolu in the French taste of this period. Fig. 327 is an even more elaborate example, playing four tunes, chiming hours and quarters, and with the arch of the dial containing movable figures, which are set in motion every quarter of an hour from the striking work. This clock is the work of Higgs & Evans of the Royal Exchange, and was made for the Spanish market, as the signature on the back plate, "Higgs y Diego Evans," shows. Spain has, until recent years, been a hunting-ground for the collector of English clocks, several notable specimens even of very early make, such as a fine Dan Quare year clock in Mr. Wetherfield's collection, having been purchased there. The workmanship of these Anglo-Spanish clocks is invariably of a high order, and there is no doubt that the Andalusian grandees were influential patrons of the more renowned makers during the whole of the eighteenth century.

The next type of case which claims our attention is the true bell-top, which, although of later introduction than the inverted bell, divides with it a place in the clock fashions from about 1760 until the middle of the next century. In a general degree the latter may be described as the walnut period of case, the former being rarely found other than in mahogany or ebonised. The inverted-bell top is, however, also made in

Fig. 335.

ANONYMOUS.

Eight-day Striking Clock.
Verge escapement. Mahogany case.

22 ins. high × 11¼ ins. wide × 6 ins. deep.
8 in. enamelled dial.

Date about 1790.

Fig. 336.

Fig. 336.

"HY. BORRELL, LONDON."

Eight-day Striking Clock.
Pull repeater.   Enamelled and painted dial.
Brass case, chased and water-gilt.

14½ ins. high × 5¼ ins. wide × 4 ins. deep.

Date about 1800.

mahogany during the last quarter of the eighteenth century; therefore this classification is only approximately true, although in its genesis the inverted-bell top is typical of the walnut period in bracket clocks, in the same way as the bell-top signalises the introduction of mahogany.

Figs. 328 and 329 are two exceptional specimens of bell-top cases of the 1770 period. The first has a well-proportioned case, veneered with mahogany of choice figure, and has its original bracket, which for space considerations is not shown here. The signing of the dial on a silvered plate fixed under the XII of the hour circle was the usual fashion of this period. The movement is an eight-day striker, with the phases of the moon in the arch and a "strike-silent" lever immediately above. Both corner-pieces and hand are typical of the period, and the persistence of the early form of minute hand will be noticed. Fig. 329 is of broader type; necessitated by the greater width to accommodate the extra train. The clock is a strike and pull repeater, chiming hours and quarters, and playing tunes from a spiked drum on eight bells. It has the detachable crutch form of pendulum, suspended from brass jaws by a flexible steel spring, which was the usual method at this date, the superiority of this type over the direct crown-wheel and fixed bob being well established. The case is veneered with curl mahogany, edged and mounted with chased and embossed brass. The repeating string is shown at the side of the case. The flamboyant minute hand indicates a prevalent fashion peculiar to high-class bracket clocks and inferior-grade long-case clocks at the same period. The design of the frets in the door and the corner-pieces is somewhat meaningless, but the close attention to minor details which is so characteristic of the earlier clocks was no longer accorded at this date.

Fig. 330 is a fine chiming and repeating clock by John Harrison, a member of

Fig. 337.

JOHN HALLIFAX, LONDON.

Eight-day Striking, Chiming, and Musical Clock, with double set of hammers. Chiming quarters on six bells and tunes on nine. Seventeen hammers for musical work. Three pulling strings.

Plays the following tunes :

    (1) A New Garot.
    (2) Geminiany's Minuet.
    (3) A Lovely Lass to a Friar came.
    (4) The "Granidear's" March.
    (5) Charming Jenny.
    (6) The Dutch Skipper.

Small dials (left), "Strike-silent" (right) regulation. Verge escapement. Mahogany case, brass mounted. Engraved scroll back plate.

2 ft. 3 ins. high (over all) × 1 ft. 2 ins. wide × 8 ins. deep.
Dial 12½ ins. × 9 ins. Hour circle 1⅝ ins.

Date about 1750.

Fig. 337.

Fig. 338.

ANONYMOUS.

Eight-day Striking and Chiming Clock, on eight bells.
Mahogany case.

2 ft. 9 ins. total height × 1 ft. 1¾ ins. wide × 7½ ins. deep.
7 in. hour circle.   3 in. day of month dial in arch.
Dial 11 ins. high × 7½ ins. wide.

Date about 1765.

a noted London family of clock-makers. The case is ebonised on mahogany, and mounted with cast and chased brasswork, and supported on feet of the same metal, in the French fashion already noticed in the inverted-bell top cases of the large musical clocks of the period. The name is engraved on the double circle immediately above the hands, and in the arch is a "chime-silent" dial. The face of the dial and the circles are completely silvered, with the spandrel corners of brass chased and gilded. The term "chasing," however, at this date had lost much of its early significance, and consisted merely of a perfunctory tooling and filing of the rough brass castings.

Figs. 331, 332, and 333 illustrate the development of these bell-top bracket clocks and the gradual departure from the earlier spade-headed hour hand to the pattern of Fig. 333, where the two closely resemble each other. The significance of this point has already been referred to at an earlier stage. Fig. 333 has a case veneered with rosewood, and a silvered dial with the spandrel corners painted, the indications of the close of the eighteenth century. In all three clock cases the differing forms of the bell-top and the ogee "Chippendale" feet are characteristics worthy of notice.

Fig. 334 is a large chiming clock in an ebonised case by Webster, probably William Webster of Change Alley. The dial is painted, with the corners in colours—a somewhat gaudy fashion—and the hands are of the most simple type, of blued steel. The case is mounted with frets and castings of brass, cleaned up and lacquered, with little or no attempt at chasing. The case is ebonised on mahogany. The movement, however, is of fine workmanship, the three trains arranged with great care and symmetry, and with a dead-beat escapement. The chiming work is on six bells, the hammers lifted from a spiked drum in the usual way.

It is rare to find a circular dial in conjunction with the bell-top bracket case where the door and its bezil are shaped to correspond. Fig. 335 is a clock of the earlier fashion, with the verge escapement, and is not signed, either on dial or back-plate. The general workmanship, however, indicates a date at the close of the eighteenth century, although the fashion of the dial and case is more in the style of the middle nineteenth.

Fig. 336 is a striking clock with a japanned dial painted with garlands of flowers, in a water-gilt brass case finely chased, and having the general appearance of a clock made for the Turkish market. The moon-headed hands are suggestive, apart from the fact that Henry Borrell was associated with Markwick Markham (probably a successor), who had a considerable trade with Stamboul. Mr. F. J. Britten illustrates in his book a miniature watch with Turkish hour

Fig. 339.

"HENRY JENKINS, CHEAPSIDE."

Astronomical Clock.
Mahogany case.

23 ins. high × 16 ins. wide × 11 ins. deep.
Dial 15 ins. high × 11 ins. wide.

Date about 1770.

numerals and the hall-mark for 1813, signed "Markwick Markham, Borrell, London," evidently by the same maker as this clock. The stars on the door and the form of the pinnacles are further suggestions that this clock was intended for Oriental exportation, probably consigned to an English official in Constantinople, judging from the Roman numerals and the Adam style of the casework. The movement is as fine as the case, and is fitted with a repeating string to sound the hours. The fretted doors on the sides are hinged to open, released by turnbuckles and knobs.

Fig. 337 is a fine musical and chiming clock by John Hallifax of Fleet Street, also made for the Spanish market in the same way as the one by Higgs and Evans, illustrated in Fig. 327. This clock has a double set of hammers, one for

Fig. 340.

"WILL^m. BULL," STRATFORD, ESSEX.

Eight-day Striking Clock.
Enamelled dial. Mahogany case.
Direct-bob pendulum. Engraved back plate.

12 ins. high (without handle) × 9¼ ins. wide × 6 ins. deep.

Date about 1780.

the chiming and the other operated from a spiked drum. There are 16 bells in all: one for the hours, six for the chimes, and nine for the tunes, of which the clock plays six from 17 hammers. The pointer in the arch is for the alteration of the tunes, the small dial on the left for "strike-silent," and that on the right for "up-and-down" regulation, the pendulum being lengthened or shortened by a cam under the suspension. The case is of solid mahogany, mounted with ormolu, and there are three pulling strings on the side, for strike, chime, and musical work respectively. The centre spire and the feet are not original, the latter being unnecessary additions. This clock is later in style and workmanship than the date of John Hallifax's bankruptcy in 1740. A noticeable feature is the cross-braces to the handles—a very necessary contrivance in the transporting of such a heavy clock as this.

Fig. 338 is a close approximation to the Chinese style of Thomas Chippendale, the case being of varnished and waxed mahogany, light in colour, and mounted with lacquered brass ornaments. The clock is a strike and chime movement, with eight bells and as many hammers, and is quite a good example of the work of this period. Neither the dial nor the back-plate are signed.

Fig. 339 is a bracket clock by the same maker as the long-case already illustrated in Fig. 242, the movement being a simplified version of the astronomical

Fig. 341.

"JNO. PYKE, LONDON."

Eight-day Striking Clock.
Mahogany case.
Pull repeater, striking hours and quarters.
Bob pendulum.   Brass and silver dial.

7½ ins. high × 5¼ ins. wide.
Height 13 ins. over handle × 7 ins. wide × 5¼ ins. deep.

Date about 1770-80.

Fig. 342.

GEORGE LEFROY, WISBEACH.

Mahogany Eight-day Striking Clock.
Brass mesh on front and sides.

18½ ins. high × 12½ ins. wide × 6 ins. deep.

Date about 1785.

Fig. 343.

ROBERT PHILP (PHILIP?),
6 New Court, St. John Street,
Clerkenwell.

Ebonised Striking Bracket Clock.

16 ins. high.

Date about 1780.

Fig. 344.

GEORGE ADDIS,
79 Cornhill, E.C.

Ebonised Striking Bracket Clock.

14½ ins. high.

Date about 1790.

Fig. 345.

JOHN FRENCH,
21 Tavistock Street,
LONDON, W.

Mahogany Striking Bracket Clock.

19 ins. high.

Date about 1795.

Fig. 346.

W. ALEXANDER,
10 Parliament Street,
LONDON, S.W.

Mahogany Striking Bracket Clock.

15 ins. high.

Date about 1830.

clock described in Chapter XI. In this example the centre of the dial also rotates, and upon it is engraved a longitudinal map of the globe, and to set the clock it is necessary to align the hour hand to the particular country in which the clock is, and the position of other localities marks the time in those

Fig. 347.

ALLAN & CAITHNESS, LONDON.

Eight-day Striking Clock.
Mahogany case.

10 ins. high × 9¼ ins. wide × 7½ ins. deep.
6 in. painted convex dial.

Date about 1800.

Fig. 348.

THOMAS BANNISTER, "Journeyman," LONDON.

Eight-day Striking and Musical Clock,
playing five tunes on twelve bells, from spiked drum.
Mahogany case.
Tune dial in arch.

2 ft. 4 ins. high over all × 12¾ ins. wide × 8 ins. deep.

Dated January 7th, 1801.

countries from the outside ring of the 24-hour numbered dial. The three subsidiary dials are for day of the month (left), minutes and seconds from two hands (centre), and time of sunrise and sunset (right). The small hole and slot on the left of the subsidiary central dial in the arch are connected with the maintaining power of the bolt-and-shutter kind, a most unusual form in a clock of this late date.

The next three examples illustrate

the beginning of the broken-arch form of case, which became very popular after about 1760. This type was usually fitted with a circular dial and brass-hinged bezil, in lieu of the arched glazed door enclosing a dial of the same shape. The earlier broken-arch cases are generally square, the arch low, and the mouldings scratched, with very small members. Fig. 340 is a very good specimen of this class, the case well made, of good mahogany, and the movement of fine workmanship, a pull repeater, striking hours and quarters. A reference to Fig. 243, in the chapter on long-case clocks, will show that a fairly close relation existed at this period between the bracket and the grandfather clock cases, the same general principles of form being observable in each. Fig. 341 is a London clock of the broken-arch type of case, with a movement of good quality.

Fig. 349.

ANONYMOUS.

Eight-day Striking and Chiming Clock.
Mahogany case.
Playing eight tunes on ten bells, as follows :

"Robin Adair."
"Barbara Allen."
"Vicar of Bray."
"Men of Harlech."
"Home, Sweet Home."
"Blue Bells of Scotland."
"Lass of Richmond Hill."
"Gavotte" (Bach).

2 ft. 1 in. high × 12 ins. wide × 7 ins. deep.

Date about 1800-10.

Fig. 342 is slightly later in date and of better proportions, somewhat marred in general appearance by the unnecessary feet, which were so frequently added to bracket clocks during the nineteenth century. This clock is quite an exceptional specimen of the work of a country maker, both movement and case being of good quality. Much of the brass meshwork is modern, but was probably of the same pattern in the original instance, as the design of diapered crescents is quite typical of this period. The dial is cream enamelled, and the hands are delicately wrought. The brass bezil is fixed to, and opens with, the door in the same way as with the previous example. Four later examples of these broken-arch cases are given in Figs. 343, 344, 345, and 346. Fig. 343 has a dial of enamel, and Fig. 345 has the painted dial of the period, the case surmounted by three spires, with the lifting handles on the sides.

Towards the close of the eighteenth century many' elaborations of these broken-arch cases were made, such as Fig. 347, for example, where the sides are arched to correspond with the front. The clock is an eight-day striker, with a domed painted dial enclosed by a solid hinged bezil of quarter-round section. The frets of the case, the ball terminals, the columns, and the feet are of lacquered brass, and the case is of solid mahogany. The general form suggests a building rather than a clock case, especially in such details as the breaking of the plinth moulding and the arching of the sides. The movement is of good quality, with a back plate engraved on the edges, or "teapot" engraved, as it is usually termed.

Fig. 348 shows, in its oval dial, a somewhat radical departure from the usual clock traditions, but dials of this form appear to have been popular, as they are not uncommon. The inscription, "Thomas Bannister, Journeyman," is peculiar, and

Fig. 350.

GEO. JAMESON, PORTSEA.

Mahogany Eight-day Striking Bracket Clock.

1 ft. 6 ins. high × 10½ ins. wide × 6 ins. deep.
8 in. dial.

Date about 1810.

Fig. 351.
Side view of movement of Fig. 350.

suggests that this clock was a "masterpiece" submitted by the maker on his application for the freedom of his Company. The dating, January 7th, 1801, still further bears out this idea. Thomas and James Bannister were afterwards established at Kirby Street, Hatton Garden. Fig. 348 is a striking and musical clock playing five tunes on twelve bells from a spiked drum in the usual way. Among these is the Hundredth Psalm, a great favourite with clockmakers of this period. The small dial, with its pointer, is for the alteration of the tunes. The clock is in original state, and is a good example of conscientious workmanship.

Fig. 349 is another elaborate musical clock of about 1800–10, playing eight

Fig. 352.

**DWERRIHOUSE & CARTER,
Berkeley Square, LONDON.**

Eight-day Recoil Striking Clock.
Mahogany case inlaid with ebony lines.
Brass ring, lion-head handles at sides.

20½ ins. high × 9 ins. wide × 5¾ ins. deep.
7 in. enamelled dial.

Date about 1810.

Fig. 353.

—— BARWISE, LONDON.

Eight-day Recoil Striking Clock.
Mahogany case.

18½ ins. high × 12¼ ins. wide × 6½ ins. deep.
8 in. convex dial.

Date about 1810.

Fig. 354.

Fig. 355.

Eight-day Striking Clock.
Mahogany case, inlaid brass lines.

12 ins. high × 7¼ ins. wide × 2¾ ins. deep.
3¾ in. enamelled dial.

Date about 1835.

Fig. 354.

Wᵐ· NICOLL, Junᵣ·, LONDON.

Eight-day Striking Clock.
Ebony case, brass mounted.

1 ft. 4¼ ins. high × 10 ins. wide
× 6¾ ins. deep.
7 in. dial.

Date about 1825.

Fig. 356.

Eight-day Striking Clock.
Mahogany case.

12¼ ins. high × 6½ ins. wide × 4 ins. deep.
4¼ in. enamelled dial.

Date about 1840.

tunes, one of which, the "Gavotte," by Bach, must have been a novelty in England at this date, as Johann Sebastian Bach, although dead some sixty years before, was practically unknown here at the commencement of the nineteenth century. The dial of this clock has the Arabic instead of the Roman numerals, and the three subsidiary dials on the arch are for "strike-silent," "chime-silent," and alteration of tune respectively. All four are enamelled in separate circles, on a ground of engraved

Fig. 357.

J. LEROUX, CHARING CROSS.

Eight-day Striking Clock.
Ebony case, brass mounted.
Enamelled dial.

21 ins. high × 9 ins. wide × 5½ ins. deep.

Date about 1760.

brass. The movement, although of good quality, is unsigned—an unusual thing with these elaborate musical clocks. The top of the case is panelled and fretted, to emit the sound from the nest of ten bells immediately underneath.

Fig. 350 is of about the same date, but of finer quality than the preceding. The escapement is a dead-beat on a knife-edge, shown in

Fig. 358.

"RIACH, LONDON."

Eight-day Striking Verge Clock.
Mahogany case inlaid with satin-wood.
"Strike-silent" lever.

18 ins. high × 10 ins. wide across base.
5½ ins. across waist.   6 ins. deep.
6¾ in. convex painted dial.

Date 1790.

a side view of the movement, the anchor of which engages with a contrate-wheel with the teeth set at right angles to its plane of rotation. The dial is a simple painted convex, the bezil of which is attached to, and opens with, the front door. The pierced brass frets are embossed in scroll and floral patterns. George Jameson was a chronometer maker of some considerable renown.

The dead-beat escapement, which has already been described in a former chapter, was a favourite one with high-class makers in clocks of great precision, after its invention by George Graham, although it has the drawback of slowing the clock by the thickening of the oil on the pallets.

Fig. 359.
EDWARD TOMLIN,
69 Threadneedle Street, E.C.

Mahogany Inlaid Eight-day Striking Bracket Clock.

In the possession of Messrs. Story & Triggs.

22½ ins. high × 11½ ins. wide across base × 5¼ ins. deep across body.

Date about 1795.

Fig. 360.

RICHARD BEST, LONDON.

Eight-day Striking Clock.
Mahogany case.

19½ ins. high over all × 10½ ins. wide over base × 6¾ ins. deep.

Date about 1835.

In clocks with a visible escapement, on the face of the dial, the pin-pallet escapement was generally substituted, especially in clocks after the French style.

Fig. 352 is a clock with the older form of recoil escapement, in a mahogany case inlaid with ebony lines. The hands are of the serpentine form, which was very fashionable in clocks of the early nineteenth century, and the edges of the back plate are engraved. The lion-head handles at the sides are a concession to the English Empire style of Thomas Hope, which at this date had supplanted the more graceful manner of Sheraton.

Fig. 353 is another recoil striking clock by Nathanael Barwise, of about the same date as the preceding, with a case veneered with the choice mahogany so characteristic of this period, and inlaid with the "key-cornered" lines of the later Sheraton style. The corners are embellished with fluted quarter columns, "stopped" with brass, and on the sides are the usual ringed lion-headed handles. The ivory escutcheoned lock releases the bezil tang, which is secured by the bolt. At the back is the usual glazed door, and the back plate is engraved on the edges in a simple running floral pattern.

Fig. 354 is another recoil striking clock in an ebony case,

Fig. 361.

ANONYMOUS.

Eight-day Verge Striking Clock.
Engraved back plate. Painted convex dial.
Case veneered with East and West India satin-wood.
Sunk panel. Ebony corner lines.

2 ft. high × 11½ ins. wide × 6 ins. deep.

Date about 1790–5.

with pierced brass frets with handle, caddy feet, quarter columns, and engraved band round the plinth, also of brass. The dial is convex, painted cream, with quarter-round bezil and elaborated moon hands, and a simple "teapot" engraving round the back plate. Figs. 355 and 356 are further examples of these "Sheraton" broken-arch cases of the first half of the nineteenth century.

The balloon case coincides with the broken-arch form, commencing about 1760 and persisting throughout the nineteenth century. Fig. 357 is an eighteenth-century example by John Leroux of 8 Charing Cross, in a French style of case, of ebony with mountings of ormolu. Mr. Wether-field has a clock by John Johnson in an almost identical case to this example. The escapement here is a direct verge, with a bob pendulum.

Fig. 358 is a more typical balloon case, of mahogany panelled with satin-wood and inlaid with holly lines; and Fig. 359 is an exceptional example of a well-proportioned case in the Sheraton style, banded with a broad line of satin-wood edged with ebony, and supported on cast brass feet. Several variations of the balloon case were made, especially when the lever was substituted for the pendulum clock, where the front of the case was shaped out to match the sides. These cases were frequently cut out of solid wood, with a hole cut through for the clock. This method of making was somewhat repre-hensible, as the veneering of the unbroken sweep of the sides over the end grain of the wood on the top of the case was impractic-able, the veneer having a tendency to blister up under the strain and the inefficient hold of the glue on the end wood.

Fig. 360 is an unusual form of the balloon case, of good mahogany, supported

Fig. 362.

EDWARD BIRD, BRISTOL.

Eight-day Recoil Striking Clock.
Mahogany case, inlaid lines.

1 ft. 9 ins. high × 10 ins. wide × 5½ ins. deep.
8½ in. painted convex dial.

Date about 1810.

on chased brass feet in the French style. The dial is painted with two subsidiary dials below the hour circle, the one on the left for the "strike-silent," that on the right showing the day of the month. The hands are very simple in form and of gilded brass. The back plate is engraved and is pierced for the bell, the hammer being short, with its tail at the bottom of the plate. The back door is fretted and glazed.

Fig. 361 introduces the arch-top case— a rare fashion until almost the close of the

Fig. 363.

THOMAS WRIGHT, DORKING.

Mahogany Inlaid Bracket Clock.

1 ft. 5½ ins. high × 10 ins. wide × 5½ ins. deep.
8 in. dial.

Date about 1800.

Fig. 364.

JOHN THWAITES, LONDON.

Eight-day Striking Clock.
Mahogany case, brass frets.

20¼ ins. high × 10 ins. wide × 5¾ ins. deep.

Date about 1810.

eighteenth century. This is an important clock, although unsigned, with the case veneered with choice satin-wood, panelled with ebony lines. The sides have panels of close brass meshwork, and the handles above are well chased. The movement is a direct verge eight-day striker of good quality, with a painted convex, or "boom" dial encased with a quarter-round bezil, glazed and hinged.

Fig. 362 is a later specimen, of similar form but with the English Empire fluting of the base and the ball caddy feet of 1800. The hands are exceptionally choice, pierced in running loops,

Fig. 365.

EDWARD NEWMAN, LONDON.

Eight-day Recoil Striking Clock.
Mahogany inlaid case.

17 ins. high × 9½ ins. wide × 5½ ins. deep.
7¾ in. painted convex dial.

Date about 1820.

and well finished. The back plate is edge-engraved in simple fashion, and the movement is of the early recoil type. Fig. 363 is the true arch top unornamented, the case of mahogany inlaid with lines of holly, and ovals and spandrels of East India satin-wood. The side handles are embossed in floral patterns, with shell-fretted panels below. The movement is an eight-day recoil striker, with a centre-piece pendulum and an edge-engraved back plate.

Fig. 364 shows the influence of the English Empire style of Hope very clearly in the sunk panel below the dial and the cresting of the case with an inlaid terracing. The back plate of this clock is edge or " teapot " engraved. The general character of the dial and hands is almost identical with the previous example. Fig. 365 is a simpler version of Fig. 364, the case of mahogany inlaid with a single box line.

Fig. 366.

Eight-day Clock.
Mahogany case, inlaid brass.

12½ ins. high × 6¼ ins. wide × 4¼ ins. deep.
4 in. enamelled dial.

Date about 1820.

The lancet top is a nineteenth-century fashion rarely found, when decorated, without an inlay of the brass marqueterie so general in the later Sheraton-Empire furniture. This form of case has the advantage of being more easily veneered than the true arch top, the veneer in the latter being laid in a state of strain which demands careful workmanship. Fig. 366, in addition to the brass inlay before referred to, has another typical English Empire or late Sheraton detail, the " milling " of the base moulding. This device was adopted as a cheap and more or less effective substitute for carving. Four lateral strips were glued together with paper between the joints, so that the glue should not hold too well, and the piece being turned in a pattern of narrow rings, was afterwards split into the four again, each of quarter-round section, and laid down on the rebate above the base. This method was frequently adopted to embellish the door framings of the pedestal sideboards of the English Empire period. It serves to indicate the decadence of English cabinet-making of the period, when carving was imitated to save expense in manufacture.

Fig. 367 is an important clock by a noted maker, in a case veneered with ebony, inlaid with stars, lines, and marqueterie of brass. The general style is the early Victorian travesty of the Gothic, which in point of ugliness vies with the efforts of Batty Langley a century before. The movement of this clock is a recoil strike and chime of fine quality, with an engraved bordered back plate. The sides have floral ring handles and Gothic frets. Fig. 368 is another brass-inlaid ebony-cased clock by Septimus Miles of 32 Ludgate Street, City, with a simple movement of somewhat early type. The date of this clock is some forty years before that of the previous example. Fig. 369 is another example of about the same date.

It is remarkable that a style with so few redeeming characteristics as that of the English Empire of "Anastasius" Hope should have become so paramount in its influence as to compel a designer of the renown and excellence of Thomas Sheraton to jettison practically all that was fine of his earlier manner, to follow

Fig. 367.

"FRENCH, ROYAL EXCHANGE, LONDON."

Eight-day Clock.
Striking, and chiming on eight bells.
Ebony case inlaid with brass lines.
"Strike-silent" dial in arch. Brass hands.

29¼ ins. high × 12 ins. wide × 6½ ins. deep.
Painted dial 12 ins. high × 8 ins. wide.

Date about 1850.

the prevailing craze. The rage for the classicalism of the Napoleonic era had extended from France to England during the first decade of the nineteenth century. This was undoubtedly the factor which won for the new manner the place which it attained in the popular favour. There is little to be said in praise of the French furniture of the period ; there is nothing to recommend the Anglicised travesty of the style. The classical manner of Robert Adam was often stiff and artificial, but there

was always present some evidences of the desire to evolve something fine. Adam was restrained, and largely influenced by the desire for comfort ; he descended from the Roman atrium to the English saloon, and often, as at Nostell Priory for example, with distinctly noteworthy results. Robert Adam was sometimes stilted, often un-technical, but never ugly. It was reserved to Thomas Hope to show to what depths of degradation the rage for the classical could be dragged. Thomas Hope was a man of considerable fortune who had travelled extensively in Europe, Asia, and Africa. He published his *Household Furniture* in 1805, a work illustrated with interiors principally from his own house in Duchess Street, Portland Place. The general character of his de-signs is one of ultra-severe classi-calism, no concessions to modern comfort being made in any way. The style was highly esteemed in his day, Hope achieving more re-nown as a designer and mentor of taste than as a novelist and

Fig. 368.

"MILES, LUDGATE STREET, LONDON."

Eight-day Recoil Striking Clock.
Ebony case, inlaid brass.

1 ft. 7 ins. high × 10 ins. wide × 5½ ins. deep.
8½ in. painted convex dial.

Date about 1810.

philosopher, in which latter his eminence was unquestioned, but acknowledged only after his death. His "English Empire" style became vulgarised in the hands of the craftsmen of his day—the inevitable fate of any highly popular manner. Its influence permeated the trade of the clockmaker almost as much as that of the joiner. In Figs. 370 to 373, four examples of this style are illustrated. Figs. 371 and 372 are of the actual period of Hope, and are therefore more pronounced. The first has such building details as the Grecian akroter superimposed on a French

Fig. 369.

HANDLEY & MOORE, LONDON.

Eight-day Striking Clock.
Ebony case inlaid with brass.

16½ ins. high × 9 ins. wide × 5¾ ins. deep.

Date 1810–20.

Fig. 370.

THOS. GOSTLING, DISS.

Eight-day Striking Clock.
Mahogany case. Brass spire, feet, and frets.

23¾ ins. high × 10½ ins. wide × 5¾ ins. deep.

Date about 1845.

Fig. 372.

WILMOT, UPPER ROSOMAN STREET.

Eight-day Recoil Striking Clock.

Mahogany case.

21 ins. high over spire × 11 ins. wide.

7 in. enamelled dial.

Date about 1810.

Fig. 371.

Wᵐ. HOLMES, STRAND.

Eight-day Recoil Striking Clock.

Mahogany case inlaid with brass.

19 ins. high × 12½ ins. width × 6¼ ins. depth of base.

6 in. painted dial.

Date about 1810.

Fig. 373.

T. & J. OLLIVANT, MANCHESTER.

Eight-day Striking Clock.

Rosewood case.

23½ ins. high × 10¾ ins. wide × 6 ins. deep.

Date about 1840.

Fig. 374.

ANONYMOUS.

Eight-day Recoil Striking Clock.

Mahogany case.　Engraved back plate.

20 ins. high × 16 ins. wide at base × 6¾ ins. deep.

9¼ in. dial.

Date about 1800.

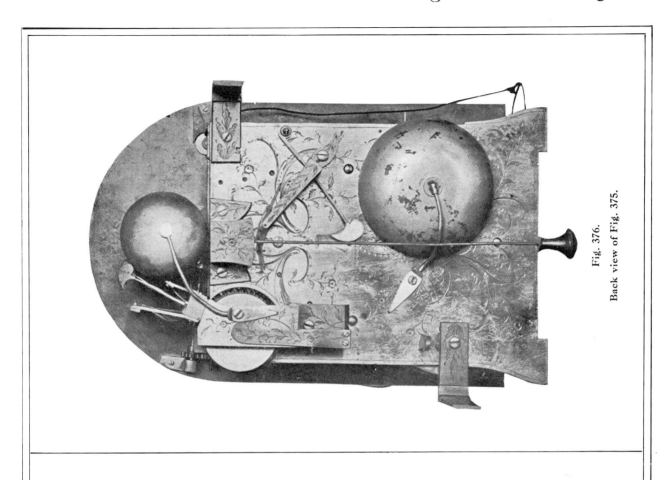

Fig. 376.

Back view of Fig. 375.

Fig. 375.

GIBBS, 38 BANNER STREET, LONDON.

Ebony Musical, Eight-day Bracket Clock.

Two pull-string repeaters.   Plays four tunes.   Chimes on eight bells.

1 ft. 4 ins. high × 9 ins. wide × 6 ins. deep.

Silvered dial 10½ ins. × 7 ins.

Date about 1840.

Fig. 377.

—— HUGGINS, LONDON.

Eight-day Recoil Striking Clock.

Mahogany case, inlaid brass.

"Strike-silent" dial in arch.

Day of month dial below hands.

22 ins. high over all × 10½ ins. wide × 6¼ ins. deep.

Dial 10¼ ins. × 6¾ ins.

Date about 1830.

Fig. 378.

—— BENTLEY, LONDON.

Eight-day Clock.

Mahogany case inlaid brass marqueterie.

16½ ins. high over all × 8⅛ ins. wide × 4 ins. deep.

6½ in. painted convex dial.

Date about 1815.

style of case. The second is almost Egyptian in character. Figs. 370 and 373 are later, with the crudities of the style somewhat toned down. The quaint mixture of Gothic and classical details in the last example shows a curious jumbling of the styles of Chippendale and Hope.

The classical manner is evident in nearly all the later nineteenth-century clock cases. Fig. 374 shows the French influence of the Directoire and the Neo-Grec in the flanking bracket-pieces, a detail very general in the marble cases of a somewhat later period.

Fig. 375 is a somewhat remarkable clock in a simple case of this period. The movement is of a much earlier type and of elaborate construction, playing four tunes from the spiked drum shown in the left-hand top corner of the back plate. There are two repeating strings for the strike and chime respectively, the three hands in the arch being for the silencing of the strike and the chime and the alteration of tunes. To accommodate the musical and chiming work, the hour bell is placed outside the back plate and low down, as shown in the illustration. George Gibbs was a well-known maker of about 1840, but this clock has an appearance of being a much earlier example, cased at a later date.

Figs. 377 to 380 show the chamfer-top style of case. The first is an arched-dial clock with a strike-silent finger above and a day-of-the-month dial below the hands, resembling the previous example. The second is merely a timepiece in a brass-inlaid mahogany case. The third is a pull repeater, the fashion for which became very rare after about 1830. The fourth has a centre-screw pendulum and the striking bell in the centre outside the back plate. All are typical early nineteenth-century cases, the strong similarity of the one to the other suggesting a common origin. This is more than a mere surmise, the clock industry at this period—that is, the actual manufacture, as distinguished from the sale to the public—being centred in the neighbourhood of Clerkenwell. With a trade so complicated, depending so largely on accuracy, not only of workmanship but also of adjustment of parts, specialisation was inevitable, and had existed from very early times. Thus makers of chronometers, of watch balances, of hands, spandrel corners and frets, and clock cases, brassfinishers and chasers, and even men whose life was spent in timing and adjusting watches and clocks, were by no means unusual. We have seen that corner-pieces were made in considerable numbers, and of the one series of patterns—a consideration dictated by the exigencies of casting from moulds, but also due to the fact that specialisation and stereotyping tend to become synonymous terms. The same

Fig. 379.

── MOGINIE, PIMLICO.

Eight-day Recoil Striking and Pull Repeating Clock.
Mahogany case.   "Strike-silent" lever.

20 ins. high × 10¼ ins. wide × 5½ ins. deep.
Painted dial 8 ins. diameter.

Date about 1825.

Fig. 380.

"THOS· RICHARDS, LONDON."

Eight-day Striking Clock.
Mahogany case with brass mouldings.
Centre-screw pendulum.

16 ins. high × 10¼ ins. wide × 6 ins. deep.
8½ in. convex dial.

Date about 1820.

Fig. 381.

ALEXANDER LEROUX, CHARING CROSS.

Eight-day Clock.

Mahogany case, inlaid chequered lines.

14 ins. high (17 ins. over spire).   Base 7¼ ins. wide × 4¾ ins. deep.

5 in. silvered dial.

Date 1790.

Fig. 382.

ANONYMOUS.

Eight-day Striking Clock.

Enamel dial.   Battersea enamel plaque inlaid.

Mahogany case inlaid with satin-wood.

15 ins. high × 9 ins. across base × 4 ins. deep.

4 in. dial.

Fig. 383.

Eight-day Clock.
Ebonised case.   Brass frets.

$10\frac{1}{4}$ ins. high $\times$ $5\frac{3}{4}$ ins. wide $\times$ 3 ins. deep.
4 in. enamelled dial.

Fig. 385.

Eight-day Verge Clock.
Ebonised case, inlaid brass.

13 ins. high over all $\times$ $5\frac{1}{2}$ ins. wide
$\times$ 3 ins. deep.

Date 1810.

Fig. 384.

— SADDLETON, LYNN.

Eight-day Clock.
Ebonised case, inlaid brass.

$9\frac{1}{4}$ ins. high $\times$ $5\frac{1}{2}$ ins. wide $\times$ $3\frac{1}{2}$ ins. deep.

Fig. 386.

ELLICOTT & TAYLOR, LONDON.

Eight-day Recoil Timepiece.
Mahogany case with brass moulding.

11 ins. high $\times$ $5\frac{1}{2}$ ins. wide $\times$ $4\frac{1}{2}$ ins. deep.
4 in. enamelled dial.

Date 1815.

Fig. 387.

Eight-day Clock.
Mahogany inlaid case.

11 ins. high $\times$ $5\frac{1}{2}$ ins. wide $\times$ $3\frac{1}{3}$ ins. deep.
4 in. enamelled dial.

Date 1800.

Fig. 388.

Eight-day Clock.
Mahogany case inlaid with satin-wood bandings.

10 ins. high × 6 ins. wide × 4¼ ins. deep.
4 in. enamelled dial.

Date 1800.

Fig. 389.

Eight-day Clock.
Mahogany case, inlaid brass.

12 ins. high over all × 6¾ ins. width of base × 3¼ ins. deep.
4 in. enamelled dial.

Date 1810.

Fig. 390.

Eight-day Ting-tang Quarter-striking Clock.
Ebonised case. Engraved brass frets.

12¼ ins. high over all × 5¾ ins. wide × 4 ins. deep.
3½ in. enamelled dial.

Date 1795.

Fig. 391.

Eight-day Clock.
Ebonised case.

9½ ins. high × 5¼ ins. wide × 3¼ ins. deep.
4 in. enamelled dial.

Date 1800.

applies to the manufacture of clock cases—nominally a branch of the furniture-making industry, but in actual fact a distinct trade. In making for stock, or for ready sale, the innovator is always more or less discounted; it is the one who follows the prevailing fashion who is successful. Occasionally we find a maker whose personality is sufficient to dominate a trade and establish a vogue, but this is rarely if ever the case with a subsidiary industry—a maker of parts as distinct from the producer, or the one who has the credit for the production of the actual finished piece. Thus the peddler of the article is nearly always more favourably circumstanced than the maker, and is frequently acclaimed as the originator of a style to which he has rendered no further assistance than the commercial one of merely buying and selling.

With the introduction of the lever escapement in lieu of the pendulum control, a fashion began for miniature mantel clocks in restricted cases too narrow to permit of the swing of a pendulum. Occasionally the same type of case was used for the pendulum-controlled clocks, the escape-wheel teeth and the release being made very shallow to allow of a small-waisted case and a narrow arc of swing. The eleven examples illustrated in the conclusion to this chapter show some of the patterns of cases current during the nineteenth century, with these miniature mantel clocks. Although they all depart, more or less, from established traditions, and some are merely variations of patterns which have been previously illustrated and described, some originality of design and considerable taste in proportion and decoration is evident in Figs. 381 and 382 for instance, and although much of the individuality of character which is so marked in the early eighteenth-century clocks had become dissipated or depraved, the general standard of workmanship was still well maintained. In this respect the trade of the clockmaker compares very favourably with that of the cabinetmaker of the same period, although even in the case of the latter, while some of the furniture produced, even during the "Golden Age" of English cabinetmaking, was poor in quality and workmanship, it was not until the era of power machinery, at the close of the nineteenth century, that the woodworking trades descended to depths unknown during that of the hand-worker, where the craftsman wrought at his bench, with simple pride in the piece produced—as much the product of brain and eye as of hand—and with no thought of the wholesale production and duplication which the following generation was to witness.

Chapter XV

Mural and Cartel Clocks

HE whole of the examples of English clocks which have been considered in the foregoing chapters may be resolved into three general types. In the first instance we have the brass lantern, essentially a wall clock, whether made to stand on a fixed bracket, or spiked to the wall itself; the long case is made to stand on the floor—no other position being possible; and the wood-cased, spring-driven clock has its proper place on a mantel-shelf, or a table. For several reasons, however, the mural clock, whether of the lantern, hooded, Cartel, "Act of Parliament," or dial kind, never entirely declined in favour, as in given circumstances the wall was the only possible place for a clock. Nearly all the celebrated makers appear to have been responsible for some specimens of wall clocks, the usual pattern being that similar to the hood of a long case, with weights and pendulum hanging below. This kind is essentially the "cottage"—one might almost say, the kitchen clock—but the type was thought worthy of the attention of makers as renowned as Joseph Knibb, and therefore demands consideration here.

There is no doubt that the origin of these hooded clocks in England was due to Dutch influences during the reign of James II. The type is a much more familiar one in Holland than in this country during the whole of the eighteenth century. Two noticeable peculiarities regarding these hood clocks may be mentioned here: the first, that their case-work does not conform to the regular traditions of the different periods, so that any general resemblance to the long-case clocks already illustrated in the foregoing pages is a very misleading indication of date; and the second, that they are invariably fitted with 30-hour movements, for no particular reason which can be discovered. It is, of course, possible to substitute the dial and movement of a true long-case clock for the original 30-hour, but it is more likely that if these hooded cases were ever fitted with eight-day movements, the reverse of this exchange has been effected in years gone by. Examples of these wall clocks are encountered, however, of date towards the end of the eighteenth century, where the movements are unquestionably original, and these are invariably of 30-hour duration, and there is little doubt that in nearly every instance hood

Fig. 392.

GERRIT STORM, AMSTERDAM.

30-hour Alarum Clock.

25 ins. high × 13 ins. wide × 8 ins. deep.
9½ in. dial.   2 in. circle.

Fig. 393.

"JOHN KNIBB, OXON., FECIT."

30-hour Alarum Clock.

Oak case veneered with ebony.

20 ins. high × 9½ ins. wide × 6¼ ins. deep.
5¼ in. dial.   ⅞ in. circle.

Date about 1690.

Fig. 394.

JOHN SPENDLOVE, THETFORD.

30-hour Alaruming Wall Clock.
Mahogany case.

20 ins. high × 11 ins. wide × 7½ ins. deep.
Engraved silvered dial 8 ins. high × 5¾ ins. wide.

Date about 1770–80.

Fig. 395.

—— **WHITEHURST, DERBY.**

30-hour Alaruming Wall Clock.
Inlaid mahogany case.

23 ins. high × 11½ ins. wide × 6¾ ins. deep.
7½ in. silvered dial.

Date about 1770.

Fig. 396.

EIGHT-DAY CARVED AND GILT CARTEL CLOCK.

2 ft. 9 ins. high × 1 ft. 8½ ins. wide.

7¼ in. silvered dial.

Date about 1760.

clocks were 30-hour, the eight-day or the month movement being reserved for the grandfather case.

Fig. 392 is a Dutch clock showing the style prevalent in Holland. The almost invariable presence of the alarum disc round the centre of the hand collet appears to suggest that these clocks were intended for servants' quarters, as in the usual apartments such a function would have been more of a nuisance than an advantage. This Dutch clock, as far as can be ascertained, dates from the last half of the

Fig. 397.

G. REASON, LONDON.

Eight-day Timepiece.
Carved and gilt wood case.   Silvered dial.

31 ins. high × 22 ins. wide.

Date about ————

eighteenth century, but is early in style as far as the design of the case is concerned.

Fig. 393 is a very early specimen, by John Knibb of Oxford, one of four famous brothers already referred to in an earlier chapter. The clock is a 30-hour, one handed, with central alarum disc, crown-wheel escapement, and short bob pendulum. The case is of oak, veneered with ebony, with twisted pillars at the side. The hood is made to slide up in the fashion of the early long cases. Apart from its simple type, this example is quite a good specimen of the work of John Knibb, the hand being well pierced, the cherub-corners chased, and the mouldings of the case of delicate sections and well finished.

It may be as well to point out that single-handed clocks, where original, lack the minute divisions on the outside of the hour circle, the hour being divided into quarters on the inside only. The presence of clocks with dials of this kind in long cases should be viewed with suspicion, unless both case and clock are of very early date. When a dial has an hour-ring lacking the minute divisions and yet fitted with two hands, it is beyond question that the clock has been tampered with. It seems hardly necessary to have to point out such an apparently obvious detail as this, but it is so usual to find these wall-clock movements fitted to long cases, provided with a pair of hands, and masquerading as grandfather clocks, even in important sales such as those at Christies', that the caution may not be so unnecessary as would at first appear.

Fig. 398.

"J. PARKES, OLD CHANGE, LONDON."

Gilt Convex-dialed Eight-day Lever Clock.

25 ins. diameter.
Dial 14½ ins.

Date about 1800.

Fig. 394 is a wall clock in a case of plain mahogany, with

an engraved silvered dial and the invariable alarum disc. The name, "John Spendlove, Thetford," is engraved on a silvered boss in the arch.

Fig. 395 has a mahogany case inlaid with flowers and tendrils of holly, and a silvered circular dial. Although of late date, the clock lacks the minute motion-work. John Whitehurst was a well-known maker, first of Derby and afterwards at Bolt Court, Fleet Street, London, E.C. He was properly a maker of turret clocks. His business was carried on, after his death in 1788, by his son. The date inscribed on the clock in "The Chauntry," Newark, to the effect that it was made in 1807 and fixed in 1808 "by Mr. John Whitehurst, Senior, of Derby," suggests that he was longer lived than the records show. John Whitehurst (junior) was one of three clockmakers invited to tender for the clock in the tower of the Houses of Parliament in 1846.

Fig. 399.

ROBERT BUNYAN, LINCOLN.

Eight-day Wall Clock.
Black lacquered case. White painted dial.

5 ft. 2 ins. high.
24 in. dial.

Date about 1780.

If the hood clock may be justly regarded as the timepiece of the servants' hall, the Cartel is the clock of the salon. Both the term and the fashion for these "Pendules à Cartel" were French in inspiration. The English Cartel clocks were usually of wood, carved and gilded, those of French origin of cast brass or bronze, water-gilt, and nearly always finely chased.

Unlike the hood clock, the English Cartel is nearly always of eight-day duration, but rarely fitted with striking work. The usual fashion of the cases was that of the French Louis XIV, evidently made to harmonise with the apartments of the middle Georgian period, where a coarse version of the same style was the prevalent one for decorations and panellings.

Fig. 396 is a bold clock in a carved gilt case of the period of 1760, the ornament clumsy but vigorous, in the French manner of the time. The eagle with outspread wings is reminiscent of the circular mirrors with distorting glass which were so general at this period. The dial has a visible pendulum disc, seen through the lunette above

Fig. 400.

MATT^{W.} HILL, DEVONSHIRE STREET.

Eight-day Wall Clock.
Black lacquer case.   White painted dial.

4 ft. 7 ins. high.
Dial 24 ins. diameter.

Date about 1790.

the hands, with a minute dial above. Although of some importance, the clock is unsigned.

Fig. 397 is another of these carved Cartel clocks of about the same date as the preceding, the dial centre painted with a grotesque head, the eyes of which move with the pendulum in its swing. Fig. 398 is a circular clock with a case similar in style to the convex mirrors of thirty or forty years earlier. The movement has a lever escapement.

It is curious to notice how a title, once bestowed, has the habit of persisting long after the occasion which caused it to arise has ceased to exist. The usual title for the long-waisted circular or octagonal-dialed clocks is that of "Act of Parliament," and the cause of the name is historical and interesting. It was in 1797 that Pitt imposed a tax of five shillings per annum on clocks, the Act stating that: "For and upon every clock or Timekeeper, by whatever name the same shall be called, which shall be used for the purpose of a clock, and placed in or upon any dwelling-house, or any office or building thereunto belonging, or any other building whatever, whether private or public, belonging to any person or persons, or Company of Persons, or any Body Corporate, or Politick, or Collegiate, or which shall be kept and used, by any Person or Persons n Great Britain, there shall be charged an annual duty of Five Shillings."

It is difficult to imagine an impost so trifling as this affecting the clockmaking industry, still less that it should have caused anyone possessing a clock to dispose of it, but such appears to have been the fact to a considerable extent. We live in the

Fig. 401.

ANONYMOUS.

Eight-day Wall Clock.
Mahogany case.
Black dial with gilt numerals.

4 ft. high × 6 ins. deep.
Dial 21 ins. diameter.

Date about 1790.

Fig. 402.

ANONYMOUS.

Eight-day Wall Clock.
Black case.
Black dial with gilt numerals.

4 ft. 5 ins. high × 6 ins. deep.
Dial 24 ins. × 28 ins.

Date about 1790.

days of dog licenses, and it seems impossible that the duty should have any effect in keeping the number of dogs strictly limited. One can, however, only judge the effect of a tax after it has been repealed. The Act relating to clocks was very unpopular, and was withdrawn in the following year. During the period of its operation, however, it became the custom for innkeepers all over the country to hang large clocks in their public rooms for

Fig. 403.

ANONYMOUS.

Eight-day Wall Clock.
Mahogany case inlaid with satin-wood flutes and bandings.

3 ft. 10 ins. high.   Waist 17 ins. × 7 ins. deep.
White dial 15 ins. diameter.

Date about 1800–10.

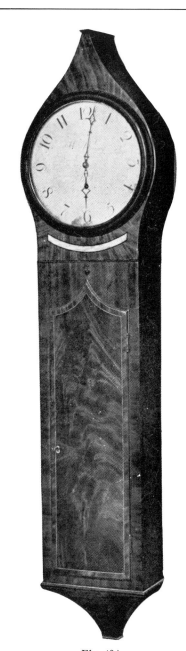

Fig. 404.

"W. YOUNG, FECIT."

Eight-day Wall Clock.
Mahogany case.

5 ft. high.   Waist 11 ins. × 7 ins.
deep.
12 in. brass dial.

Date about 1800.

Fig. 405.

CLOCK BAROMETER.

Eight-day Clock.

4 ft. 5 ins. high × 1 ft. 2½ ins. wide
× 3 ins. deep.

8 in. convex painted dial.

Fig. 406.

CLOCK BAROMETER.

Eight-day Clock.

4 ft. 3 ins. high × 1 ft. 3 ins. wide
× 3 ins. deep.

6 in. convex enamel dial.

Fig. 407.

CLOCK BAROMETER.

Eight-day Ting-tang Quarter-
striking Clock.

4 ft. 2 ins. high × 1 ft. 3½ ins. wide × 5 ins.
deep.

7 in. silvered dial.

the benefit of such customers as had disposed of their watches to escape the duty. These were known as Act of Parliament clocks, and the custom persisted long after the Act was repealed. Even at the present day these large mural timepieces are usually to be found in the public rooms or halls of inns in the southern counties of England.

These so-called " Act of Parliament " clocks are generally very similar in form to each other, with circular or octagonal dials, without glass or bezil, and long trunk cases. The clocks are nearly always fitted with pendulums of seconds' length. Another curious point is that the cases are usually lacquered in gold on a black or dark green ground. These facts appear to point to a limited period of manufacture apart from the evidence of the Act of Parliament itself, but the truth is more probably that these mural clocks were in existence prior to the passing of the Act, but that the tax caused them to be removed from private dwellings and to be fixed in public places. A period between 1760 and 1780 is a much more likely one for the manufacture of these lacquered cases, many of which are of quite respectable quality. The mural timepiece at the India Office is similar to these Act of Parliament clocks, and is certainly not later than 1780. Lacquer was probably chosen as the protecting surface as being better able to withstand inequalities of temperature than polished wood.

Figs. 399 and 400 are typical "Act of Parliament" clocks, in cases of black lacquer and with white painted dials. The important size of these cases will be noticed, that of Fig. 399 being 5 feet 2 inches in height. In Fig. 401 the dial is black with the numerals in gold, with a case veneered with good curl mahogany. Fig. 402 has an octagonal dial and black case, all lined and decorated with gold. In all four examples the pendulums are of seconds' length. Figs. 403 and 404 are of the period of Sheraton, with cases of mahogany inlaid and banded. These are typical wall clocks of the period, made for domestic, as compared with public use.

One further type of clock remains to be considered : that enclosed in a case together with a barometer and thermometer. Three examples are given in Figs. 405, 406, and 407, which may be taken as typical. All three have mahogany cases, the first inlaid with satin-wood bandings and lines, the second having ivory knob and spire, and the third brass mounts and columns. These clock barometers are invariably of late date, generally of the last decade of the eighteenth century. They may be described as being in the style of Sheraton. They belong to the history of English domestic clocks in somewhat perfunctory fashion, and may be described as being on the border line between clocks and watches. The so-called " Sedan-chair " watches of the early eighteenth century are not very far removed from them in point of size.

List of Makers illustrated in the Volume

GOULD, CHRISTOPHER, London, C.C. 1682, a celebrated maker of fine long-case clocks. Mr. Percy Webster had recently an eight-bell chiming miniature long clock by him, with the case elaborately inlaid with marqueterie. Several notable specimens of his work are in the Wetherfield Collection   Fig. 191.

GRAHAM, GEORGE, London, a very eminent maker; C.C. 1695, Master 1722; died 1751, aged seventy-seven. Buried in Westminster Abbey. Was in the service of Tompion, and succeeded him in business in 1713. Mudge and Dutton followed Graham at the Dial and One Crown in Fleet Street. Graham remodelled the cylinder escapement and invented the mercury pendulum. He was buried in the Abbey with his master, Tompion. Graham appears to have confined his attention almost exclusively to watches and bracket clocks, long cases by him being exceedingly rare   Fig. 307.

GRANT, RICHARD, London; about 1765 ..   ..   Fig. 328.

GRETTON, CHARLES, London; The Ship, Fleet Street; apprenticed to Lionel Wythe in 1662, C.C. 1672, Master 1701. A celebrated maker   ..   Figs. 181, 294.

GRIGNION, DANIEL AND THOMAS. "From the late Mr. Quare." The two appear to have been finishers to Quare, and evidently attempted, after his death, to obtain as much of his trade as possible. About 1730–40   ..   ..   Fig. 306.

HALL, THOMAS, London, apprenticed 1675 to George Hambleton, C.C. 1690   ..   ..   Fig. 101.

HALLIFAX, JOHN, Fleet Street, London, maker of musical and chiming clocks. He figures in the Gazette as a bankrupt in June 1740   ..   ..   ..   Fig. 337.

HANDLEY & MOORE, London; apprentices of John Thwaites, of Clerkenwell Close, 1798; 1810–20   ..   ..   Fig. 369.

HARRIS, ROBERT, London; about 1745–50   ..   ..   Fig. 212.

HARRIS, THOMAS, in Ye Strand; about 1680–90   ..   ..   Fig. 281.

HARRISON, JOHN, Newcastle; about 1780   ..   ..   Fig. 330.

HASSANIUS, JACOBUS, London (probably James Hassenius, admitted C.C. in 1682 as an alien)   Fig. 168.

HAWTHORN, D., Darlaston; about 1705 ..   ..   Figs. 138, 139, 140.

HIGGS & EVANS, Royal Exchange (7 Sweeting's Alley), makers of musical clocks for the Spanish market, usually inscribed "Higgs y Diego Evans" ..   ..   Fig. 327.

HILL, MATTHEW, Devonshire Street, London; about 1790. Maker of Act of Parliament and mural clocks   ..   ..   Fig. 400.

HILTON, EMANUEL, Portsmouth; about 1775   ..   ..   Fig. 257.

HOCKER, JOHN, Reading, apprenticed to John Martin, afterwards to Edward Joslin; C.C. 1729   ..   ..   Fig. 200.

HODGES, NATHANIEL, "In Wine Office Courte in Fleete Streete"; C.C. 1681 ..   Figs. 37, 287.

HOLMES, WILLIAM, 56 Strand; about 1810   ..   ..   Fig. 371.

HOSKINS, DANIEL, London; about 1630 ..   ..   Fig. 33.

HUBERT, DAVID, London; C.C. 1714, Master 1743; 1714–48   ..   ..   ..   Fig. 183.

HUGGINS, London; about 1830 ..   ..   Fig. 377.

HUGHES, THOMAS, Broad Street Buildings, London; C.C. 1712–35   ..   ..   Fig. 309.

IRVING, ALEXANDER, Westminster, C.C. 1695   ..   ..   Fig. 125.

ISREALS, JOSEPH, London; about 1775 ..   ..   Fig. 226.

JAMESON, GEORGE, Portsea, formerly of 33 Charing Cross, London, maker of chronometers and elaborate clocks; 1800–10   ..   ..   ..   Fig. 350.

JEFFREYS & JONES, London, makers of regulator clocks and fine watches; about 1800 ..   Fig. 246.

JENKINS, HENRY, 68 Aldersgate Street, London, 1756–83; maker of elaborate astronomical clocks ..   ..   Figs. 242, 339.

JOHNS, THOMAS, London; about 1700–5 ..   ..   Fig. 124.

JOHNSON, THOMAS, London; about 1680; maker of long-case clocks. One in Mr. R. Hoffmann's possession with $1\frac{1}{4}$ seconds pendulum ..   ..   Figs. 99, 143.

KIRK, JOSEPH, Nottingham; about 1740 ..   ..   Fig. 205.

KNIBB, JOHN, Oxford; about 1680   ..   ..   Fig. 393.

KNIBB, JOSEPH, of Oxford and afterwards of London, C.C. 1670, one of a famous family of makers—Samuel, Joseph, John, and Peter. Joseph was the most renowned. He made all kinds of clocks—lantern, long-case, bracket, or mural—and his work is invariably of high quality. His address is given in advertisements as at the Dial in Fleet Street. Mr. Wetherfield has a clock by him signed as from Hanslope, a Buckinghamshire village, and from its late date was probably Joseph Knibb's place of retirement .. .. Figs. 81, 82, 109, 279.

KNOTTESFORD, WILLIAM, London, C.C. 1663, Master 1693, an early maker, and, from his work, of considerable skill .. .. Fig. 275.

LANE, JOHN, Fetter Lane, maker of clocks of the later regulator type .. .. Fig. 245.

LEES, T., Bury, maker of clocks in the Yorkshire style; about 1790 .. .. .. Fig. 261.

LEFROY, GEORGE, Wisbeach; about 1785 .. .. Fig. 342.

LEROUX, JOHN, 8 Charing Cross; C.C. 1781 .. .. Figs. 357, 381.

LOWNDES, JONATHAN (often engraved "Loundes"), Pall Mall, C.C. 1680, Steward 1696
Figs. 280, 285, 293.

LYONS, RICHARD, London; apprenticed 1649, C.C. 1656, Master 1683 .. .. Fig. 93.

MACHAM, SAMUEL, London, maker of long-case clocks of some note, judging by the number of dials met with bearing his name. The general quality is above the average, although much beneath that of makers like Knibb, Quare, or Tompion. About 1700–10 .. .. Figs. 122, 161

MARKHAM, MARKWICK, Royal Exchange; 1720-60. Markham appears to have done considerable business with the Turkish market, judging from the number of his signed dials painted with Turkish hour numerals. At a later date he probably factored more than he made, and this may account for the fact that Markham's name is often coupled with that of another maker—e.g. "Markwick Markham, Hy. Borrell" .. Fig. 207.

MARTIN, EDMUND, London, a maker of long-case clocks of good quality; about 1760–80 Fig. 235.

MASSY, HENRY, London, probably near Leicester Fields (name usually engraved "Hen Massy"). A noted maker, son of Nicholas Massy, a Huguenot refugee, who migrated to this country during the last three or four years of the reign of Charles II. Henry Massy obtained his freedom in 1692, and was in Charles Street, Haymarket, in 1707 .. .. Figs. 111, 290.

MILES (SEPTIMUS), 32 Ludgate Street, London, 1794–1824; Livery C.C. 1810; 8 Little Carter Lane, E.C., 1825–42 .. .. Fig. 368.

MOGINIE (SAMUEL), 1 Prince Row, Pimlico; 1820–42. His regulator clocks are especially fine in workmanship .. .. Figs. 252, 379.

MUDGE, THOMAS, Fleet Street, London; born 1715, died 1794. A noted maker, who succeeded George Graham in business (he was Graham's apprentice), and afterwards continued in partnership with William Dutton (q.v.). Mudge invented the lever escapement, and devoted much of his later life to perfecting watches and chronometers. He obtained his freedom in 1738, and the livery in 1766 .. .. Fig. 243.

NEVE, HENRY, in Ye Strand, also engraved "NEUE," one of the Huguenot refugees from France. His clock work is characterised by great precision. About 1700–20 .. .. Fig. 291.

NEWMAN, EDWARD, London; about 1820 .. .. Fig. 365.

NICHOLAS, C., London; C.C. 1685 .. .. Fig. 141.

NICOLL, WILLIAM, Junior, 117 Great Portland Street, London, W.; 1790–1835 .. Fig. 354.

OLLIVANT, T. AND J., Market Street, Manchester; 1832-6 .. .. Fig. 373.

OOSTERWYK, ABRAM, Middelburg, Holland; about 1710. A Dutch maker of clocks very much in the English style .. .. Fig. 170.

PAINE (or PAIN), WILLIAM, Trowbridge, Wilts; about 1785–90 .. .. .. Fig. 223.

PARKES, JOHN, Old 'Change, London, E.C.; 1800 .. .. Fig. 398.

PAYNE, WILLIAM, "In East Smithfield," an early maker of lantern clocks; about 1610–20 Fig. 24.

PHILP (PHILIP), ROBERT, 6 New Court, St. John Street, Clerkenwell, 1779–88, maker of musical clocks .. .. Fig. 343.

PILLING, JOHN, Boothfold, maker of Yorkshire clocks; about 1800 .. .. .. Fig. 262.

POISSON, HENRY, London (Royal Exchange); about 1695–1720 .. .. .. Fig. 153.

PUCKRIDGE (JOHN?), 72 Snow Hill, London, E.C., 1790–1815, Livery C.C. 1814 .. Fig. 231.

PURDEN, JOHN, London; about 1795 .. .. Fig. 250.

PYKE, JOHN, Newgate Street, London, E.C.; about 1730–55 .. .. Figs. 203, 341.

QUARE, DAN., St. Martin's-le-Grand, afterwards at Exchange Alley, born 1649, died 1724. Brother C.C. 1671, Master 1708. A celebrated maker, whose work is characterised by careful finish and exactness of detail. Quare is credited with the invention of the repeating watch. Partner in later life with Edward Horseman, the business being continued under the title of Quare & Horseman. Dan. Quare appears to have divided his attention equally between long-case, bracket clocks, and fine watches. Quare was a strict Quaker .. .. Fig. 304.

QUARMAN, JOSEPH, Temple Cloud. There appear to have been three brothers of the same address—Samuel, Joseph, and George. Samuel was the best known. About 1780–90 .. .. Fig. 224.

RAVEN, SAMUEL, London; about 1795 .. .. Fig. 237.

REASON, G., London; cartel clock; about 1770–80 .. .. Fig. 397.

REID, THOMAS, London; about 1780 .. .. Fig. 332.

RIACH, London; bracket clock; about 1790 .. .. Fig. 358.

RICHARDS, THOMAS, 17 Bridgwater Square, Barbican, 1804; 96 Shoreditch, 1830 .. Fig. 380.

RICHARDSON, HENRY, London; about 1700 .. .. Fig. 197.

ROBINSON, DAN., apprenticed 1681; about 1690–1720 .. .. Fig. 163.

ROOKER, RICHARD, Chelsea; C.C. 1728 .. .. Fig. 303.

SADDLETON, Lynn; about 1820–30 .. .. Fig. 384.

SADLER, ROBERT, "Red Lyon Fields," London; about 1725 .. .. .. Fig. 301.

SCHOLEFIELD, JAMES, London; about 1760 .. .. Fig. 210.

SCHOUTEN, H., Amsterdam, Dutch maker .. .. Fig. 164.

SCRIVENER, RICHARD, London; C.C. 1639 .. .. Fig. 155.

SHELLY, JOSEPH, London; C.C. 1717 .. .. Fig. 190.

SMALLWOOD, Lichfield; bracket clock; about 1740 .. .. Fig. 317.

SMITH, JAMES, 115 Fleet Street, London; 1760–80 .. .. Figs. 244, 329.

SMITH, JOHN, 143 Houndsditch, London; Livery C.C. 1776–90 .. .. .. Fig. 331.

SPEAKMETT, E., London; about 1700 .. .. Fig. 130.

SPENDLOVE, JOHN, Thetford; about 1770–80 .. .. Fig. 394.

STAUNTON (STANTON), EDWARD, Leadenhall Street, London, E.C., a noted maker; apprenticed 1655, C.C. 1682, Master 1696. Maker of long-case and bracket clocks .. .. Fig. 88.

STOPPES, AYLMER, London; about 1735–40 .. .. Fig. 204.

STORM, GERRIT, Amsterdam, Dutch maker .. .. Fig. 392.

STUBBS, THOMAS, London; about 1695 .. .. Fig. 114.

THWAITES, AYNSWORTH, Rosoman Street, Clerkenwell, 1740–80, maker of a remarkable pair of clocks now in the India Office .. .. .. Figs. 240, 241.

THWAITES, JOHN, London, continued business of above at same address; Master C.C. 1815, 1819, 1820; 1786–1816 .. .. Fig. 364.

TOMLIN, EDWARD, 69 Threadneedle Street, London, E.C.; 1770–98 .. .. Fig. 359.

TOMPION & BANGER, London, continued business of Thomas Tompion. Watches of 1700–4 were often signed " Tho. Tompion, Edwd. Banger " .. .. Fig. 308.

TOMPION, THOMAS, Dial and Three Crowns, Fleet Street, London, the most renowned of all the English clockmakers ; born 1638, died 1713 ; buried in Westminster Abbey ; Brother C.C. 1671, free in 1674, Assistant 1691, Warden 1700, and Master 1704. Tompion was a prolific maker of watches, lantern, long-case, and bracket clocks. He presented to the Pump Room at Bath, in 1709, a fine month clock, with an arched dial and of elaborate construction .. .. .. Figs. 77, 79, 90, 159, 297.

TRAFFORD, THOMAS, London ; about 1660-70 .. .. Fig. 29.

UNDERWOOD, WILLIAM, Westminster ; about 1720–5 .. .. Fig. 157.

UPJOHN, THOMAS, Exeter ; about 1760 .. .. Fig. 318

UPJOHN, T. J. (J. & T. ?), 5 Chandos Street, Strand, London ; about 1805–15 .. .. Fig. 247.

WEBSTER, WILLIAM, Exchange Alley, London ; C.C. 1710. One of a noted family of clockmakers .. .. Figs. 193, 319, 334.

WENHAM, D., Dereham ; about 1750 .. .. Fig. 206.

WESTT (WEST), THOMAS, London ; about 1710 .. .. Fig. 162.

WHEELER, THOMAS, " near Ye French Church," London. Apprenticed 1647 to Nicholas Coxeter, C.C. 1655, Master 1684, died 1694 .. .. .. Fig. 36.

WHEELER, THOMAS, 114 Oxford Street, London ; about 1700 .. .. .. Fig. 132.

WHITCHURCH, SAMUEL, Kingswood ; about 1765 .. .. Fig. 211.

WHITEHURST, JOHN, Derby, afterwards of Bolt Court, Fleet Street, London ; well-known maker of turret clocks ; died 1788 .. .. Fig. 395.

WICKSTED, EDWARD, 9 Fore Street, London, E.C., 1768 ; 114 Bunhill Row, 1795 ; maker of musical clocks .. .. Fig. 326.

WIGHTMAN, THOMAS, George Yard, London ; about 1800 .. .. Fig. 251.

WILLS, RICHARD, Truro ; about 1780 .. .. Fig. 233.

WILMOT, Upper Rosoman Street, London ; about 1810 .. .. Fig. 372.

WILSON, JOSHUA, London, apprenticed to William Fuller, 1688 ; about 1700-10 .. Fig. 172.

WINDMILLS & BENNET, London ; about 1720–30 .. .. Fig. 179.

WINDMILLS & ELKINS, London ; about 1730 .. .. Fig. 202.

WINDMILLS & WIGHTMAN, London ; about 1725 .. .. Fig. 185.

WINDMILLS, JOSEPH, St. Martin's-le-Grand, after in Mark Lane, London ; C.C. 1671, Master 1702. A celebrated maker of clocks and watches .. .. Fig. 283.

WISE, JOHN (WYSE), London ; C.C. 1683 .. .. Figs. 112, 119.

WOODMAN, JOHN, London ; about 1700 .. .. Fig. 323.

WRIGHT, THOMAS, Dorking ; about 1800 .. .. Fig. 363.

YOUNG, W. ; wall clock ; about 1800 .. .. Fig. 404.

Index